EXPLODING ENGLISH

EXPLODING ENGLISH
Criticism, Theory, Culture

BERNARD BERGONZI

CLARENDON PRESS · OXFORD

1990

Melbourne Auckland
and associated companies in
Berlin Ibadan

Oxford is a trade mark of Oxford University Press

Published in the United States
by Oxford University Press, New York

© *Bernard Bergonzi 1990*

British Library Cataloguing in Publication Data
Bergonzi, Bernard 1929–
Exploding English: criticism, theory, culture
1. Great Britain. Universities. Curriculum subjects:
English literature
I. Title 820.7'1141
ISBN 0–19–812852–5

Library of Congress Cataloging in Publication Data
Bergonzi, Bernard
Exploding English: criticism, theory, culture / Bernard Bergonzi.
p. cm.
Includes bibliographical references.
*1. English philology—Study and teaching (Higher)—Great Britain—
History—20th century. 2. English philology—Study and teaching
(Higher)—United States—History—20th century. 3. English
literature—History and criticism—Theory, etc. 4. Criticism—Great
Britain—History—20th century. 5. Criticism—United States—
History—20th century. 6. English teachers—Great Britain—
Biography. 7. Bergonzi, Bernard. I. Title.*
PE68.G5B47 1990
420'.71'141—dc20 89–37448
ISBN 0–19–812852–5

Set by CentraCet, Cambridge
Printed in Great Britain by
Courier International Ltd.
Tiptree, Essex.

FOR ANNE

PREFACE

I am not sure how best to describe this book, since it crosses boundaries. It attempts to bring together elements of critical theory, intellectual history, and the sociology of knowledge, together with a touch of autobiography. In essentials it is an account, from within, of a changing culture and form of life: the academic study of English Literature as I have been involved in it for the past thirty years, with a backward glance at its earlier history. The focus is primarily on events in Britain, though there is frequent cross-reference to the American scene, where theory has become a major industry, both for home consumption and for export. Interesting and disconcerting things are happening, but the phrase 'crisis in English', has become something of a cliché on both sides of the Atlantic, and I have tried to avoid using it, inclining towards Graham Hough's view, 'In a world full of sin and misery what happens in the arts departments of universities rarely deserves the name of crisis.'

Throughout the book I refer to the 'academy' more often than to the 'university', since in Britain significant intellectual developments have taken place elsewhere in higher education, in polytechnics and colleges. Where I do speak of the 'university' it should be understood as a general construct, drawn from many sources, and not referring just to my own university.

There are frequent quotations from other writers, sometimes in agreement, sometimes in disagreement. This may, at times, look like an instance of the excessive reliance on established authorities that I deplore in the book. I cannot rule this out, but my conscious practice was governed by a number of considerations: my own ideas are often sparked off in reaction to other people's, who may, in any case, put things better than I can myself; and, in Bakhtinian terms, polyphony is preferable to a monologue.

I have been working on this book for several years (though the final version was all written in 1987–8), after thinking about it for several more. During this time I incurred more intellectual debts than I can hope to acknowledge, not only to other writers, but to innumerable contacts and conversations with friends, colleagues, and students; as well as to more formal academic activities, particularly classes in criticism that I have taught at Stanford and Warwick. Out of so many, I shall refer specifically only to my wife, to whom I owe so much, and who read through the drafts with a keen eye and gave me much valuable criticism and advice. Finally, I want to express my thanks to the University of Warwick, for study leave and many other things; and to the Warden and Fellows of New College, Oxford, where I was a visiting fellow in the Michaelmas term of 1987, and where I found much kindness, and a congenial environment in which to work on this book.

B.B.

University of Warwick

CONTENTS

LIST OF JOURNALS

Like Hales, and unlike our nation in general, Falkland concerned himself with the *why* of things as well as the *what*. 'I comprise it all,' says Hales, in two words: *'what* and *wherefore*. That part of your burden which contains *what*, you willingly take up. But that other, which comprehends *why*, that is either too hot or too heavy; you dare not meddle with it. But I must add that also to your burden, or else I must leave you for idle persons; for without knowledge of why, of the grounds or reasons of things, there is no possibility of not being deceived.'

MATTHEW ARNOLD, 'Falkland'

'That comes from having a literary education,' Walter burst out in his old-style raucous vein. 'You think a bloody sight too much of criticism if you put it as high as second-hand. Our infernal college' (he turned to me) 'after we'd cleared out elected some damn fool who'd written a thesis on the Criticism of Criticism. Instead of electing him they ought to have kicked his bottom down the Cury.'

C. P. SNOW, *Last Things*

1. ANECDOTAL INTRODUCTION

I refer to myself and my experiences more explicitly in this introduction than in the rest of the book, but the whole of it has an autobiographical dimension. If every generation hankers after a lost unity of being, mine was located in the 1950s. At the beginning of the decade I was recovering from a severe, almost fatal illness, and was without any occupation, or the apparent qualifications for one, though I had a strong desire to be a writer. My formal education had been interrupted by wartime displacement and long periods of ill health in childhood. I left school in 1945, just before my sixteenth birthday, and went to work as a junior clerk in a small City firm publishing children's books. A year later, I fell ill again. Being in hospital gave me the opportunity for wide though quite undirected reading, and I emerged as an autodidact with aspirations to high culture, a latter-day version of E. M. Forster's Leonard Bast. Eventually my health recovered: at that time there was work of a sort for anyone who wanted it, and I got another clerical job, becoming a member of the white-collar proletariat, just as Leonard had been in 1910. I wrote poems, and some were published in little magazines. I had the advantage of living in London—I was a second-generation Londoner—though in the unfashionable southern suburbs, and I went to poetry readings and met writers. I developed aspirations, or pretensions, to the literary life, though I had little idea of how one started leading it. I was too timid for bohemianism, and clung to the security of my parents' suburban home. I started to write novels, and soon abandoned them. I published a book review in *Our Time*, which was a cultural organ of the Communist Party, and others in *Nine*, which was edited by Peter Russell, a passionate admirer of Ezra Pound, who shared Pound's political as well as his literary attitudes. An involuntary ideological balance was thus maintained.

In 1950 I bought what proved to be the final issue of *Penguin New Writing*. Without realizing it, I had encountered both a cultural and a personal turning-point. John Lehmann's paperback miscellany, *Penguin New Writing*, had flourished during the Second World War, when there was an enormous public appetite for reading matter of every kind, and poetry reached a wider audience than ever before, or since. Lehmann published articles, stories, and poems by lonely men and women who were in the armed forces or engaged in other kinds of war work, as well as poetry, fiction, criticism, and cultural surveys by established writers. It was pre-eminently the organ of what Arthur Koestler called the 'Thoughtful Corporal belt'. Lehmann himself was a scion of Bloomsbury—sometime assistant to Virginia Woolf at the Hogarth Press—who combined cultivated literary taste and proletarian sympathies, and *Penguin New Writing* was a successor to his earlier, more decisively left-tending publications, *New Writing* and *New Writing and Daylight*. During the war it sold very widely, and afterwards it struggled on for another five years. I used to buy it, and longed to be published in it. But people did not read so much in peacetime, the circulation dropped steadily, and in 1950 *Penguin New Writing* ceased publication, just as its more mandarin competitor, *Horizon*, had done the previous year. Yet the last issue contained a portent of things to come, indicating a shift in taste, and the arrival of a new literary generation. This took the form of an essay on William Empson, by a twenty-five-year-old poet, critic, and academic, John Wain. The Empson essay must have been one of his first pieces of criticism to appear in an established publication, even if in its valedictory number. Wain later became a well-known man of letters, who worked in many literary genres, and was Professor of Poetry at Oxford in the 1970s. He was then a protégé of Lehmann's, who had broadcast Wain's poems in a radio magazine he edited called 'New Soundings'. One generation shortly trod another down, and in time Lehmann's programme was taken off the air to be replaced by one edited by Wain himself, called 'First Reading', which was supposed to be more responsive to the work and attitudes of an emerging new literary generation, subsequently to be dubbed 'The Movement'. The initial performance of 'First Reading', in the spring of 1953, contained extracts from Kingsley Amis's still unpublished first novel *Lucky Jim*, and, among other items, two poems by me. (A reviewer of the programme in the *Observer* expressed satisfaction at what he called the 'simplicities' of my poems, but deflated any possible hubris by thoroughly garbling my name.)

That is looking ahead a little. One result of Wain's article on Empson, who was at that time a neglected figure, was to prompt me—as it did other readers—to seek out his remarkable poetry. It came to enjoy an intense if brief vogue in the early fifties: Wain himself, A. Alvarez, George MacBeth, and the late Jonathan Price all wrote poems in the Empson manner, and so did I. Yet I believe that the brief account of Wain in the 'Notes on Contributors' had as much of an influence on me as his article. He was there described as teaching at the University of Reading the English Literature he learnt at the University of Oxford. At that time I did not know very much about universities. My family background was respectable working-class and lowest middle-class and no one I knew had ever been to one, apart from a cousin on my father's side. But it seemed a fine way of earning a living for someone who was keen on literature, and the seed of my later career was implanted. Leonard Bast was attempting to turn into Rastignac or Lucien de Rubempré. Looking back on my life, I find that everything important in it seems to have been the result of pure chance (which in some moods I am prepared to regard as the careful manœuvres of Providence). I used to attend convivial evenings of talk and poetry reading at the Chelsea flat of the poet and critic, George Fraser, who became a good friend. There, about the time my poems were broadcast on 'First Reading', I met the Scottish poet, Tom Scott, who had been asked by Edwin Muir to try to find students to attend Newbattle Abbey, a residential college for adults near Edinburgh, where Muir was warden. Scott asked me if I would be interested in going there. It seemed a good idea to me, as I felt thoroughly in a rut in my office job, and wanted time to read and write and think. It seemed a thoroughly alarming idea to my parents, though in retrospect they may have come to believe that it led to something they could warily approve. The London County Council, as it used to be, agreed to pay my fees for a year's study at Newbattle, and gave me an extra £15 as pocket money. I was able to supplement this with some money I had been left in a legacy several years before and had prudently saved against the proverbial rainy day, which I decided had now arrived. In practice, a rainy day proved indistinguishable from a lucky break. In the autumn of 1953 I went to Newbattle. It proved in many respects a liberating as well as an educative experience. Apart from anything else, living in Scotland for a young Londoner who had never been further north than Buckingham was half-way to living in a foreign country. Edwin Muir was tutor in literature as well as warden, and under his relaxed tutelage I embarked on some extensive reading of English classics that up to that time I knew only by repute. I also got to know young academics from Edinburgh University who came out to Newbattle to take classes, and through them came to frequent some drawing-rooms of that dramatic city. This encouraged a Balzacian taste for the amenities of upper-middle-class life.

Edwin Muir was gentle, withdrawn, and quizzical. His personality seemed to embody—which is a contradictory way of putting it—the Platonic spirit of his poetry. He was too involved in his own inner life to make a very effective lecturer. But there was a quiet radiance about him, and I saw in him an inspiring model of what a life dedicated to literature could be like. He was a good man, not altogether in the right job at Newbattle—where he did not last very long—and I owe him a great deal. I returned to London on 16 June 1954: Bloomsday, fifty years on. I was stimulated and restless and ambitious. I spent some weeks writing a novel, which remained unpublished, and rightly so; I could never bear to reread it, and the only typescript is now in Georgetown University Library. Then I took another clerking job, with the London Brick Company. At the end of 1954 I published a collection of poems called *Descartes and the Animals* under the imprint of the little magazine, *Platform*, edited by Frederick Woods, of which I was associate editor. I can regard these early poems, mostly written in the tight, formal, Movement manner, with more equanimity than my early fiction. Some of them appeared in anthologies, and in 1984 I was pleasantly surprised to find a stanza from the title poem quoted in Christopher Ricks's book *The Force of Poetry*.

One of the things I learnt at Newbattle was that it was still possible to go to university in one's mid-twenties, or at an even more advanced age. In fact, the college did a useful job in preparing potential mature students to enter degree courses. One of my fellow students, Alex Reid, went on to take degrees at Edinburgh and Oxford, and then returned to Newbattle as tutor in philosophy. In time, he became Principal. I now attempted to continue my formal education. Oxford and Cambridge provided competitive scholarships for mature entrants; I applied to both, submitting an essay on Richardson's *Clarissa*. Both universities offered me an award, but the Oxford deal looked better, so I elected to go there. I was admitted to Wadham, and in the autumn of 1955 went up to read English Language and Literature. I enjoyed Oxford enormously, in a way that is familiar to mature students (and perhaps only to them), who are able to appreciate the privileges and freedom of university life all the more because they know the world outside. A sense of being grateful for privilege, even an underlying anxiety that it might be snatched away, has tended to affect my later attitudes, not always fortunately. (It was reinforced by my mother's anxiety; she felt that there was something inherently fraudulent about my going to Oxford, and that sooner or later I would be found out.) Among other things, this sense tended to make me peculiarly unsympathetic to the student revolts of the 1960s.

At Oxford, where F. W. Bateson was my tutor for a time, and my friends included Martin Dodsworth, Roger Lonsdale, and Christopher Ricks, the ghost of Leonard Bast was finally laid to rest (I lately came across a vivid evocation of those years in Judith Grossman's novel about a scholarship-girl in Oxford in the fifties, *Her Own Terms*.) I became less of a struggling individual, and more of a type, the ambitious, upwardly mobile scholarship-boy, famously commemorated in Richard Hoggart's *The Uses of Literacy*, which came out in 1957, in the middle of my time at Oxford. Without fully realizing it at first, I entered an institution, where I still remain. I am not now referring to college or university, but the institutional system of English Literature as an academic subject, whose later fortunes I look at in this book. It was a

Anecdotal Introduction

good moment to move into it. In the immediate post-war years English had expanded rapidly as a subject, and, most significantly, had drawn closer to the production of literature. I liked to think of myself as a poet and critic, and the university seemed a very suitable location for that dual role. The mid-fifties saw the brief heyday of the Movement, as described in Blake Morrison's excellent book. Several of its representative figures combined the roles of university teacher of English, literary critic, and writer of fiction or poetry; notably, John Wain, my original role-model, Kingsley Amis, and Donald Davie; Philip Larkin was also located in the academy as a librarian. In fact, Wain gave up teaching to become a full-time writer at about the time I went to Oxford, just as Amis did a few years later. But the ideal remained feasible and attractive. Admittedly it was Cambridge, whose offer I had declined, which placed literary criticism at the centre of English study. Oxford English was notoriously suspicious of criticism, and primarily concerned itself with scholarship—historical, linguistic, biographical, bibliographical—lightly pervaded, where appropriate, with belletristic appreciation. However, the prevailing order of things gave me and a group of like-minded friends a taste for the pleasures of intellectual opposition. The idea of literary criticism—in effect, a blend of Leavisite, Empsonian, and New Critical approaches—was upheld by the Oxford University Critical Society, which A. Alvarez had founded as an undergraduate in the early 1950s. I became an active member, along with Martin Dodsworth, then a Wadham undergraduate, now well known as a critic and a Professor of English in the University of London. Among the dons, one of the supporters of the Society was F. W. Bateson. He was a scholar and a literary historian, but also, unusually for Oxford, a firm believer in the value of criticism. He admired Leavis, though he lamented Leavis's scholarly deficiencies, and attempted to draw him into constructive debate, but the admiration was not returned. Bateson was an engaging man, eccentric in personality and opinions, with a taste for intellectual mischief that made him a stimulating though not invariably responsible tutor.

Another senior member of the Critical Society, who has remained a friend, was W. W. Robson, then a fellow of

Lincoln and subsequently Masson Professor at Edinburgh. At that time he was the only Leavisite in the Oxford English Faculty, which made him a lonely figure, a missionary *in partibus infidelium*. He was later to lose faith in Leavis as decisively as other people lose faith in Communism; the shift is apparent if one compares Robson's *Critical Essays* of 1966 with his *The Definition of Literature and Other Essays* of 1982. The English Faculty regarded Leavis as an oppositional figure, malign but curiously inescapable. He was derided, usually without being named, in the writings of its senior members, and in the tart asides of Faculty lecturers. The Critical Society, though not officially Leavisite, used Leavis as a kind of patron, and he came once a year from Cambridge at the Society's invitation to lecture to a large audience. The lectures, as I recall them, were not intellectually distinguished; Leavis took the opportunity to dwell on and vindicate his own achievements in combating, without due recognition, the forces of academic and cultural darkness; the tone was generally querulous. Nevertheless, these occasions had a certain symbolic force. I did not think of myself as a Leavisite—whether I would have become one if I had gone to Cambridge is a good question—and I disliked his dogmatic exclusions and the Puritan tradition he embodied. I was more inclined to identify with the American New Critics who were then beginning to be read in England. For instance, I wrote enthusiastic reviews of the English editions of R. P. Blackmur's *Language as Gesture* and Allen Tate's *The Man of Letters in the Modern World* for a long-vanished weekly called *Truth*. *Theory of Literature*, by Wellek and Warren, which I read about this time, left a firm impression. Nevertheless, I took more from *Scrutiny* than I was prepared to admit. In 1958 I published in another now defunct magazine, the monthly *Twentieth Century*, an attack on Ian Fleming's new kind of sex-and-violence thriller (this was before the film versions launched the global James Bond cult), modelled on Q. D. Leavis's *Scrutiny* essay on Dorothy Sayers. This piece of mine provoked some interest, and was even referred to in *Time* magazine.

I stayed on at Oxford after Schools to embark on a research degree on H. G. Wells's early writings. In 1959 I was appointed an assistant lecturer in English at the University of Manchester to teach the English Literature I had learnt at the University of Oxford (and elsewhere); or so I thought.

Traditionally, criticism and literature were part of a unified cultural activity, and most of the major English critics were also poets. With the global growth of English as an academic subject, criticism has proliferated. It is often said that most of the scientists who have ever lived are alive and working in the world today, and something similar must be true of literary critics. Most of them, nowadays, are not poets. In the past few decades, in America and Britain, criticism has shifted its adherence and location from one social institution, literature (interpreting that term in a broad and accommodating sense), to another, the university, which is much more formally structured. I have been quite well placed to observe this process over the past thirty years. I have enjoyed my life as a university teacher of English, first at Manchester, and since 1966 at Warwick, with periods as a visiting professor in American universities. I have to add, though, that the longer I do it the harder teaching seems to get, rather than the reverse. I have written a lot of criticism, mostly on modern literature, which is something I came to with an uncluttered mind, as in my day the Oxford English syllabus stopped in 1830. At the same time, the influence of Bateson and other people I encountered at Oxford impelled me towards the writing of literary history. (I occasionally think that, if I had my time over again, I might prefer the study of history, where the subject is more defined and the method more coherent. But academic historians often pursue such boring topics.) I have also written a great deal of literary journalism; more, probably, than was good for me. It can be insidiously undermining of the time and attention required for sustained scholarship; but I am by temperament a sprinter rather than a long-distance runner, and writing reviews put me in the way of a lot of books I might not otherwise have read, and stopped me from ever quite needing an overdraft when I was bringing up my family. I have also continued, in a small way, to generate literary texts; in other words, to write fiction and poetry, though less often than I would like. Still, I suppose it gives me what Hilary Corke, reviewing my first collection of poems in 1955, called a 'critic's credential'; that is, I have some idea of what it means to produce the stuff. In 1981 I published a novel, *The Roman Persuasion*. I found writing it both harder and more interesting than writing criticism.

I have taken on various administrative jobs in the academy, including running a department, and was for three instructive years a pro-vice-chancellor at Warwick. Whether this was time well spent I am not sure, but it provided me with experiences that contrasted interestingly with, and were in some respects less demanding than, the business of teaching and writing. At least, I have a fairly good idea of how a modern university is run, and of what odd people work there. My years of service on a Promotions Committee have shown me how academic productivity—otherwise known as 'research'—is assessed and rewarded. This process has implications which are peculiarly relevant, if mostly unwelcome, for the academic institution of English. Looking back at the fifties, I now see how utopian was the idea that I—and others—then entertained of a unified existence centred on English Literature: writing it, writing about it, teaching it. In fact, teaching and writing seem to me to go badly together and I would advise young aspiring writers to seek some quite other mode of employment. Thinking about my younger self, I believe I might have written more poetry and fiction if I had remained a white-collar proletarian, and might in time have made it as a professional writer. But I suppose I wanted a comfortable middle-class way of life as much as I wanted literary success, and this the university has provided. Looking at more persistent and committed writers who have taught in English departments, one observes that sooner or later most of them do what Wain and Amis did and get out. I am thinking now of those British writers who attempt to combine literary production with the academic teaching of mainstream literature. The American system of employing poets and novelists on campus to teach 'creative writing' offers the writer a different relationship with the academy; on the face of it a more direct and sustaining one, even a form of patronage, though with its own attendant dangers. Instead of achieving an ideal unity, we have suffered from the Chinese curse of living in interesting times. I attempt to describe them in this book.

2. BITTERNESS IN THE EARLY EIGHTIES

Academic debates are not invariably peaceful, but in the 1980s arguments about the state of English studies became unusually angry and peculiarly public. They should perhaps be called polemical occasions rather than arguments, since often the contestants did not share the minimum common ground that makes argument possible; and differences in principle were involved with personal issues and dramas. I look at some of these collisions in this Chapter. I find them full of human interest, with elements of dark comedy and occasional farce. But they also raise serious questions about criticism and higher education. First, there was the 'MacCabe Affair', which burst out of Cambridge early in 1981. It had the remarkable effect of filling the columns of the more literate newspapers with talk about literary theory. For a week or so, the question, 'What *is* structuralism?' seemed to be on everybody's lips. Dr Colin MacCabe, a thirty-one-year-old university assistant lecturer in English was, it appeared, being sacked for professing 'structuralism', a new and exciting approach to literary study, favoured by the students and the younger dons, but opposed by the fuddy-duddies who ran the English Faculty. Thus, an instant myth was born. The facts were more complicated.

The University of Cambridge was, and is, the only British university which still appoints assistant lecturers for a limited period, with no certainty of being kept on. MacCabe was one of three assistant lecturers in English who applied for a single established post; and he was unlucky. Some observers, invoking the perennial human wisdom of 'some you win, some you lose', believed that MacCabe should have taken his disappointment stoically, and moved on to pastures new. But there were others who thought that MacCabe was so brilliant that his non-appointment was a scandal, and outrage was correspondingly stirred, or stirred up. MacCabe and his friends had press contacts, and a campaign on his behalf took off, though only, I suspect, because it was rather a slack time for news. (Before long the MacCabe affair was overtaken by the foundation of the Social Democratic Party.)

A few facts emerged. The English Faculty had narrowly voted for MacCabe to be appointed to the new post, but the Appointments Committee of the Faculty voted the other way. Two of MacCabe's supporters were the distinguished senior professors, Frank Kermode and Raymond Williams, who at that time were aged around sixty, indicating that this was no simple matter of youth versus age. They were shortly voted off the Appointments Committee. It was widely believed that one of MacCabe's principal opponents was another eminent professor, Christopher Ricks, who was still in his forties. Ricks kept very quiet in the affair, refusing to attend a protest meeting called by students, quoting Leavis's words, 'to come would be to condone'. He did, however, tell a reporter that the real issue was 'MacCabe's intelligence', not Dr Johnson versus Jacques Derrida. Yet MacCabe's intellectual and ideological allegiance was not so easily dismissed. He was not, indeed, a 'structuralist' in the proper sense. Structuralism, inspired by the anthropology of Lévi-Strauss, the linguistics of Saussure, and the critical theory of the Russian and Czech Formalists, had arisen in Paris in the early sixties. It became more influential in American academic life than in British, and it seemed for a time to provide comprehensive formulae for the understanding of all kinds of human activity. It did not sustain this early promise, and by the eighties it was moving into history, having shown that much of our experience can be understood in terms of binary oppositions, and leaving literary critics with some useful devices for the analysis of narrative form.

MacCabe is better described as a 'poststructuralist'. His allegiances were, indeed, French; he had studied in Paris, and his Cambridge mentor was Stephen Heath, a member of the English Faculty who was a disciple of Roland Barthes and had written a book on him, in French. MacCabe inherited the residual Marxism that still possessed French intellectuals in the 1970s. But his major frame of reference was psychoanalytic, specifically that of the rebarbative revisionist Freudian,

Jacques Lacan. MacCabe was very interested in cinema, which was itself a cause of suspicion to some people in Cambridge, and he had written on Jean-Luc Godard. But his main claim to academic advancement was his book *James Joyce and the Revolution of the Word*, published in 1978, and well received by some Joyceans; the late Richard Ellmann said it was 'an important book', and likely to prove a focus for subsequent critical discussion of Joyce. However, another Joyce scholar, Michael Mason, was hostile to the book. He described it as,

a tremendously aggressive piece of writing. Its aggression is directed both at current literary criticism, and at certain texts or traditions in English Literature itself. For MacCabe the two targets are connected: the literary criticism he attacks is that which makes the same assumptions about language and reality as the literature he dislikes.

Read symptomatically and historically, MacCabe's book reveals the attitudes and interests of radical young literary academics in the mid-1970s, when it was hoped that a cloudy but potent mix of poststructuralist, psychoanalytic, and Marxist approaches would subvert established methods of studying English Literature. Like much of their writing, MacCabe's book proceeds by hunches and jumps, and tracing analogies and homologies, rather than by demonstration and sustained argument. The reply to any such objection would be that the concepts of evidence and logic were themselves repressive ideological forces. The admired models of French thought tended to do without them, whilst maintaining a wide intellectual influence.

James Joyce and the Revolution of the Word provides a stimulating performance rather than a coherent argument. To describe a critical book as a 'performance' is common enough, but it begs the question of truth. Marking undergraduate essays and examination papers we give good marks for the cogency, skill, and knowledge with which a position is advanced, not for the extent to which we personally agree with it (I would far rather encounter the lively expression of a position which I do not accept than the dull presentation of one which I do). And what is true of undergraduate work may be broadly true of doctoral theses—which MacCabe's book originally was—since they too are basically enabling exercises, albeit at an advanced level. Do we extend the same liberty to established critics and scholars? Works of scholarship can, of course, be found to be faulty by the criteria of evidence. Criticism is less easily dealt with. A major critic can be 'wrong' in his judgements, as Johnson was on Milton, yet rewardingly perceptive in the way he reaches them. Academic liberals like to think that they can admire and respond to what they disagree with, in terms of its style and performance. Sometimes, however, an absolute 'No!' may be called for, setting the limits to receptive pluralism. It appears that in the 1981 crisis, MacCabe's book and his other writings transgressed those limits. At least, his work provoked a two-hour discussion at the Faculty Board, which Raymond Williams ironically described as 'the first intellectual discussion that I had ever heard on the Faculty Board of English . . . a very serious and engaged debate, although of not very high quality and not particularly well informed.'

One of MacCabe's identified opponents openly took the position that his intellectual approach was in itself a barrier to academic advancement. This was Howard Erskine-Hill, fellow of Jesus College and a respected eighteenth-century scholar. When the affair erupted he declared he was in favour of standing up for the interests of science in the broadest sense, rather than standing up for rhetoric. He uncompromisingly argued that the new approaches with which MacCabe was associated

might be thought to go so far as to deny the relevance of evidence and probability in academic enquiry. It is an extraordinary decadence of literary studies. In so far as that is a question then I think that anybody who encourages that sort of position is not likely to be at the top of the list for an appointment.

On 3 and 4 February 1981 the Cambridge University Senate debated the MacCabe case, and the larger problems of the English Faculty. The transcript of the debate makes good reading, melancholy and diverting in turn. One of its most impressive episodes was the resounding attack on the Faculty Board made by Frank Kermode, the Edward VII Professor of English Literature:

it is extraordinarily longwinded and extraordinarily inept. It is so far from being an effective instrument of administration that it would be fairer to describe it as a forum for the display of stubborn self-regard, and occasionally as an instrument of mischief. It is a great wonder that a body of scholars, some of them very distinguished and the rest presumably at least able, should, on coming together for the purposes of administration (and they come together for virtually no other purpose), present so striking an image of corporate vacuity and vanity.

Stephen Heath, MacCabe's supporter and ally, in his opening speech expressed what he called his sincere belief that, 'in the present conjuncture of interests and struggles the current King Edward VII Professor himself would not have been upgraded.' Kermode undoubtedly had his opponents in the Faculty. Two years before, Erskine-Hill had published an article which called him to account for his dangerous relativism and subjectivism in critical matters. The results of the MacCabe affair for Kermode were radical. Shortly after it he severed his connection with English at Cambridge, resigning his chair to take up a post at Columbia. Looking back at those events in 1985 he still expressed himself with some bitterness: 'Cambridge, of course, is exceptionally hostile to any kind of thought at all, as far as the English Faculty is concerned.' He deplored the state of mind that believed the entire French critical effort could be demolished by simple common sense. MacCabe himself, Kermode told an interviewer, had been the object of bitter opposition for several years: 'People had undertaken as early as 1976 to get rid of him. It wouldn't have mattered if he'd written six wonderful books, instead of one indifferently decent first book.'

Erskine-Hill, for his part, made an impassioned plea in the debate for traditional standards of knowledge and judgement. He said of an unnamed 'recent Cambridge book', 'this strand of structuralism denies the concept of testing. In so far as such positions have found their way into academe they must be regarded merely as a passing folly.' He believed that press reports had greatly exaggerated the bitterness in the Faculty, and called for good will so that it could continue in its academic work. Nevertheless, when one reads through the substantial transcript of the two-day debate the notes of bitterness and bewilderment are inescapable.

Many of the difficulties raised were local and structural, not directly connected with MacCabe, or with matters of literary principle. There were complaints of a disastrous division of responsibilities between Faculty and colleges, and the lack of competent teachers for the ever-growing number of undergraduates who wanted to read English. The temporary nature of assistant lectureships was a further source of discontent. It is evident that academic politics of a fairly fundamental kind were also involved; some of the arguments recalled F. M. Cornford's *Microcosmographica Academica*, published seventy years earlier. It has been suggested that MacCabe's ally, the gallophile Stephen Heath was the real target of the conservatives, though as an established member of the Faculty he could not be easily removed. At the time of the affair Kermode described him as 'one of the truly brilliant people on the Faculty'. Such praise can sound provocative. Heath survived, but he later confessed that the affair had taken up a year of his life. MacCabe came out of it rather better. He moved from Cambridge to the University of Strathclyde in Glasgow, to become the youngest professor of English in the British Isles. After four years he moved on to be a visiting professor in America and Director of Production at the British Film Institute.

One of the most quietly significant contributions to the debate came from John Beer, fellow of Peterhouse and at that time Chairman of the Faculty. His speech was thoughtful, if a little complacent. Beer acknowledged the practical and organizational problems of Cambridge English, but maintained there was nothing wrong with the content of the tripos itself. He then made an interesting concession:

If there are difficulties they lie, I believe, less in the syllabus itself than in certain problems created by the evolution of the Faculty itself over the last sixty years. One can trace at least five layers of interest among our teachers, dating from various periods.

Beer described these five layers, which I summarize in the following way:

1. Traditional scholarship: historical, biographical, linguistic.

2. Close reading, with an implicit human value discovered in the act of reading.

3. The study of literature in its social and cultural contexts.

4. An international approach to literary study, invoking structuralist, poststructuralist, and other foreign critical modes.

5. The aligning of literature with other, more popular modes of signification, notably television and films.

In one sense, such pluralism is admirable, a fine instance of the multiplicity of interests and the free play of mind which one expects in a great university. Yet not all approaches can easily coexist; choices may have to be made, and choices imply exclusions. It is precisely these exclusions which underlie recent and current debates about the nature of English studies. Experienced academics will make their own accommodations among different approaches, but students will find it less easy. What looks like desirable diversity from inside a subject can seem mere fragmentation and incoherence to those outside it, or not very securely within it.

Such was the reaction of some speakers from other disciplines at the Senate Debate, who suggested that faced with such incompatibilities students might suffer a confusion of mind whose effects were not merely intellectual. The point was firmly made by Dr G. H. Wright, a University lecturer in Anatomy, who said he attended because he wanted to raise an issue of more than narrowly professional interest:

I ask for an enquiry into the incidence of breakdown among undergraduates. Ever since my return to Cambridge in 1946 the Faculty of English has seemed to me and to many others to be a relatively unhappy part of our University. One could afford just to be amused, as long as the feuds appeared to affect only the dons: but in recent years there has been disquieting evidence of strain among undergraduates—not the healthy strain of thinking deeply and achieving new understanding, but the destructive strain that leads to mental breakdown, to the need to go away from the University for a year or two, and to a flight from English to another subject. There is an urgent need to find out whether or not there is more such breakdown in the English Faculty than in others. If indeed there is, then we should try to find out if there are identifiable contributory causes within the Faculty.

There is anecdotal and impressionistic evidence to suggest that what Dr Wright found at Cambridge may be true elsewhere. Cambridge had particular problems, though. Long before the MacCabe affair the English Faculty had been divided between the supporters and opponents of F. R. Leavis.

Outside Cambridge popular interest in the affair soon died down, and many people never did find out what structuralism was. For some weeks the *Guardian* ran a generally bad-tempered correspondence about the MacCabe affair and English studies in general, which produced a welter of opinion from all possible positions, including those who thought that English ought not to exist at all as an academic subject. The most thoughtful comment occurred in an editorial in the *Times Higher Education Supplement*, which reflected on the problems facing what it called 'fissiparous disciplines', where there was little or no agreement on fundamentals. (There had been a similar case to MacCabe's, though less publicized, concerning a Cambridge psychology lecturer.) The editorial writer suggested that there were three possible options: (i) to encourage diversity, and thereby risk losing intellectual coherence, with negative implications for the quality of teaching; (ii) to cling to a preferred intellectual doctrine, at the risk of being insular and intolerant; (iii) to accept an institutional split, and so hasten the process of disintegration. The writer acknowledged that all three possibilities were unsatisfactory. Nevertheless it was useful to have the stark choices so clearly described. The implications of this analysis remain relevant, and I shall return to them.

Further bad temper was aroused when a book called *Re-Reading English* appeared in 1982, in the Methuen 'New Accents' series. This was a collection of essays edited by Peter Widdowson of Thames Polytechnic; the contributors were mostly Marxist, or at least of leftist inclination, and they addressed themselves to the problems of defining and teaching literature, the nature of literary canons, and the effect of academic institutionalizing on critical practice. *Re-Reading English* had a generally bad press, but whatever the contributors' biases, and the high level of nonsense in some essays, they were addressing themselves to real issues, which have become exigent since the book first appeared. Widdowson's introduction, it is true, ends on a vulnerably prescriptive note:

'if English is necessarily a site on which social meanings are constructed, and if this has been the case within and on behalf of the dominant ideology, then let it now become such for a materialist poetics.' The last phrase has lately become a common coded term for 'Marxist readings of literature'. What does not emerge from Widdowson's book, and from later works written from a similar position, is how the Marxist teacher reckons to deal with the student who is consciously committed to the 'dominant ideology'—through impenetrable false consciousness—and believes in the virtues of the market economy and parliamentary democracy. Elsewhere, though, a more tentative note emerges, particularly in the essay by Tony Davies, who nicely presents the familiar predicament of the literature teacher:

Whatever I write or think, however pure, rigorous and systematic my discourse may be on such occasions, when once again I sit down to tutorial or seminar, with *Lycidas* or *Middlemarch* open in front of me, and turn, in that expectant pause, to the surrounding faces, what comes out of my mouth then is likely to sound, by the highest standards of discursive rigour, decidedly limp: 'Well, what do you think of this, then?'

A recurring theme in the book is the ideological desirability of shifting the emphasis of literature teaching from individual texts and authors to larger matters: the problematical nature of literature as a constructed entity, and the historical and cultural forces which determine it. Davies has the honesty to admit that however desirable such a shift may be in theory, in practice it is unlikely to occur: 'it is extraordinarily difficult to imagine, still more to imagine *teaching*, a literature syllabus whose points of reference are not textual and authorial.' Conflicts between the desirable and the feasible emerge at intervals in the book, as though it invited its own deconstruction.

In June 1982 *Re-Reading English* was fiercely attacked in the *London Review of Books* by the Ulster poet and Nottingham academic, Tom Paulin, who produced some good polemical phrases—one contributor, Anthony Easthope, was said to make the experience of reading a sonnet by Sidney sound like a spell in a forced-labour camp—but never seriously confronted its arguments. Paulin's final comment was, 'culture must be in a terminal condition when teachers of English preach the destruction of their discipline and offer little more than attitudinizing in its place.' Paulin's rage was not rooted in any definable critical position. Although upholding a traditionalist approach to English Studies, he took the opportunity at the end of his piece to dismiss with contempt another recent book, of a quite different persuasion from *Re-Reading English*. This was Ian McGilchrist's *Against Criticism*, a carefully argued attack on the concept of critical theory, which on the face of it Paulin might have been expected to sympathize with, as subsequent correspondents pointed out. But on this occasion there was no pleasing him. His review provoked a sustained and tetchy correspondence in the *London Review of Books*, written from many points of view, though none of them wholly favourable to Paulin. Some letters were from contributors to, or admirers of, *Re-Reading English*, defending the book. Some agreed with Paulin's attack on Widdowson's book, but defended McGilchrist. Others disliked both *Re-Reading English* and Paulin's way of dealing with it. Paulin himself wrote in to condemn what he called 'institutionalized nihilism', and argued that English needed to become 'a rigorous and dryer subject, like history: otherwise, it will disintegrate into a flabby and monstrous non-subject.'

Widdowson had the last word in a long and eloquent letter. What Paulin wrote, Widdowson tolerantly observed, 'was not, of course, a review at all: rather it was an exhibition of his own deepest hopes and fears.' Paulin's deepest hope, Widdowson concluded, was to become a successful man of letters; his fear was that *Re-Reading English* might stop that happening. After more in this knockabout vein, Widdowson turned to the practical implications of his book:

A number of points arise here—directed more to those who have supported us in these columns than to the paranoid few. First of all, there should be a much fuller exploration of what we have in mind to replace a moribund 'English'. Is it 'Cultural Studies', or 'Media and Communication Studies', as people keep darkly hinting? Is it an 'alternative canon'? Is it the existing canon differently 'read' and 'taught'? What is meant by a 'socialist pedagogy'? What is a 'materialist criticism'? These questions demand discussion.

One might have thought they demanded answers, not just discussion. Here the crisp prescriptions of Widdowson's introduction give way to the limpness that Tony Davies acknowledges. The discussion is presumably still continuing, for no firm answers have yet emerged.

In December 1982 another attack on *Re-Reading English* appeared, this time by Claude Rawson in the *Times Literary Supplement*. It was more precise than Paulin's. Rawson pressed hard on the book's implicit contradiction between aim and possibility, finding it enacted in the wavering and orotund style of some contributions, where there was a 'note of self-doubt, rattled bossiness thrashing about in an intellectual void'. Rawson's attacks on what he called the 'billowings of sheer untalented modishness' in the weaker contributions went home, though I believe he was too hard on the book overall. He does at one point acknowledge that there are things wrong with the current state of English, referring to 'symptoms of a disorientation none of us has any right to be complacent about, though we might murmur, perhaps with more hope than conviction, that "it's not all like that".' Rawson added that whatever was wrong was not likely to be put right by Widdowson's contributors, and that such books made a principled defence of the humanities harder to sustain. Unlike Paulin's, this review did not provoke much correspondence, though Anthony Easthope wrote to the *TLS* to complain of Rawson's 'liberal paternalism', now unmasked as sheer authoritarianism. The review did, however, have a curious aftermath.

Nicolas Tredell contributed a review of *Re-Reading English* to *PN Review*, which was as unfavourable as Paulin's and Rawson's but more measured in its tone and careful in its analysis. The book, he concluded, 'does not, as its proponents naively imagine, break with the supposedly repressive critical discourses of the past; it maintains and extends them. It is a continuation of hegemony by other means.' But Tredell agreed that it represented a challenge to liberal humanists which must be met. He developed his argument in a subsequent article in the magazine, 'The Politicization of English', which provoked another letter from Easthope. This remarked, in passing, that Rawson's *TLS* review of *Re-Reading English* was the second to have been commissioned, an earlier one having been suppressed as too favourable. The editor of the *TLS*, Jeremy Treglown, when asked for a comment, denied, with supporting evidence, any hostility to the Newest Criticism in general. The earlier review of *Re-Reading English*, had, he insisted, been turned down because it was 'irredeemably weakly argued and badly written'. In a later issue the author of that original review, Roger Poole, wrote to give his side of the question. His view of *Re-Reading English* had, he said, been very favourable as far as the book's analysis of the state of English was concerned, though he rejected the contributors' mostly Marxist conclusions and prescriptions. He was convinced that his review had been rejected, not because it was badly written, but because it was ideologically unacceptable. The correspondence ran and ran, with further contributions from the irrepressible Easthope; in a subsequent letter Poole described the changes made in his typescript before it was returned to him, which, he argued, were of an ideological rather than a stylistic nature. Regarding the evidence as dispassionately as possible, I would say that Poole's case looks stronger than that of the *TLS*. We are not likely to know the truth, unless one day, far in the future, it emerges in someone's literary memoirs. But the point of the story, if it has one, is not the truth about a minor scandal and mystery, but the revelation that such seemingly abstruse matters as critical theory and literary education should have so much blood in them.

Nineteen eighty-two also saw a sharp and more intellectually significant confrontation between two eminent senior scholars: Frank Kermode and the late Dame Helen Gardner, formerly Merton Professor at Oxford. In that year she published *In Defence of the Imagination*, which included the Charles Eliot Norton lectures she had delivered at Harvard in 1978–9. The book made a fighting defence of liberal humanism, as Helen Gardner understood it. In her opening chapter she presented herself as a 'kind of literary Rip Van Winkle': for about ten years, because of the pressure of professorial duties and scholarly commitments, she had fallen behind in reading academic journals and critical books, other than those on Donne and Eliot. After her retirement from the Merton chair, and the easing of other burdens, she began to catch up on recent critical writing, only to find herself in a 'strange disturbing world', where there was an extraordinary new vocabulary, ransacked from other disciplines like linguistics, psychology, philosophy, and theology, or loosely coined from Latin and Greek. There were also words which the critic 'had made up for his own pleasure in a mood of high spirits or "playfulness", a word which for some appeared to be a synonym for critical activity.' More serious were the abolition of the author as the creator of a text, and the denial of the text's objective status. Instead, the 'reader' became paramount, an abstraction covering an infinitude of readers, all generating different readings endlessly. Not liking this new world, Helen Gardner went to attack it, with a series of polite but damaging onslaughts on named opponents: critics such as Frank Kermode, Stanley Fish, and Harold Bloom; and theatre directors of Shakespeare such as Peter Brook and John Barton. Gardner's impatient polemics are enjoyable, but her aim is frequently wayward. One of Rip Van Winkle's difficulties in waking in an unfamiliar world would have been in recognizing and understanding what he was looking at. Where strange critical approaches were concerned, Gardner was more concerned to hit out than to comprehend.

Her attack on Kermode had a certain piquancy, since it was largely directed at *The Genesis of Secrecy*, which comprised the Norton Lectures he had delivered at Harvard the year before she gave hers (though she also gave unfavourable attention to things in his earlier books). Reviewing Gardner's book in the *TLS*, Denis Donoghue expressed unease at the decorum of a distinguished lecturer attacking her equally distinguished immediate predecessor from the same platform. But Howard Erskine-Hill wrote to the paper, applauding Helen Gardner's defence of her discipline, saying that where fundamental values were at stake it was right to override the fear of indecorum. Events in Cambridge the previous year were still sending out ripples, and Helen Gardner's objections to Kermode were substantially the same as those earlier addressed by Erskine-Hill: that his criticism lacked objective values and was disablingly sceptical and relativistic. She also accused him of inaccuracies in his reading of St Mark's gospel as a narrative. Kermode, she remarked, 'has a very strong

sense of his own historical position and makes many statements about what "we" today must necessarily feel and
think.' This is true of critics other than Kermode; Lionel
Trilling was much given to using the first person plural, and
the usage suggests a reaching from isolation towards an idea
of community rather than any certainty that such a community exists. Gardner makes a fair point about Kermode as a
critic when she refers to his historical self-consciousness. This
is evident in the 'Prologue' to his *Essays on Fiction 1971–82*,
where Kermode looks back with nostalgic pleasure at the
seminars on structuralism which he conducted at University
College London, in the early seventies, as if they took place in
some remote vanished era. A sense of rapid periodization is,
in fact, common in recent critical theory. Kermode remarks
that his *The Sense of an Ending*, published in 1967, suffered
because it was written in ignorance of structuralism: 'I
remember feeling rather dismally that quite a lot of work had
gone into a book which became antediluvian almost on
publication.' This is to take far too historicist a view of one's
own career, or to assimilate intellectual developments to
technological ones. *The Sense of an Ending* remains an acute
and suggestive study of the nature of narrative, and in no
sense 'antediluvian'.

In this same 'Prologue' Kermode looks in an informed but
moderate way at recent critical developments, notably deconstruction. His remarks on the subject are fair-minded, making
it clear that he is not a deconstructionist, and giving good
reasons for not being so. The contrast with the panicky and
ill-informed attack in Gardner's book is heavily in Kermode's
favour. He made a detailed reply to her charges, but did so,
perversely or quixotically, in *Raritan*, an American quarterly
with few readers in England. So the opinion persisted that
Kermode's reputation had been in some sense demolished:
The Times, for instance, said he had been reduced to 'a heap
of cardboard ruins'. His article, called 'On Being an Enemy
of Humanity', is both a solid defence and a stylish polemic,
more effective than Gardner's because more exact and
directed. He begins by saying he had been reluctant to read
In Defence of the Imagination, partly because of the calibre of its
admirers: 'I confess to doubting that a book capable of

eliciting the unstinted admiration of Peter Conrad can be worth reading, and Erskine-Hill's communication only made me wonder at Shakespeare's genius in coining, so far in advance of its imperative occasion, the epithet "forcible-feeble".' Nevertheless, he finally agreed to read it on being told by a London editor that it appeared to have left him covered in blood. In the rest of the article he goes on to show that Gardner misunderstood many of the things she wrote about with so much confidence: not only deconstruction, but hermeneutics, and much of Kermode's own argument; he refers to 'Dame Helen's curious tactic of admitting that she knows very little about a subject before making authoritative pronouncements about it.' Gardner had claimed that Kermode's understanding of scriptural exegesis is faulty; he rebuffs her charges and makes a vehement counter-attack:

> To be blunt, everything she says about my treatment of types and testimonies is either superfluous or false . . . the whole parade of superior learning and wisdom is comically shabby and in the end I thought I should wash off the stage blood and say so.

Apart from the particular points at issue between Gardner and Kermode, one notices an element of contradiction in her argument, concerning the extent to which plurality.of interpretation is admissible, a question about which Gardner was, I believe, always uncertain. There are places in *In Defence of the Imagination* where she seems to want to tie interpretation to a particular, given historical meaning. But she concludes her chapter on Kermode by asserting:

> If it were really possible for 'interpretation' to arrive at a final, completely adequate interpretation of the 'meaning' of an imaginative text, or fiction, the text would be no longer worth reading. Its meaning must always lie beyond an interpreter's power, if it is to retain its power over the imagination.

Kermode seizes on this uncertainty of aim and uses it to point to a larger lack of direction in the lectures:

> I sometimes suspect that apart from a general intention to give me and some other wretches a bad time she is not altogether clear what she *is* trying to do. I felt this particularly when she announced, as if in opposition to me, that 'The interpreter can cast light here and there . . . but he can never become the text's master.' Of course! Yet it is for expounding this view and for trying to explore its implications that my book so offends her.

Apart from the particular arguments, there is a clash of world-views and of temperaments. Kermode's temperament, particularly as expressed in *The Genesis of Secrecy*, is undoubtedly sceptical and relativistic, in a Montaigne-like way, whereas Gardner inclines to impatient, bracing cheerfulness. In the first of her lectures, she remarks briskly, 'Those afflicted by the difficulty of arriving at ultimate answers to large general questions about the universe might benefit by taking to heart the advice Sidney Smith gave to melancholics: "Take short views".' Such attitudes are familiar enough in the academic environment which Gardner inhabited. It takes some discernment to see in them just where a sensible empiricism ends and an insular philistinism begins. Gardner objects to Kermode's 'final cheerless conclusion', in *The Genesis of Secrecy*, 'that books, like the world, are "hopelessly plural, endlessly disappointing".' Gardner was an Anglican used to seeing a decent order in things, and no doubt had good personal reasons for disliking this attitude. Kermode is an agnostic; yet a sense of reality as 'hopelessly plural, endlessly disappointing' could accommodate itself to the religious vision of Ecclesiastes or Pascal's *Pensées*.

The bitterness of the early eighties has to be seen as a sign or symptom of unprecedented strain in literary education. It is a commonplace that scholarly arguments can be extremely fierce, and may become wounding. Yet they were traditionally played, however fiercely, according to agreed rules; in Wittgenstein's terms, within a shared form of life. If tempers sometimes rose high, and there were fouls and infringements, it was still evident what rules were being broken. Recent conflicts in the academic study of literature resemble the anger and confusion that would arise if a group of players found themselves on a field, without any agreement as to whether they were playing rugby or soccer or hockey or baseball; or some other game, whose precise nature and rules were still slowly emerging; or no game at all, with the added implication that the whole concept of games was an empty one. In such a situation common-sense injunctions to stop all the arguing and simply get on with the game are likely to sound unhelpful or even stupid.

3. FOUNDATIONS

I

In its origins 'English' was, and remains, a synthetic subject, comprising several elements. A large university English department will contain experts on many things; from, as the phrase goes, *Beowulf* to Virginia Woolf; from Icelandic sagas to black women poets; from Elizabethan stagecraft to post-structuralist narratology. From time to time, areas have dropped away from English departments, to pursue their own autonomy, as has happened with linguistics, theatre studies, and, most recently, with film studies. Nevertheless, the diversity of what goes on in English departments is, I believe, greater than in other academic areas. Many teachers, however, still have a loose sense of what is involved in the basic pedagogy of the subject, at least in undergraduate teaching. This might be roughly described as the close reading of texts, inserted in a literary-historical-biographical continuum. Syntheses, like coalition governments, can have a long life, provided there is a general agreement about keeping them together. In recent years the English synthesis has been increasingly under strain, with the bitter consequences described in the previous Chapter.

The word 'English' in itself conveys potent emotions, but has no immediately obvious referent. It can refer to (i) a nation, (ii) a language, (iii) a literature, (iv) an academic subject. England is the largest of the ancient nations comprising the British Isles, or the North-West European Archipelago; or, more narrowly, the United Kingdom of Great Britain and Northern Ireland. Foreigners, of course, persist in using 'English' as synonymous with 'British', but it should mean something more specific. English national identity exists, if in less intense and historically conscious forms than Irish or Scottish or Welsh; indeed, one constituent of it may have been the continuing effort to subdue the weaker neighbouring nations. Sense (i) of 'English' now refers to the nation as a cultural rather than a political entity, but it keeps a specific reference. This is not at all true of sense (ii). The English language developed in Britain over the centuries as a blend of Teutonic and Latinate elements, simple in grammar, complex in idiom, and perverse in phonology and orthography; it has now become, not altogether suitably, the world's first global language, universally studied and spoken in one form or another. It is the first language of a dozen or so countries, the second language of many more; the medium used by international congresses and airline pilots, by Japanese tourists travelling in Italy and Polish engineers working in Sweden. The situation, dangerously convenient for the British, arises from the growth of American power and not from any intrinsic qualities of the language.

How, then, does sense (iii), as in 'English Literature', relate to a small, ancient nation and a global language? It is a complex relation. The literature has always extended beyond narrowly English national identity, since Irish and Scottish writers have contributed so much to it. That they are included in it can be seen—has been seen—as an act of imperialistic appropriation, but if so, it is one that the objects of it have found convenient. A minimal definition might be that English Literature is the literature in English of the various peoples of the British Isles. One says 'in English' so as to exclude work in Gaelic and Welsh. Even so, too much might be left out. Anglo-Saxon keeps a prominent place in many English departments, under the tendentious title of Old English, though it is no more like modern English than Dutch. And what of the work of the cosmopolitan medieval poet, John Gower, who wrote in English, French, and Latin? Or the Latin poetry of the Renaissance humanists? Or Milton's writing in Italian, and Wilde's and Eliot's in French? Definitions finally break down with Samuel Beckett, who belongs simultaneously to English, Irish, and French literature. And there are the texts written in other countries, in other languages, that have somehow adhered to 'English', such as the plays by Sophocles and Racine and Ibsen which are often included (in translation) in drama courses. It is evident that 'English Literature' is an unstable, if substantial, concept,

and has become far more so since the language burst the
bounds of a single nation, or a particular geographical region.

Sense (iv) of English, as the name of an academic area,
includes aspects of the other usages, in ambiguous or confus-
ing ways. This usage is of quite recent origin, recorded in the
Supplement to the *Oxford English Dictionary* as first occurring
in 1889, when the subject itself was appearing on the cultural
map. The history of English as an academic discipline has
been well documented since Stephen Potter's pioneering
work, *The Muse in Chains*, came out in 1937. There have been
a number of useful books, including interesting recent work
by Marxists, who tend to see the establishment of 'English' as
the imposition of cultural unity at the expense of class
solidarity. Given the existence of these studies, I shall not
provide a historical recapitulation of the growth of the subject,
though it may be useful to set down a few salient dates and
events. An important figure in its prehistory, well before the
concept of 'English' had emerged, was Hugh Blair, professor
of rhetoric and *belles-lettres* at Edinburgh University in the late
eighteenth century; his *Lectures on Rhetoric and Belles-Lettres*,
first published in 1784, became an influential textbook. The
first chair of English proper was established at University
College London, in 1828 (to be held by a 'language' man,
who regarded literature with hostility). This was followed by
chairs at other London colleges, and at provincial universities
as they developed later in the nineteenth century; the study
of English Literature was often combined with other 'national'
subjects, such as history, geography, or philosophy, demanding diverse skills from the original professors. An Honour
School of English Language and Literature was established
at Oxford in 1893, with a strong linguistic bias to make the
subject seem intellectually respectable. Sir Walter Raleigh
became the first Merton Professor of English Literature, and
Sir Arthur Quiller-Couch was appointed to the Regius chair
in the subject at Cambridge in 1912, though the Cambridge
English Tripos was not finally launched until 1917, and did
not cover both parts of the degree until the mid-1920s.

I believe that five constituents, separate but clearly inter-
twined, can be traced in the historical emergence of 'English',
sense (iv). They are the nationalistic, the religious, the ethical,

the aesthetic, and the rhetorical. I shall make brief comments on each in turn.

II

To British-born English-speakers the study of the literature of their own language might seem the most natural thing in the world. But the process whereby the classical texts of English literature replaced, or at least complemented, the classics of Greece and Rome as a major constituent of humanistic education was argued warmly and at length. It was part of a major change in the landscape of European culture from the eighteenth century onwards, when vernacular literature became a powerful instrument in forming national consciousness. Patrick Parrinder has observed of Johnson's Dictionary, 'Johnson implicitly connects the genius of our language and literature to the "spirit of English liberty". The emergence of the modern sense of "literature" is indeed part of the rise of cultural nationalism.' Isaiah Berlin has summarized Herder's thinking on national culture in these words:

what German epic poetry has in common with German family life, or German legislation, or German grammar, determines the pattern of these activities—runs through them more deeply—than that which German poetry has in common with Hindu or Hebrew poetry.

The association of vernacular literature with national aspiration, and sometimes with a sense of sacred mission, was most marked in those countries where national sentiment was subject to foreign oppression. I encountered this vividly on a recent visit to Poland. In the crypt of Cracow cathedral, itself part of the ancient palace of the Polish kings, one finds the huge stone tombs of the two great poets, Mickiewicz and Slowacki, who rest there in an ambience of sainthood. Here the literary, the patriotic, and the religious are brought into a single focus. Poets' Corner in Westminster Abbey offers a far weaker gesture of a similar kind. English rhetoric on the subject may have been more subdued than Continental European, but the emergence, in consciousness and institutions, of English Literature was an act of cultural nationalism.

Charles Kingsley said that English literature was the autobiography of a nation, and F. D. Maurice, Professor of English
at King's College, London, wrote, 'we cannot safely separate
our literary pursuits, even our literary recreations, from the
history and life of our nation.' Gerard Manley Hopkins made
the point more pungently: 'A great work by an Englishman is
like a great battle won by England.'

Cultural nationalism pervades a remarkable Government
publication of 1921, *The Teaching of English in England*, usually
known as the 'Newbolt Report', from the name of the
chairman of the committee which produced it, the patriotic
poet, Sir Henry Newbolt, famous as the author of 'Drake's
Drum'. The report was the outcome of a particular historical
circumstance: it had been commissioned during the First
World War, and prompted by a patriotic concern with
national unity. (It shows, too, a harsh animus against the
supposed excesses of Germanic scholarship.) It also represents the culmination of several major Victorian tendencies: a
Wordsworthian commitment to joy and an Arnoldian belief
in the value of poetry; a conviction that English should
replace Classics as a humanistic discipline (though without
involving their total disappearance), and that teachers of
English are missionaries with a heavy and unique cultural
responsibility. In the Report the 'nationalistic' and the 'religious' elements in the English synthesis are interwoven.

Its introduction invokes Arnold in the sentiment that
'Culture unites classes', and is confident that English can play
a central unifying role; for this reason the Report has been
denounced by Marxists, who see it as instrumental in helping
to avert revolution in England. Although the Report is mostly
written in the bureaucratic prose normal in such productions,
the tone regularly rises to quasi-mystical flights; underlying
the rational, earnest proposals about the teaching of English
in schools, colleges, and universities, is a sense of the sacred
unity of English language, literature, and speech, bringing
together the separate senses of 'English' described above:
'English is not merely the medium of our thought, it is the
very stuff and process of it. It is itself the English mind, the
element in which we live and work.' The following longer
extract shows the Report's rhetoric at its least inhibited:

To every child in this country, there is one language with which he must necessarily be familiar and by that, and by that alone, he has the power of drawing directly from one of the great literatures of the world. Moreover, if we explore the course of English literature, if we consider from what sources its stream has sprung, by what tributaries it has been fed, and with how rich and full a current it has come down to us, we shall see that it has other advantages not to be found elsewhere. There are mingled in it, as only in the greatest of rivers there could be mingled, the fertilising influences flowing down from many countries and from many ages of history. Yet all of these have been subdued to form a stream native to our own soil. The flood of diverse human experience which it brings down to our own life and time is in no sense or degree foreign to us, but has become the native experience of men of our own race and culture.

The fluvial metaphor is remarkably sustained, but it invites a deconstructive reading. Rivers are notable images of flux, carrying everything without discrimination away to the sea. Time, like an ever-rolling stream, bears all its sons away. The watery element is insubstantial, and Keats dreaded the oblivion of one whose name had been 'writ in water'.

There is an Arnoldian element in the Report's conviction that certain things are better ordered in France. It admires the way the French have made their language and literature a focus of pride and national unity, and urges the English to take their own literary heritage with equal seriousness. The main thrust is directed at the teaching of English, particularly in schools. The responsibility of the teacher of English is twofold. One aspect is to foster a love of literature; the other is to teach the pupil to write clearly, forcibly, and correctly. The concern with literature was continued and amplified by later developments, notably at Cambridge in the 1920s and 1930s; the Report's ideas were taken up by *Scrutiny*, though in a different idiom, modernist rather than late-Romantic, Eliotic rather than Wordsworthian. An emphasis on the purity and intensity of English experience can be found in the Scrutineer John Speirs, and the latter-day Leavisite, Ian Robinson. But the approach to language teaching now seems remote. It is openly prescriptive, inspired by an ideal of correct speech and writing as an embodiment of national unity which seems to derive from the French model. We are now sceptical of such an approach, given the non-prescriptive bias of modern linguistics and our sense that the ideals of correctness in language are at best relative. Still, some of the Report's proposals seem pragmatically sensible, even if they are not in line with current educational theory, such as the recommendation that schoolchildren should be taught standard speech and that dialect-users should be bilingual, not for reasons of social superiority, but to ensure mutual intelligibility between speakers from different regions. The historical context is relevant. During the First World War British soldiers from different parts of the country had difficulty in understanding each other.

The Report was prescient in recognizing that English was already on the way to becoming an international language, with a corresponding need for general intelligibility. It did not, however, face the implications that the internationalizing of the language would have for its central concept of English as a mystical fusion of nation, language, and literature. Throughout the Report the approaches to language and literature tend to pull in different directions, and its nationalism is very provincial. It does at one point acknowledge the perplexing possibility that English literature might be written outside England, that is, in America, but postpones possible difficulty by referring to American literature as something no doubt potentially interesting and important, but which did not yet exist. This was at a time when the canon of classical American literature, now studied throughout the world, had long been in existence. Though, to be fair, Americans had not yet recognized it either.

III

As I have said, the Report was marked by a religious as well as a nationalistic view of English, though it did not advance it so openly. The religious dimension of literary study is a larger, vaguer concept, harder to define and locate in history. It is so large that in the present context I shall deliberately treat it briefly in order to treat it at all. One can say that at some time in the eighteenth century the human imagination and the emotions associated with it began to assume a semi-divine power and authority, in ways explored and commemorated by the major Romantics, and in our own day by

Wallace Stevens: 'We say God and the imagination are one.' Imagination, and poetry, in which it was manifested, did not necessarily exclude religion; it could supplement or revivify it, as in some strands of European Romanticism. But increasingly poetry was thought of as having the power to provide the emotions associated with the receding Sea of Faith. Nineteenth-century literature provides many examples: one of the most famous is John Stuart Mill's account of how Wordsworth's poetry helped him in a major crisis of his life. In latter-day language, it provided great therapeutic support in dealing with a nervous breakdown brought on by the aridities of rationalism and utilitarian thought. Mill's language recalls that of traditional religious experience, but his solace did not come from supernatural sources. It came from poetry: not from the doctrine contained in the poetry, as a believer might find in reading Dante or George Herbert, but from the imaginative power of the poetry itself. Matthew Arnold argued in *Literature and Dogma* that what was valuable about religion was its poetry, and in his late essay, 'The Study of Poetry' he set down a celebrated statement of the attitude I am considering:

More and more mankind will discover that we have to turn to poetry to interpret life for us, to console us, to sustain us. Without poetry, our science will appear incomplete; and most of what now passes with us for religion and philosophy will be replaced by poetry.

The 'most of what now passes' was a prudential qualification, allowing for the possibility that *true* religion and philosophy, whatever they might be, could retain their status unaffected. But this apparent concession is no more than an Arnoldian stylistic trick: the purport of his argument is clear enough. In 1926, in the new Cambridge English School, I. A. Richards quoted Arnold's words as the epigraph to his *Science and Poetry*. Richards re-expressed Arnold's sentiment in his own terser words; in an age when religious belief was fading and science had become dominant, 'Poetry can save us'.

Few apologists for literature have been as explicit as Arnold and Richards. The Newbolt Report, for instance, nowhere suggests that imaginative literature has taken the place of religion, or should do so. It would have been a most imprudent suggestion. Yet the Report often uses religious, or

religiose, language and imagery. It discusses the responsibilities of the professors of English Literature in the expanding
or newly founded provincial universities. In an echo of
Coleridge's Clerisy, each of them is to be 'an ambassador of
poetry in every important capital of industrialism in the
country.' They are to be missionaries as well as ambassadors,
and will need 'propaganda work, organization and the building up of a staff of assistant missionaries.' But the foremost
need is a right attitude of mind, a conviction that literature
and life are inseparable, that literature is not just a subject
for academic study, but 'one of the chief temples of the human
spirit, in which all should worship.' It was this aspect of the
Report that George Gordon, Merton Professor at Oxford,
singled out for attack in his inaugural lecture in 1923:

I observe, and not only in this Report, the growth of a religious jargon
about literature and literary genius, and I observe it with regret as an
affront to life. We must be modest to be believed. Here in Oxford we have
plenty to do without saving the State.

Scrutiny, which was launched in the early 1930s, represented
the convergence of lines drawn from Arnold, Richards, and
the Newbolt Report. Attitudes to religion were mixed at
Scrutiny. Leavis seems to have been somewhat anti-christian,
and his wife more so; but a number of contributors were
believing Christians, including Catholics such as James
Smith, Martin Turnell, and Derek Traversi, and Anglicans
such as George Every. The division, not exacting in critical
practice, lay between those who found the values espoused by
Scrutiny to be sufficient for the conduct of life, and those who
found them to be insufficient, but pointing in the right
direction; that is, towards transcendence. L. C. Knights, a
generally tough-minded Scrutineer and an agnostic, engaged
in quasi-mystical praise of the creative power of the imagination in the contribution he made in 1963 to a *TLS* symposium:
'as a unifying power it simultaneously works towards the
integrity and wholeness of the person and the creation of a
cosmos from the world of mere experience which, without it,
would remain fragmentary and deceptive'. For Leavis, the
modern world was ravaged by industrialism and utilitarianism, and many connections with the traditional, life-
sustaining, organic order of human existence had been
severed. Yet imaginative literature remained to preserve the

values that were threatened by social and scientific innovation; so, the study of literature, or, in other words, literary criticism, remained a supremely important activity. In *Revaluation* Leavis uses the word 'religious' to refer to the values he sees as ultimate, in a discussion of Wordsworth which also invokes Lawrence. In his later criticism it frequently recurs in discussion of the two major canonical authors, Blake and Lawrence. One recalls Paul Tillich's assurance that the 'religious' is whatever is of ultimate concern to one. It is a matter of fundamental seriousness, the seriousness with which Wordsworth in the 1800 Preface to the *Lyrical Ballads* reprobated those who would indulge a 'taste' for poetry 'as if it were a thing as indifferent as a taste for rope-dancing or Frontiniac, or sherry.'

IV

The religious concept of literature, and of the life of the imagination, is a product of Romanticism. What I call the ethical concept is, by contrast, ancient, as well as simple. It was fundamental to the classical humanism which the study of vernacular literature has so largely displaced. Virtuous behaviour was learnt by contemplating and imitating the conspicuous images of virtue to be found in great poets. It could also be learnt from philosophers and historians, who, together with poets, were traditionally studied in the Oxford School of Literae Humaniores. But as Philip Sidney observed, poetry—by which he meant more than metrical composition—was more doctrinal than history and more specific than philosophy. Sidney described poetry as providing notable images of virtues and vices, to be followed or shunned, but in either event learnt from. The ethical conception of literature was mimetic, whereas the religious and aesthetic conceptions were expressive. The former underlay the art and poetry of the Renaissance, and presupposed Christian belief, though often in a muddled or contradictory fashion, as in revenge tragedy. The High Renaissance was prepared to find doctrinal lessons as well as a dangerous beauty in the coexistence of pagan imagery and Christian truth, though in ways that regularly scandalized Christian moralists, Catholic or Protestant. Milton, in the 'Nativity Hymn', sadly concluded that the nymphs and gods had to go, while Browning in 'The Bishop Orders His Tomb in Saint Praxed's Church' is fascinated by the enormity of the juxtaposition. Later in English culture it declined into the incongruous spectacle of Anglican clergymen flogging a knowledge of pagan antiquity into recalcitrant schoolboys.

In principle, the ethical poetics of Renaissance humanism were sustained by the Horatian precept of *dulce et utile*, where the reward of learning was a sober sweetness, of a more restrained order than Wordsworthian joy or Barthesian *jouissance*. The Newbolt Report is predominantly inspired by the Romantic-religious model of poetic value, but there are places where the ethical-mimetic one makes an appearance:

> Good poetry does undoubtedly tend to form the soul and character; it tends to beget a love of beauty and of truth in alliance together, it suggests, however, indirectly, high and noble principles of action, and it inspires the emotion so helpful in making principles operative.

The classical ideals survived to form a lesser but by no means unimportant strand in the English synthesis, particularly in invocations of the moral power of literature.

V

The emergence of the 'aesthetic' as a distinct concept in the late eighteenth century, at approximately the same time as cultural nationalism, was a major innovation in European thought. One of the most direct approaches to it is via Schiller's letters on aesthetic education, where the aesthetic represents an ideal of liberation from the demands of physical necessity and moral law:

> In the midst of the fearful kingdom of forces, and in the midst of the sacred kingdom of laws, the aesthetic impulse to form is at work, unnoticed, on the building of a third joyous kingdom of play and of semblance, in which man is relieved of the shackles of circumstance, and released from all that might be called constraint, alike in the physical and the moral sphere.

Schiller's elevated sentiments suggest political utopian possibilities rather than the retreat from the world characteristic of late-nineteenth-century aesthetes. Elsewhere he emphasizes the value of form in words that have been often echoed in discussions of aesthetics and critical theory: 'In a truly successful work of art the contents should effect nothing, the form everything; for only through form is the whole man affected, through the subject-matter, by contrast, only one or other of his functions.'

In the criticism and teaching of literature we have become accustomed to thinking in terms of formal harmony and, in Coleridge's words, of the coexistence of unusual order and unusual diversity. The literary text is a work of art, an aesthetic monad, a verbal icon or well-wrought urn for contemplation rather than instruction or impulsion to action. The word 'beauty' is no longer used much, but harmony, unity, order are acceptable substitutes. Wellek and Warren provide a succinct statement of the ideal in their *Theory of Literature*:

In a successful work of art, the materials are completely assimilated into the form: what was 'world' has become 'language'. The 'materials' of a literary work of art are, on one level, words, on another level human behaviour experience [*sic*], and on another, human ideas and attitudes. All of these, including language, exist outside the work of art, in other modes; but in a successful poem or novel they are pulled into polyphonic relations by the dynamics of aesthetic purpose.

Such sentiments, or something like them, still underlie the practical activity, particularly in teaching, of many academics who would be uneasy about explicitly invoking them. A conservative academic such as Helen Gardner, who was suspicious of the New Criticism for its lack of historicity, had no hesitation about appealing to what she called 'the receptiveness and disinterestedness which are the conditions of aesthetic experience'.

For purposes of analysis I have treated separately foundational categories which have different historical and cultural origins, but which usually coexist and overlap. Indeed, readers and teachers often proceed with unselfconscious and confident eclecticism, invoking the 'Englishness' of a poem here, the affective power of its language (in short, its beauty) there, its moral insight elsewhere. However natural such an approach seems, we have to recognize that the four categories

I have so far examined are all involved with values. These values are no longer accepted by many readers, and have been specifically rejected by some participants in recent debates about the discipline of English. I return to the implications of this rejection in due course. Meanwhile, I should add that though I have described these strands in a spirit of deliberate detachment, this does not mean that I do not have my own adherencies among them.

VI

The fifth category, the rhetorical, is, in comparison, straightforward. At the very least, it is not so obviously involved in questions of value as the preceding ones. I interpret it as referring to the close study and analysis of the verbal and structural elements of texts. Gerard Manley Hopkins provided an admirable definition in a letter: 'By rhetoric I mean all the common and teachable element in literature, what grammar is to speech, what thoroughbase is to music, what theatrical experience gives to playwrights.' Rhetoric as a concept and practice goes back to antiquity, and existed long before the idea of imaginative literature emerged; its original object was oratory and other forms of public discourse. It dealt with effects and how they were achieved, and the assumption was that the process was deliberate and could be studied and learnt. Hugh Blair's Edinburgh lectures on rhetoric made an important early contribution to the development of English as an academic subject; they were widely read and studied; not only in Britain but also, as Gerald Graff has pointed out, in the United States. Alastair Fowler has said, 'Blair's lectures discussed good style and attempted close description (in effect, "practical criticism") of texts of many kinds—including histories, sermons and legal orations as well as poetry. He served his society's needs by encouraging clear expression . . .'. In so far as Blair anticipated later developments they would have been in comparative or general literature rather than in English, for he examined passages in Greek, Latin, French, and Italian as well as English. He was an excellent close reader, but his interest was in devices rather than value; this much is apparent if one compares his treatment of particular passages with Arnold's approach to his 'touchstones'.

Rhetorical analysis is not the same as literary criticism, and has a much larger subject-matter. There is, though, a substantial overlap. One fruitful development of the work of Richards in *Practical Criticism* was the application of rhetorical techniques to the textual artefacts of mass culture as carried out by Leavis and Thompson in *Culture and Environment*. Rhetorical analysis of culture does not restrict itself to writing; it can be readily applied to visual and other signifying modes, as was done by Roland Barthes in his *Mythologies*, and in much recent work on mass culture.

Hopkins's definition of rhetoric as the 'common and teachable element in literature' has been taken up in creative writing programmes, despite their misleading title. Creativity cannot be taught, but rhetoric can. As a teachable operational device, rhetoric is always potentially in conflict with the post-Romantic religious and aesthetic perspectives, in which literature cannot be taught, only experienced. Such contradictions surface at intervals in the Newbolt Report. At one point, we read, 'Another difficulty is that literature, not being a knowledge subject, cannot and should not be *taught*'; a difficulty indeed in a document whose title is *The Teaching of English in England*. Even where language teaching is concerned the Report is marked by a tension between the expressive and communicative functions of English. These difficulties are still with us.

4. *LEAVIS, LEWIS, AND OTHER OPPOSITIONS*

I

Like many English people, I acquired an early sense of binary oppositions from the Oxford and Cambridge boat race. As a child I entered into the excitement of this annual event without any sense of the real issues involved, apart from the pleasurable possibility that one of the boats might sink, as was sometimes said to happen. But I did not know what Oxford or Cambridge were; if, as I was told, they were universities, I did not know what universities were, nor, for that matter, what a boat race really was. In those pre-television days one could not see what was going on though one could hear a radio commentary, and the encounter was for me a pure structuralist opposition, a difference without substance, save for the arbitrary dark and light blue which differentiated the opponents. The Oxford–Cambridge polarity has long been familiar in English culture, though for most of the population it is an entirely empty and formal one, and easily collapsed into the compound entity of 'Oxbridge'. Applied to the development of English in higher education, however, the contrast has some substance, and represents opposed conceptions.

The Oxford Honours School of English Language and Literature was established before the turn of the century, after a campaign which lasted several years. A prime mover in it was John Churton Collins, best known for having been described by Tennyson as 'a louse on the locks of literature'; in fact he was an honourable and energetic crusader for vernacular literary education. His part in the Oxford campaign was not wholly disinterested, as he was ambitious to become the first professor of English Literature. He was disappointed in this aim, and had to retire, a broken man, to a chair at Birmingham and suicide a few years later. Some of the arguments advanced in favour of the new School were, at best, backhanded; in the debate in Congregation, William Sanday, Professor of Theology, supported the proposed School because, he said, 'there were the women to be considered, and the third rate men who would go on to become schoolmasters.' It is the permanent dilemma of schools of literary study to be denounced for either offering soft options—'chatter about Shelley' was the phrase invoked at Oxford—or for presenting a liberal and humane subject in a barbarous, would-be scientific terminology and method. From the beginning Oxford English was determined to appear tough and intellectually respectable. It was modelled on Classical Moderations, and the emphasis was heavily historical and philological, not altogether surprisingly, in view of the fact that there had been a chair of Anglo-Saxon since the eighteenth century, and the university housed the eminent lexicographers Murray and Craigie. But the new School was not conspicuous for Arnoldian sweetness and light, and did little to fulfil the dreams of the idealistic pioneers of English in education, like Churton Collins.

The Merton Professorship of English Literature was established, but could not be filled until an incumbent philologist died; Walter Raleigh was eventually appointed in 1904. He was neither a scholar nor an idealist, though he seems to have been a competent lecturer and administrator. He did not particularly enjoy teaching, as he admitted with honest cynicism in his letters:

The worst of it is, I can't read Shakespeare any more, so I have to remember the old tags. Not that I think him a bad author, but I can't bear literature. The distaste must be watched, or they'll turn me out. It's their money I want, so I suppose I've got to go on and on and be an old mechanical hack on rusty wires, working up a stock enthusiasm for the boyish lingo of effusive gentlemen long since dead.

The mood is, I daresay, not unknown among teachers of literature of a later generation.

Elsewhere Raleigh explains how he came into the profession:

I am a teacher by accident. I had not enough money for the Bar, or anything else, after graduating—second class. I had read a good deal of English literature and philosophy while I was supposed to be reading history, so I got a chance early in the movement for teaching English.

This, clearly, was not the spirit looked for in the Newbolt Report. The English School expanded under Raleigh, but still had little prestige. Evelyn Waugh's Charles Ryder, narrator of *Brideshead Revisited*, went up to Oxford in the early 1920s, and was interrogated by his pompous cousin Jasper, a fourth-year undergraduate: 'You're reading History? A perfectly respectable school. The very worst is English Literature . . .'. Few writers read English at Oxford until the Second World War; Aldous Huxley, who graduated with a First in 1916, was one of the earliest, and was followed in the twenties by Henry Green and W. H. Auden. Sir Walter Raleigh, as he became in 1911, nursed hankerings for a more active life than the academic, and he was able to indulge them after the First World War, when he was commissioned to write the history of the Royal Air Force. On field-work for this task in the Middle East he caught cholera and came home to die of it in 1922.

Raleigh's successor in the Merton chair was his former pupil, George Gordon. His inaugural lecture, naturally enough, gave no hint of Raleigh's pococurantism, but paid decent tribute to his achievements and aspirations; he also used the occasion to attack the Newbolt Report. Gordon's tribute to Raleigh and the English School at large was permeated by a characteristically Oxonian form of complacency: 'He looked forward to a time, not necessarily remote, when the Oxford School, with the Clarendon Press behind it and the Bodleian at its elbow, should be the headquarters of English Studies for the English-speaking world.' A similar trumpet call was sounded many years later, in 1967, when Helen Gardner was elected to the Merton chair and paid tribute in her inaugural to her predecessors, Raleigh and Gordon prominent among them. But despite Gordon's confidence, the action, in the early 1920s and for a long time to come, was not at Oxford but at the younger of the ancient universities.

II

English came to Cambridge much later than to Oxford and by a less direct route. For a time it was lodged with the recently established Modern Languages Tripos (dismissively known as the Couriers' or Interpreters' Tripos). The King Edward VII Chair of English Literature was established, and the first professor was appointed in 1912. He was Sir Arthur Quiller-Couch, well known as a novelist and man of letters; it was a political appointment by the government of the day, to reward Sir Arthur for services to the Liberal cause in the West of England. He remained professor, though a frequent absentee, until his death in 1944. Eventually an English Tripos was proposed and agreed to in 1917, when, it was remarked, many of the dons who might have opposed it were away at the war. The ensuing Golden Age of Cambridge English has been widely commemorated in myth and memoir. The reputation is justified; the performance-indicators, as modern bureaucrats would put it, are manifest, in such books as I. A. Richards's *Principles of Literary Criticism* (1924), *Science and Poetry* (1926), *Practical Criticism* (1929); William Empson's *Seven Types of Ambiguity* (1930); F. R. Leavis's *New Bearings in English Poetry* (1932), *For Continuity* (1933), *Revaluation* (1936); and Q. D. Leavis's *Fiction and the Reading Public* (1932). Oxford had nothing comparable to show, but it looked askance at criticism, and may not have considered such works worth producing.

The Cambridge story has been told and retold in accounts by, or of, its originators: Mansfield Forbes, I. A. Richards, E. M. W. Tillyard, Basil Willey, the Leavises. Whereas English at Oxford was institutionalized as 'English Language and Literature', indicating a strict programme, the Cambridge degree was called 'Literature, Life and Thought', which was larger and vaguer and might exclude nothing at all. The new English Faculty, when it was launched just after the First World War, took every advantage of this freedom. The effective founders were three young dons, Forbes, Richards, and Tillyard, who came from, respectively, History, Philosophy, and Classics. It was a blissful dawn, filled with promise, though Richards failed in his attempt to recruit T. S. Eliot as a teacher. Eliot responded, to Richard's consternation, that he had had enough of universities and preferred working in a bank. Nevertheless, Eliot remained a powerful force in Cambridge, where his poetry and criticism were studied and admired. In 1926 he delivered the Clark Lectures there, though they have never been published. James Reeves recalled that on arriving at Cambridge he was handed Eliot's *The Sacred Wood* rather as one is handed a hymn-book on going into church. M. C. Bradbrook has left an interesting account of those years. She points out that as the English Tripos, unlike the degrees at Oxford and London and the civic universities, was not historical in structure there could be more discussion of modern literature. The Faculty itself had little central organization or directive power (a state of affairs that was to become troublesome in later years), and the dons, who were securely based in their colleges, could offer lectures on whatever they pleased. In Professor Bradbrook's words, 'The briefest definition of Cambridge English would be "Contemporary, Comparative, College-based".' It was a small, intimate, and intense world. There was particular fascination in the interaction of a new educational programme and literary modernism:

Richards helped to strengthen the ties with America; the study of Pound and Eliot brought Paris closer. These connexions were felt to be more important than those with traditional schools of English in other universities. I remember the excitement of sitting under a willow tree on the Backs and reading R. P. Blackmur on Eliot in an early number of *Hound and Horn*; in 1931 Edmund Wilson's *Axel's Castle*, with its studies of Yeats, Valéry, Eliot reached us . . .

Richards lectured on Eliot and Yeats, and Leavis lectured on Joyce, brushing with the law by importing a copy of the then-banned *Ulysses*. Raymond Williams has claimed that the most important defining feature of the English Tripos was 'Practical Criticism', as devised and propagated by Richards; without it, he believes, a project based on something as vague as 'Literature, Life and Thought' might soon have declined into a bland, traditionalist humanism. He denies that Cambridge English was ever a 'distinctive and *coherent* course and method of study. The Golden Age was golden only in its beginnings, it searchings, its open and free speaking and for some years tolerant experimentation and inquiry.'

In time, the charisma weakened. More students meant more organization and control, the early rapture faded into common day. The Faculty became weakened by internal dissension, and it lost two of its founding fathers: Forbes by early death, and Richards by departure for America. Another loss, which had significant negative implications, was that of the young William Empson, who, as a research student, was required to leave Cambridge when contraceptives were discovered in his college room. Empson was a man of immense intellectual power and originality, who might have decisively affected the later course of English in Cambridge if he had stayed there. Instead, Empson went to China and Leavis became the dominant figure. Even as I write that sentence, I realize that it calls for qualification. In Leavis's own account, he and his wife were subject to neglect and humiliation and even active persecution. Official Cambridge was undoubtedly slow to acknowledge or reward him. He had a temporary lectureship in the late twenties which was not renewed, just as long afterwards Colin MacCabe's was not. For several years Leavis's only foothold was as a fellow of Downing College, without a Faculty post. He was finally made a Reader in 1959, not long before his retirement; but his wife, the gifted scholar and critic Q. D. Leavis, never had an institutional post. Leavis's own explanation for this neglect, official malignity, may cover some of the facts but not all of them. Prophets are often without honour in their own country, and the Leavises made enemies easily. Still, the university's slowness to recognize Leavis when he had emerged as one of the leading critics in the English-speaking world does not reflect particularly well on Cambridge. In realistic terms, Leavis might have been short-sighted in insisting on staying there at all costs, with or without a university appointment. He might have done better to have followed the example of his younger collaborator, L. C. Knights, who left Cambridge to teach in a number of provincial universities—very much in the spirit of the Newbolt Report—before eventually going back as King Edward VII Professor. But Leavis, having been born and having grown up in Cambridge, seems unable to have conceived of living anywhere else. In his thought there were two Cambridges, rather like the King's Two Bodies of medieval political theory. There was the day-to-day institution of fools and knaves and time-servers, and the ideal academic community, Platonic or Newmanian, to which he often appealed in his criticism.

Leavis himself was something of a double man, both historical and mythic. The historical Leavis was a fascinating and complex personality, who would make a challenging subject for a biography. He is to be encountered in a volume edited by Denys Thompson, *The Leavises: Recollections and Impressions*, though it is not easy to get a coherent picture from the memories and anecdotes it contains. Leavis was widely believed to have been gassed in the First World War, which was said to explain some prominent features of his self-presentation, such as his inability to bear the constriction of a tie round his neck, or to eat much food at a time. Yet one of the contributors to Thompson's book, Michael Tanner, quotes Leavis as saying, apropos of his small appetite, 'It was convenient for people to think it was because he had been gassed in the First World War, but actually it was because of the state of tension in which he lived . . .'. Leavis remains contradictory. There are many accounts of his gentleness and consideration in personal dealings, yet his public utterances in later life were painfully rancorous and vindictive about supposed or real enemies. Such venom is far more punishing to the bestower than to the recipient.

The place of Q. D. Leavis in her husband's life is problematical: he appears to have relied greatly on her judgement, and on her reading, which was wider than his. Her own distinction as a critic is only now becoming apparent with the publication of her collected papers. It has been suggested that she wrote, without acknowledgement, parts of Leavis's *The Great Tradition*. One or two of the contributors to *The Leavises* write warmly of Mrs Leavis, but the general impression one gets from Thompson's book is of a snobbish and spiteful personality. It seems as if she encouraged her husband in one of the most disturbing features of his later career: the dismissal and excommunication of former friends and colleagues on *Scrutiny*. Yet there was a tragic dimension in her personal life. When she married, her Orthodox Jewish parents disowned her and she severed all connections with them. During the war she heard without apparent emotion the news that they had been killed in an air-raid. Such tensions in the inner life suggest the material of fiction; inevitably any biography would have to be of both Leavises.

Leavis emerged as the dominant figure of Cambridge English, not inside the university, where he had enemies and his progress was slow, but in the larger world. And here we encounter not the historical but the mythic Leavis. Although many modern critics have doctorates, Leavis is the only one who has been consistently referred to by his title: 'Doctor Leavis' has his place in cultural history alongside that other mythic figure, 'Doctor Johnson'. The myth was based to some extent on the impact of his personality and appearance: the stern, handsome, aquiline features, the open shirts, the frugal mode of life, the athleticism, the unflinching integrity, the gentlemanliness of manner. This was the impression preserved by many who were supervised by him, and attended his lectures. George Steiner has recalled Leavis's last lecture at Cambridge: 'No ceremony. Only a don, spare of voice and stature, but unforgettable in his intensity, leaving a lectern in a Cambridge hall and brushing out the door with a step characteristically sinuous, lithe and unheeding.' Yet Leavis was admired and venerated by many who had not been his pupils and had never known him personally. Only Ezra Pound, among twentieth-century writers, has inspired a comparably intense discipleship and devotion.

Cambridge English, in its original Golden Age, was full of intellectual excitement; but it was also inward-looking. Leavis, though much preoccupied with his own idea or ideal of Cambridge, conveyed the practices and attitudes of its English School to a wider audience, via his books and his editorship of *Scrutiny*. That journal never had a wide circulation, but it found a receptive readership among people engaged in the study and teaching of English, in civic universities, in colleges of education, and in grammar schools. There were also overseas audiences for *Scrutiny* and its ideas, particularly in Australia. By the 1940s Leavis had become, perhaps without fully realizing it, that most potent of educators, a teacher of teachers. Young men whom Leavis taught at Downing became lecturers or schoolmasters, and some went to teach in colleges of education (I say 'men' advisedly, as there appear to have been no female Leavisites, apart from

Mrs Leavis). So strong was Leavis's influence that his disciples formed a recognizable type, with a marked social and intellectual manner. John Wain has left a sharp account of the typical Leavisite, as he observed him in the 1940s and 1950s; such a person is not aggressive or argumentative, but will probably appear as bland, quiet, and slyly genial. In conversation he does not advance his own ideas and positions, but devotes himself to drawing out as thoroughly as possible those of his interlocutor:

> His sole interest in talking to you has been to feed you with questions so that you scamper from topic to topic, throwing off judgments, each of which he receives with a polite nod and a further question. At the end of your talk he goes away with a complete dossier on you: which was, of course, the object of the exercise. Leavisites do not emerge from their fortress with the idea of mingling with literary people in general, since one of their basic articles of faith is that such people, unless they happen to be very neglected and unsuccessful, are either insolent charlatans or corrupt dilettanti.

Wain is careful to distinguish Leavis from his disciples, for whose excesses and deformations he cannot be held responsible, though they underline his remarkably strong influence as teacher and exemplar. In some cases this extended beyond ideas and intellectual style to the imitation of his personal mannerisms. Of Leavis himself Wain remarked, 'If there is one man who almost single-handed, turned the university study of "English" from a placid, rather stagnant ornamental lake to a choppy and sometimes tempestuous sea, it is F. R. Leavis.' That was an accurate comment for the early 1960s.

Leavis was born in 1895 and there is a sense in which he was the last of the Victorian Sages; *Scrutiny* represented a vigorous late flowering of their concern with the Condition of England question. The review addressed itself to the problem of keeping alive true values in a positivistic, industrialized, commercial culture. In ways foreshadowed by the Newbolt Report, *Scrutiny* believed that the teaching of English was central to this task. And it followed Arnold and Eliot and the editors of *The Calendar of Modern Letters* in emphasizing the importance of literary criticism, a subject about which the Newbolt Report had curiously little to say. Leavis's name did not appear on the masthead of *Scrutiny* until the third issue, and from then on he appeared as one name only in an editorial board of three or four. The early issues, though inspired by Cambridge English, were surprisingly eclectic. M. C. Bradbrook and others contributed articles, and there were reviews by the former editors of the *Calendar*, Edgell Rickword and Douglas Garman, and by W. H. Auden, who soon became a *bête noire* of *Scrutiny*. There was even some original poetry, though the magazine later restricted itself to critical prose. Throughout the 1930s it was a journal of seminal power, with a wide range of interests: it was concerned not only with English Literature, but with foreign writing and the other arts; it was interested in sociology and psychology and, above all, education. At that time *Scrutiny* was justified in its claim to be considered a journal of general concern with civilization, and although Leavis became an increasingly prominent contributor, there seems to have been genuinely collaborative editorial direction. In the 1940s, when many of the contributors and members of the editorial board were away at the war, the Leavises took on more and more of the running of the journal, and continued to do so until its demise in 1953. The range of interests narrowed, the contributors became fewer, and 'Scrutineering' and 'Leavisite' became more or less synonymous. The history of *Scrutiny* and its place in the cultural and intellectual contexts of its time have been admirably described in Francis Mulhern's book, *The Moment of 'Scrutiny'*, which is Marxist in approach but even-handed in argument.

Scrutiny was indebted for its title, and the spirit and style of its criticism, to Edgell Rickword and the contributors to *The Calendar of Modern Letters* which he edited from 1925 to 1927 (Rickword edited two volumes of critical essays, which had appeared in the *Calendar* or elsewhere, under the title of *Scrutinies*). Leavis, for all the immense influence he exerted, had little originality as critic or thinker; much less so than Rickword or Empson. His achievement, which was considerable enough, was to fuse a wide range of eclectic intellectual influences into a powerful force for cultural propaganda and persuasion. He drew on a central Romantic tradition for the conviction that poetry, and the imagination at large, can heal and restore the soul. Newman inspired his idea of a university, and James and Eliot and Lawrence helped him to become the kind of critic he was (though Leavis's relations with Eliot, which I have discussed at length elsewhere, were to prove tortuous). The Newbolt Report provided arguments for the centrality of English, while Leavis's debt to Richards was certainly greater than he was ever prepared to acknowledge. His wife, Q. D. Leavis, seems to have influenced him in considerable if incalculable ways.

Many diverse elements intersect in Leavis: Romanticism, the English puritan tradition, Victorian cultural criticism, modernism, and several strands of twentieth-century anti-positivist and anti-scientific ideology. But if Leavis's thinking was unoriginal, his tone was unmistakable and very personal. More was involved than a successful act of assimilation of different sources. Leavis's mental world was unified by a passionate mystique or metaphysic. Like many twentieth-century intellectuals he was inspired by a myth of catastrophe. Though he never refers to a single abrupt act of severance— unlike Eliot, who was inclined to see the English Civil War as the source of dissolution and disorder—Leavis was haunted by the idea of a world and a set of values which had all but vanished. They were mythically exemplified in the opening pages of *The Rainbow*: once there was a genuine community, man was close to nature, working with the rhythm of the seasons, genuinely creative in his work and crafts, unreflectingly religious. Now, all is changed, by industrialism, technology, Benthamism, mass civilization, egalitarianism, the suburban state of mind. This approach recalls a familiar sociological opposition: *Gemeinschaft* versus *Gesellschaft* and sundry variations on that theme. But it is given a particular tone by the cultural nationalism which was always close to the surface in Leavis. George Steiner has observed of a characteristic passage where Leavis writes of the 'strength of English':

It belongs to that complex of agrarian autonomism, of *la terre et ses morts*, which ranges from Péguy and Barrès to Allen Tate and the Southern Fugitives in America. Behind it shimmers an historical vision (largely fanciful) of an older order, rural, customary, moralistic.

Leavis found support for this vision in Eliot as well as Lawrence, antithetical writers though they are usually assumed to be. There is common ground between aspects of the *Scrutiny* ideology and the *Volkisch* elements in European right-wing thought.

For Leavis, the old values were fast vanishing, but they persisted in one important area: great literature, or a certain selected canon of it; they could be rediscovered and re-enacted in the process of responsive critical reading. Whilst literature, and the criticism which was the key to it, remained then all was not lost. Hence Leavis's characteristic note of urgency. The values in question were by no means 'literary' or 'aesthetic', as scholars or *littérateurs* customarily assumed, but a matter of Life itself. Leavis draws selectively on Romantic tradition; one implicit source for his beliefs is the 1800 Preface to the *Lyrical Ballads*, which affirms the moral and socially unitive power of poetry, with its roots in ordinary human affections and speech. It exemplifies a powerful English tradition, which leads on to Mill and Arnold, but it is a narrow line. It stands in contrast to the dimension in European Romanticism, notably exemplified in Schiller's letters on aesthetic education, which makes the 'aesthetic' a central force in human life, related to play and freedom and imagination. Leavis invariably substitutes the 'moral' for the 'aesthetic'; his so-called puritanism may have been in evidence here, finding the idea of play and pure contemplation insupportable in a serious context. (Milton had an analogous difficulty in convincingly presenting the free aesthetic existence of Adam and Eve before the Fall.) The belief in specifically literary and aesthetic values recurs in the major developments and transformations of Romantic theory and practice: in French symbolists and English aesthetes, Russian Formalists and American New Critics. One finds it, too, in an idiosyncratic latter-day Leavisite, the late Geoffrey Thurley. If Leavis and the *Scrutiny* writers rejected this way of thinking it may have been, as Francis Mulhern has remarked, because they looked at the whole of history and society in a mythicized and literary way.

For Leavis, the values on which civilization depended were far too important to be called 'literary'. They were not to be called unqualifiedly 'religious' either, but they had a religious weight and seriousness. Literature, the right literature, was indeed a form of sacred scripture, and the critic and teacher was a hierophantic interpreter. Yet critical reading was valuable in itself, even when not directed at great literature, in ways suggested by the Newbolt Report and made explicit by Richards's work of the 1920s. That is to say, the process of close, attentive reading involves the reader in choices and discriminations and judgements akin to those we continually make in our day-to-day living, and so strengthens and refines our capacity for them. Richards had presented this process in the language of a materialistic neurology; Leavis transposed it to an older vocabulary of moral choice.

The concept of morality involved would have been unintelligible to a great moral critic of the past, that earlier Doctor, Samuel Johnson, for whom the ethical values which governed life were not immanent in literature, but external to it in Christian tradition; one did not draw such values from literature, one judged it by them. Such attitudes are far from extinct today, especially among those unaffected by a modern literary education, and have surfaced in the recent past in trials for literary or dramatic obscenity. Indeed, an interesting and unexpected development within the academy has been the revival of a form of direct, external ethical valuation of literature, though its points of reference are not Christian but Marxist or feminist. Yet the idea of the moral power of the imagination is too firmly rooted in post-Romantic tradition to be easily overthrown or abandoned. Richards had tersely paraphrased Arnold as 'poetry can save us', and Leavis reinterpreted this doctrine as 'criticism can save us'. In Mulhern's words, 'Literary criticism was culture's gift of wisdom to a blinded civilization.' *Scrutiny* bravely took up the burden of trying to save civilization, a task much discussed in the 1930s; see the excellent account in Lucy MacDiarmid's book of 1984, *Saving Civilization: Yeats, Eliot and Auden Between the Wars*. In the early years *Scrutiny*'s mood was optimistic, and though opposed to the literary Marxism of the time, inclined towards the Left. Later the mood became pessimistic and, at times, apocalyptic. Leavis's later criticism and cultural commentary was assertively conservative, in ways which separated him from the 'Left Leavisite' tendency associated with Raymond Williams.

Scrutiny's combination of moral urgency and supposedly 'ordinary' critical language produced an idiolect which was easily recognizable. It has been analysed by an American academic, Howard Felperin, who encountered it at the University of Melbourne, once the leading Antipodean outpost of Leavisism. At Yale Felperin had made the transition from the New Criticism to nascent structuralism, and had come to terms with forms of apparent jargon which could be defended as the contending discourses of a technical discipline. At Melbourne the idiom seemed lucid and straightforward in a middle-class British way, though he soon learned it was less straightforward than it seemed:

What I discovered was that an author's prose can be 'crisp', or if he is not careful, 'brittle'; his moral outlook 'buoyant' and 'life-affirming' (unless of course it is 'life-denying'); his work 'central' or 'essential' or 'marginal'. (To what and from what was not made explicit, unless it was 'life' or the 'great tradition'.) The only authors who seemed to be consistently regarded as 'central' and 'essential', for whatever it is worth, were Shakespeare and Jane Austen. The critic, in turn, supposed himself to write out of his 'inward possession' of the work, to seek a 'realized experience' of it, to strive for 'completeness of response' to it, but most often seemed to entertain 'worries' about its artistic, and especially, its moral status until he could finally dismiss it as 'easy' or 'unearned' or 'self-indulgent'. He thereby proved himself a reader or critic—never an interpreter or scholar or even student—of 'sensibility' and 'judgement', superior by implication to the author he had just put in his place.

My own 'worries' with this school of criticism—and allowing for the economy of caricature, I think I have offered a fair sample of its characteristic terms and procedures—had to do with its curious combination of self-proclaimed democracy and undeclared authoritarianism. Here was a 'natural language', a critical idiom drawn from common parlance and apparently aimed at an audience of 'common readers'; yet its vocabulary was deployed in such a way as to create a tone as dreadfully earnest and a protocol as predictable and formulaic as a religious ritual.

Felperin's account is of more than merely anecdotal interest; as an outsider he was quickly able to get a sharper impression of Leavisism than many British people could. Americans have always been puzzled by Leavis. In the 1940s he was regarded as a special English kind of New Critic, and the first selection to be made from *Scrutiny*, *The Importance of Scrutiny*, edited by Eric Bentley, was published in America in 1948. There have been one or two American Leavisites, such as Seymour Betsky and Marius Bewley. But Leavis's quasi-mystical invocation of 'Englishness' naturally seemed alien to American readers, and his influence in the United States was not deep-rooted or sustained. So Felperin, in his chapter called 'Leavisism Revisited', can refer to Leavis as a past phenomenon in cultural history.

In Britain the situation is more complex. Leavisism may be declining, but it is still a visible presence in parts of higher education; not only in some English departments, but particularly in education departments and teacher training colleges, and in the books and periodicals devoted to the teaching of English in schools. In this area *Scrutiny*'s strong early commitment to education has born fruit, in ways described by Margaret Mathieson. At Cambridge, John Harvey, critic and novelist and fellow of Emmanuel, preserves a strong attachment to Leavis. Fred Inglis, an educationist at Warwick, is one of the few surviving Left-Leavisites; Right-Leavisites are more common, such as Ian Robinson of University College, Swansea, and Duke Maskell, of Newcastle Polytechnic. The right-wing philosophers John Casey and Roger Scruton have also written admiringly of Leavis. Robinson, author of *The Survival of English*, is an ideologically hard man and a formidably intelligent critic, whose judgement has certainly been disturbed by his devotion to Leavis, whom he regards not just as a major critic, but as a great creative writer. Nevertheless, *The Human World*, which he founded and edited for several years in the 1970s, was a serious-minded and provocative journal, which tried to recapture the extended interests of early *Scrutiny* and to establish a conjunction of ideas drawn from Leavis and from Wittgenstein. On one occasion Robinson did attempt a reasoned criticism of Leavis, who responded harshly, accusing him of 'some automatism that intervenes in his thought and works havoc.' But Leavis did not, I believe, repudiate Robinson, as he did the editorial board of *The Cambridge Quarterly*, a broadly Leavisite journal established in the 1960s.

These marginalia of cultural politics stand somewhat apart from Leavis's real importance for criticism and literary education in Britain. He was, of course, attacked in his lifetime, and has been attacked since his death. He had domestic enemies at Cambridge, such as F. L. Lucas and E. M. W. Tillyard, and he was always coolly regarded at Oxford, as I shall shortly go on to discuss. More recently, attacks have come from Marxist-poststructuralists. Nevertheless, it is easier to attack Leavis than to dismiss him. His importance remains, whatever one thinks of him. English studies in Britain, and in other parts of the anglophone world, would certainly have developed differently without Leavis. He always regarded himself as a critic, in his own special and exalted sense, and refused all dealings with philosophy. In his famous debate with René Wellek in 1937 he declined to reflect on and justify his critical assumptions, saying that to do so would turn him into a philosopher. He retained this stance throughout his career, as indicated in the title of a posthumous collection of essays, *The Critic as Anti-Philosopher*. Nevertheless, there are those who have seen an implicitly philosophical dimension in the late phase of Leavis's criticism, when he was concerned to establish a 'human world' of collaboratively created value, between the merely personal and the apparently objective. As Wellek has written, nearly forty years after his controversy with Leavis:

Leavis's assertion, not unique to our time, of the claims of culture against civilization, of a value-charged understanding against scientific explanation, buttressed by a recognition of affinities with some philosophers in the phenomenological and exsitentialist tradition, remains a necessary task for every humanist.

Trying to assess Leavis as a literary critic, I believe that his best work was done in the 1930s, in his early books, *New Bearings in English Poetry*, *For Continuity*, and *Revaluation*, in some of the essays later collected in *The Common Pursuit*, and in the first phase of *Scrutiny*'s existence. In this work Leavis was sensitively and acutely applying modernist insights—notably those drawn from Eliot's criticism—to literary texts, and redrawing the map of English poetic history. Leavis is indeed, as his admirers assert, an exemplary close reader, and he is generally a better critic of poetry than of the novel, where too often he has no method but the quotation of enormous passages accompanied by unspecific, copiously adjectival commendation. The book on D. H. Lawrence, influential though it has been, seems to me unsatisfactory as criticism. Although Leavis always asserted that literary criticism was a collaborative activity, involving discussion and dialogue, his customary tone was monologic. Even without the anecdotal evidence collected in Denys Thompson's book, one would assume that Leavis was a proud man who found it difficult to tolerate disagreement. Indeed, it was the stiff moral grandeur of the personality which captivated the Leavisites. It also made him unable to accept the compromises and periodic defeats that are unavoidable in institutional life; this, certainly, was a cause of many difficulties for him at Cambridge.

If Leavis is ultimately important it is not because he was, as his admirers claim, a great literary critic; if one gives that phrase its proper weight then, in our century, in England, only Eliot and James seem to me to deserve it, whatever qualities one finds in Leavis, who took so much from those masters. Leavis was supremely a publicist for criticism and the idea of criticism. The Leavises and their original collaborators on *Scrutiny* realized the implications of a particular moment in intellectual and cultural history, when English was an expanding subject in schools and the academy but had no clear rationale. Leavis placed literary criticism, as it had emerged and developed at Cambridge in the 1920s, at the heart of English studies; historical scholarship became marginalized, a matter for specialists only (though there were able scholars on the *Scrutiny* team, such as Mrs Leavis and H. A. Mason). In the recent past criticism had been part of the profession of letters; after Leavis it seemed to be firmly rooted in the academy. An important historical transition had been effected. The Newbolt Report and Richards had claimed, in rather muffled ways, that English was educationally special, and not just one more subject to be studied. Leavis amplified this claim with prophetic energy; for *Scrutiny* English was the central discipline of the humanities, just as theology had been queen of the sciences in the Middle Ages. Historians and philosophers might want to resist the claim, but its point was its boldness. English was no longer a weak parvenu subject, of use only to women and third-rate men who wanted to become schoolmasters. In the academy a subject claiming central importance is sure to be resisted; but, as in any negotiation, if you start off with an impossibly large claim you are still likely to end up with something substantial. So with the *Scrutiny* view of English. If universities could not accept it as the discipline at the heart of all others, they were still prepared to grant its importance. The Newbolt Report's sentiments about the spread of the missionary spirit in literary education were well on the way to being fulfilled. *Scrutiny* provided a rationale that had to be acknowledged even where it was not accepted. By the early 1950s, when the journal ceased publication, academics teaching English Literature were either in sympathy with its mission, or had good reasons for not being so.

III

Meanwhile, what of Oxford, where the degree included a good deal of Old and Middle English, and literature stopped in 1830? Under the unadventurous guidance of George Gordon, Oxford English wanted no part in the Arnold–Newbolt–Cambridge line. It shunned the dubious excitements at the junior university, and devoted itself to scholarship, securely resting on the twin foundations of the Bodleian Library and the Clarendon Press. In 1926 the *Review of English Studies* was founded as an organ of strict academic professionalism, untainted by the missionary spirit. Otherwise, to extract a line from one of Pound's late *Cantos*, 'For 30 years nothing of interest occurred in that country.' Then, in 1936, something of great interest occurred, when C. S. Lewis published *The Allegory of Love: A Study in Medieval Tradition*. It is a remarkable contribution to literary history, and like everything Lewis wrote, beguilingly readable and persuasive in its rhetoric. In her British Academy obituary of Lewis, Helen Gardner said of *The Allegory of Love*:

Whether one agrees or disagrees, in detail or in large, with its thesis, after reading this book one's whole imagination of the past has been extended and changed. Lewis recovered for the ordinary reader what had been lost for centuries, the power to read allegory and to respond to the allegorical mode of thinking. He was able to do so because he was a born allegorist himself. His imagination was stirred by ideas and concepts and their congruity, and they came to life in his mind almost as persons. He was, besides, a moralist to the depths of his being, and was deeply moved by allegory's power to embody moral concepts and illuminate moral experience. But, in addition, *The Allegory of Love* is written by a man who loved literature and had an extraordinary power of stimulating his readers to curiosity and enthusiasm. In his first book Lewis revealed his two supreme gifts: a range of wide and exact learning with a power of imaginative response to individual works that continually sets them in a fresh light.

This was certainly my own response to *The Allegory of Love* when I first read it as an undergraduate. It remains a classic of critical scholarship, or scholarly criticism.

In 1936 Leavis also published his own major contribution to literary history, *Revaluation*. More than half a century on, Leavis and Lewis seem to me the most substantial figures their respective English schools produced, embodying antithetical views not only of literature and culture, but of life, worthy opponents for each other, though they never engaged in open intellectual debate. The perception of differences is possible only within a framework of resemblances; things must have something in common before they can be compared at all. Leavis and Lewis, in fact, had quite a lot in common, beginning, to be not wholly serious, with their similar names, which might be indistinguishable in bad handwriting or mumbled speech. More important was their generational experience and service in the First World War. Leavis, who was born in 1895, served throughout the war as a non-combatant stretcher-bearer; Lewis, born in 1898, was at the Front as a subaltern for some months in 1917–18 before being wounded by a British shell and sent home. Both men were deeply attached to their respective universities, so much so that they could not consider going elsewhere, and they did not find it easy to establish themselves in an academic career in them. Once established they found that honour was slow to come; Leavis became a Reader only towards the end of his career, and Lewis was twice passed over for a chair of English Literature at Oxford.

As personalities they were lonely men, but ready to socialize, Leavis at tea-parties at his house in Bulstrode Gardens, Lewis in Oxford pubs with the kindred spirits of the Inklings. Both men were insular in their attitudes, resolute non-travellers, and both were devoted to an ideal of Englishness in literature. In *The Allegory of Love* Lewis argued that as well as seeing Spenser as 'Elfin, Renaissance, voluptuous, courtly, Italianate and decorative' we should also see him as 'English, Protestant, rustic, manly, churchwardenly, domestic, thrifty, honest'; the latter string of epithets is one that Leavis's more devoted admirers might well have applied to him. Both Leavis and Lewis were honourable, old-fashioned, middle-class Englishmen, and it is not altogether surprising that when Lewis moved to a chair at Cambridge in the 1950s he and Leavis became on friendly terms. Indeed, Donald Davie recalls being part of a conversation between Lewis and Leavis, who were in firm agreement that 'there could not be in any serious sense universities on American soil' because the United States was not a democracy but a plutocracy. 'Sagely nodding and capping each other's observations, Lewis and Leavis would hear nothing from me, or from another of the company lately returned from a year in the States.'

One of the ways in which Lewis did differ from Leavis was in not being averse to theoretical discussion. He did, after all, have an Oxford Greats training in philosophy behind him, and he liked to argue. His ideas about literature were set out in essays collected in *Rehabilitations*, and in his debate with E. M. W. Tillyard, *The Personal Heresy*, both published in 1939; and in a remarkable late book, *An Experiment in Criticism*, which came out in 1961, two years before his death. Lewis was totally opposed to the Arnold–Newbolt–Cambridge conception that poetry could in some sense 'save us', or save civilization, by its preservation of values. This may have been partly because Lewis was an Anglican Christian—like other prominent figures in Oxford English, such as David Cecil, Nevill Coghill, and Helen Gardner—and wanted no part in any substitute religion. That accounts for a good deal, but not everything; some Scrutineers, after all, were also Christians, and a Catholic monk, Sebastian Moore, wrote one of the most unreservedly admiring pieces in Thompson's compilation on the Leavises. Something has to be attributed to Lewis's temperament, which made him at worst mistrustful of and at best uninterested in institutions and large cultural questions. Leavis, inspired by Newman, was much concerned with the idea of a university, and its role in transmitting values and preserving civilization at large. Lewis had a view of universities which even for his day was, as he sensed, impossibly narrow. As he saw it, universities were for learning, not for education, which was the business of schools. Training should not be the primary concern of either, though Lewis acknowledged that somehow surgeons and engineers had to be trained, without being very interested in how it was to be done. He carried the attitudes of traditional humanism *à outrance*. He did accept the importance of education, in ways that have something in common with Arnold and *Scrutiny*, but he took a pessimistic view of its prospects:

If education is beaten by training, civilization dies. That is very likely to happen. One of the most dangerous errors instilled into us by nineteenth-century progressive optimism is the idea that civilization is automatically bound to increase and spread. The lesson of history is the opposite: civilization is a rarity, attained with difficulty and easily lost. The normal state of humanity is barbarism, just as the normal surface of our planet is salt water.

Lewis is writing here in a tradition of Christian-conservative pessimism about man and society, given greater urgency by its historical moment, the eve of the Second World War. To *Scrutiny* it would have seemed like unacceptable quietism and defeatism, though Leavis was eventually to express a comparable pessimism. Both men, we may be sure, would have reacted with horror to the triumph of an anti-intellectual utilitarianism in Thatcherite England.

Although Lewis was a university teacher of English for most of his life, he had little faith in institutionalized culture. He took a lonely and individual approach to literature, and was more concerned with private joy encountered in exploratory reading than with readily communicable cultural satisfactions and values. There is an important clue to his attitudes in his spiritual autobiography, *Surprised by Joy*. At school the young Lewis discovered that other children had enjoyed the same books as he had done, and that public merit might be gained from reading the right books:

What had been 'my' taste was apparently 'our' taste (if only I could meet the 'we' to whom that 'our' belonged). And if 'our' taste, then—by a perilous transition—perhaps 'good' or 'the right taste'. For that transition involves a kind of Fall. The moment good taste knows itself, some of its goodness is lost. Even then, however, it is not necessary to take the further downward step of despising the 'philistines' who do not share it.

'Philistine' was an Arnoldian concept; here we see Lewis consciously distancing himself from the idea of approved values in literature, and the ensuing enterprise of raising literary standards, erecting canons of excellence, engaging in fine discrimination, excoriating the inferior and the attitudes of its producers and consumers; the enterprise, in short, which culminated in *Scrutiny*. This inchoate response of the young Lewis was to lead to some of his most provocative and interesting theoretical writing.

I can think of only one place in Lewis's writing where he mentions Leavis by name. This is in *A Preface to Paradise Lost*, in a discussion of the surging, kinetic effect of Milton's verse movement, which Leavis objected to, since it seemed to carry the reader forward against his will. Lewis remarked that he and Leavis were pretty well in agreement on the way the verse worked, but their responses were totally different: 'He sees and hates the very same that I see and love.' The brief comment provides a useful crux in critical theory, showing how judgements ultimately depend on values and discourses outside themselves. Generally Lewis's opposition to the *Scrutiny* programme and ideal is left implicit, but is none the less pronounced, particularly in *An Experiment in Criticism*. *Scrutiny* believed that literary judgements were cultural judgements, and that ultimately the future of civilization itself depended on the exercise of appropriate discriminations. Lewis is committed to ethical values of a traditional kind, but is quite agnostic about the desirability, perhaps the possibility, of cultural values, and of using literature to shore up a threatened civilization. At the end of *An Experiment in Criticism* he specifically denies that literature is to be valued (*a*) for telling us truths about life, and (*b*) as an aid to culture. Believing that literature should be surrendered to rather than interrogated, Lewis thought it positively harmful that undergraduates should be trained to make value judgements: 'Here, plainly, are young people drenched, dizzied and bedazzled by criticism to a point at which primary literary experience is no longer possible.' This was written in about 1960 when Cambridge, to which Lewis had removed, was still pervaded by Leavisism.

Lewis's stance was a deeply personal one, expressing his individual sense of what literature was, which excluded the easy making of judgements of good or bad, worse or better (though he was quite prepared to make them if he felt it necessary; they are not uncommon in his critical writing, though usually implicit rather than explicit). He represented an Oxford tradition of aversion from value judgements, which perhaps stemmed from the absence of culturalist underpinning to literary study there, in contrast to the prevailing attitudes at Cambridge. Immediately after the First World War the newly demobbed and still shell-shocked Robert Graves attempted to take a degree course in English at Oxford. In time he received a complaint that the essays he wrote for his tutor were 'temperamental'. A spokesman for his college said, 'it appears, indeed, that you prefer some authors to others'. In later years, Helen Gardner argued that the making of judgements was no necessary part of an English degree; she believed that reading literature was indeed concerned with values, but that value was to be intuited separately from each work, without any need to make comparisons or erect hierarchies. More recently, her successor in the Merton chair, John Carey, has been vehemently dismissive of the possibility of making value judgements. This is a paradoxical position for Carey, since in his work as a reviewer he frequently makes judgements, often of a sharp and combative kind. But he may believe that such judgements are appropriate in literary journalism but not in academic discourse. This is a tenable position, to which I shall return.

Lewis had no interest in cultural politics, but he left a substantial body of work in scholarship, criticism, and theory which does not accept the premises of what I shall call for brevity the Cambridge ideology. Indeed, it provides a critique of that ideology; and even some anticipations of the ideas of the radical critics of the 1970s and 1980s. For Lewis the value of literature was aesthetic not moral, and he resisted any attempt to try to bring these two concepts together. In *The Personal Heresy* he defended an 'objective or impersonal theory of poetry', which finds its easiest application in drama and epic. Lewis illustrates the theory in a virtual paraphrase of Eliot's 'Tradition and the Individual Talent': 'The man who cries out with pain is not the same as the man who vividly expresses to us the blood-curdling nature of the cry.' The belief in impersonality led Lewis to a New Critical kind of formalism; the poem is to be read in its own terms, without reference to the poet's biography (here Lewis places himself at odds with the Oxford scholarly tradition). Poetry advances, not propositions, but, in effect, what Richards called 'pseudo-statements':

> Poetry is an exploitation of language to convey the concrete; one of the means by which it does this is a free use of propositions which have logically only the remotest connexion with its real utterance. What it 'says' is the total, concrete experience it gives to the right reader.

The emphasis on 'total, concrete experience' sounds Leavisite, but elsewhere in *The Personal Heresy* Lewis rejects a central Leavisite—and ultimately Romantic—concept by asserting that 'sincerity' and 'insincerity' have no meaning as evaluative terms. Lewis argues that they raise irrelevant questions about the poet's state of mind, rather than address themselves to the question, 'What, in this series of words, excites a feeling of hostility which prevents enjoyment?' In this book Lewis adopts a strongly anti-intentionalist position, which is another aspect of his commitment to impersonality. He remarks that 'misunderstandings, or mistranslations, can produce poetry that no poet wrote. Indeed, to be encrusted with such poetless poetry is the reward, or the penalty, of every poem that endures.' Lewis's belief in the possibility of 'poetless poetry' has interestingly radical implications, even hinting at the 'free-floating signifiers' of poststructuralist theory. It would not, I think, be accepted by a theorist who shares some of Lewis's views, E. D. Hirsch jun.; nor by the advocates of the New Pragmatism.

Lewis's formalism continues in the later work, *An Experiment in Criticism*. There he makes a distinction between 'substance' and 'story' which closely parallels that of the Russian Formalists (whose work Lewis is unlikely to have known) between 'fabula' and 'szujet'; roughly, between the raw material of

narrative, and the accumulated devices of style and structure
that make it interesting and pleasurable to read. Lewis values
literature, not for its truth-telling qualities, but for its capacity
to provide pleasure and enjoyment; qualities which anticipate
the *jouissance* and *plaisir du texte* of the later Roland Barthes.
At the end of *An Experiment in Criticism* Lewis does move
beyond hedonism to a justification of literature as providing
the capacity to move into alien kinds of life, or the enlarge-
ment of experience by seeing through others' eyes. 'Literature
heals the wound, without undermining the privilege, of individuality', as he finely puts it; the formulation acquires greater
resonance if one does what Lewis would not wish one to, and
relates it to his own rather solitary personality. Such a
criterion is still aesthetic, but it arguably approaches the
moral, in so far as it recalls the extension of community by
affection and sympathy that Wordsworth looked for in the
1800 Preface. But the emphasis is more contemplative than
active.

Lewis is particularly at odds with Leavisite assumptions in
his remarks on fantasy and realism. *Scrutiny* contributors
tended to regard the former with suspicion—lapsing into day-
dreaming was a grave critical offence—and to privilege the
latter, implying that all literature would be *Middlemarch* if it
could. Lewis carefully distinguishes between levels of fantasy;
in ascending order of interest there is (*a*) delusion about
reality; (*b*) day-dreaming as consolation; and (*c*) 'Normal
Castle Building', which may be egoistic or disinterested. This
third entity leads to fiction, motivating both the production
and the reception to it. As a reader and writer of fiction
himself, Lewis preferred fantasy to realism, but he goes on to
make a judicious examination of the different modes of the
latter, outlining a valuable distinction between 'realism of
content' and 'realism of presentation'. French classical tragedy has the former and not the latter; medieval romance has
the latter and not the former; *War and Peace* has both; the
Orlando Furioso and *Rasselas* have neither. Lewis's taste for
fantasy and his relative coolness about realism chime with
recent literary opinion, both creative and critical.

The central argument of *An Experiment in Criticism* is a
challenging and original essay in what is now known as

'Reader Response' criticism, though I doubt if that phrase was current in 1961. Lewis begins by positing, not different kinds of book, but different kinds of reading, literary and non-literary. The former is receptive, attentive, concerned with form and the devices that bring pleasure, and always ready to look back, and reread; it is, in short, reading for its own sake, not as a means to an end. Non-literary reading is something we all have to do on occasion, when we are faced with the prose of information: official reports, office memoranda, most newspaper articles. Some readers, the 'non-literary' read like this all the time; they cannot think of invention as legitimate, they 'have no ears', they are unconscious of style; they like non-verbal narrative such as strip-cartoons and films, and in fiction they want rapid narrative, concentrating on a succession of events. They form the large majority of readers, Lewis says, adding that the distinction between literary and non-literary readers has nothing to do with moral virtue. Even people who are professionally concerned with literature may sometimes read in non-literary ways, like academics needing to advance themselves in their careers, or hard-pressed reviewers.

Lewis then proposes that books should not be divided and assessed in terms of their intrinsic qualities, as proposed by all critics since Aristotle, but by how they can be read. A work has a claim to 'literary' status if it can be read in a literary way, no matter by whom, or how unlikely the text in question. Lewis's account of the two kinds of reading provokes much reflection, though I am not sure how far it would stand up to probing analysis. 'Literary reading' is, I suspect, based on the way Lewis read himself, with its origins in his childhood discoveries in his father's book-filled house. For Lewis the ideal reader was the solitary enraptured child, finding in books an entrance to private enchantment. He wrote in *The Allegory of Love* that his ideal happiness would be convalescing from an illness, seated in a window overlooking the sea and reading Italian romance epics for many hours a day; the adult apotheosis of childhood experience. The model of literary reading was primarily receptive, even passive, though it also called for serious involvement with the pleasures of the text. Lewis makes little allowance for intentionality, the initial set of expectations with which we approach a text, which may be guided by an awareness of generic or other contextual considerations. Elsewhere, though, he shows himself aware of the way in which context defines meaning; in *The Personal Heresy* he wrote, 'every perception is what it is by virtue of its context'. One wonders if Lewis was here reflecting the beginnings of speech-act philosophy in Oxford in the late 1930s.

My present intention is not to give the argument of *An Experiment in Criticism* the careful consideration which it deserves and has not so far received. I am more interested in relating it to other aspects of Lewis's thought about literature, and to see what implications they hold for critical theory. Lewis's call for literary works to be defined by the way in which they can be read and not by any intrinsic elements is simultaneously élitist and egalitarian. It is élitist in that the number of people capable of the slow and time-consuming process of literary reading is likely to be small. The élite need not, however, be confined to those professionally concerned with reading literature. Lewis's idea is egalitarian in that the traditional divisions between literature and non-literature break down; *any* book can be claimed for literature if even one reader reads it in a genuinely literary way. The concept is developed from an earlier essay, 'High and Low Brows', first published in *Rehabilitations* in 1939. There Lewis divides books into two categories, 'A' and 'B'. The former are books written with a purpose, to make money, to preach, to console, to instruct, to entertain; the latter are written to provide disinterested pleasure and satisfaction; they are 'literature'. In the rapid processes of pedagogy, 'B' books may be praised as 'good' and 'A' books condemned as popular or 'commercial' or simply 'trash'. Lewis argues against such evaluative distinction, saying the categories are simply different and no more. (There may, indeed, have been a kind of deconstructive intent in calling the supposedly inferior category 'A', which would look like the higher mark in educational contexts.) Lewis argued for books to be located in vertical generic categories, which cut across the culturally loaded 'A'/'B' distinction. As an example he describes a genre called 'Simple Adventure Story', which would have the *Odyssey* at the top, followed in descending order by Scott, Stevenson, Morris, and Rider Haggard, with Edgar Wallace somewhere near the bottom. The proposed model was elaborate and not very satisfactory, since although it removed the distinction of value between 'A' and 'B' books, it reinserted it within the hierarchical generic structures. His later attempt on the problem, in *An Experiment in Criticism*, was simpler and more radical.

What characterizes both versions is Lewis's basic unease with the idea of literature as a privileged category; and this is what provides interesting alignments with recent theorists. In 'High and Low Brows' Lewis remarks, uncontroversially enough, that many of the 'B' books of our age were the 'A's of an earlier generation; not only Scott and Dickens, who were popular entertainers, but Fielding, Malory, and Shakespeare, and many others, back to the writers of metrical romances, and to Ovid:

What survives from most ages is chiefly either the work that had some religious or national appeal, or else the popular, commercial work produced for entertainment. I say 'chiefly' because the work of the 'pure' artists is not always ephemeral; a little, a very little, of it survives. But the great mass of literature which now fills class B is the work of men who wrote either piously, to edify their fellows, or commercially to earn their living by 'giving the public what it wanted'.

Lewis's implicit target here, and in similar arguments, is the *Scrutiny* school, and particularly, I believe, Q. D. Leavis's *Fiction and the Reading Public*, which posited an absolute distinction between 'good' books, which were literature, and 'bad' ones, which were a threat to civilization. As I have said, Lewis rejected the socio-cultural assumptions on which such distinctions were based; his own position was a form of Christian egalitarianism which hesitated to deny worth to any created thing.

Elsewhere Lewis expresses scepticism about the concept of literature itself:

discussions about 'Literature'—as if literature were a single homogeneous thing like water—are discussions about a non entity. Poetry is not a low nor a lofty, a useful or a mischievous, a grave or a trivial, a 'true' or a 'false' activity, any more than 'saying' is. In that sense there is really no such thing as literature—only a crowd of people using concrete language as well as they can to talk about anything that happens to interest them.

Is that a conservative or a radical sentiment? It is certainly a non-Arnoldian one. The Marxist Terry Eagleton concludes his *Literary Theory: An Introduction* with the conviction that literature does not exist, while the metatheorist Elizabeth Bruss has written of literature: 'When one is made to look at the category long enough and hard enough, it begins to come apart, with no attributes that are always and only literary, and few, if any, that are absolutely debarred.' The independent-minded conservative theorist, E. D. Hirsch, has expressed similar sentiments in *The Aims of Interpretation*:

literature has no independent essence, aesthetic or otherwise. It is an arbitrary classification of linguistic works which do not exhibit common distinctive traits, and which cannot be defined as an Aristotelian species. Aesthetic categories are intrinsic to aesthetic *inquiries*, but not to the nature of literary works . . . The idea of literature is not an essentialistic idea, and no critical approach can, without distortion, make essentialistic claims upon literature.

For Lewis the major underlying category in his aesthetic thinking was not 'literature' but 'myth', as we can see from his autobiography and other personal writings, as well as from his fiction.

Lewis was not a wholly consistent thinker about literature and literary experience. In a weak essay in *Rehabilitations* in defence of the Oxford English School, he adopts the reifying approach to the subject rejected in the passage quoted above. He presents English Literature as a 'tract of reality', a great rough countryside where the student sets forth with gun and fishing tackle, and is told to get himself a dinner. In this rather bizarre image Lewis engages in special pleading, in opposition to the more selective approach of the Cambridge English Tripos. It is hard to imagine that what he elsewhere presents as an empty concept could prove so fertile in nourishment. Oxford students who disagreed with Lewis's conviction that someone who does not know Anglo-Saxon is all his life a child among real English students (a childlike condition that has applied to nearly all English writers, and a great many scholars) and who wanted to study Victorian literature instead, would not have found the countryside as open as Lewis suggested. As L. C. Knights put it in his *Scrutiny* review of *Rehabilitation*: 'It seems to me that cutting off a hundred or two hundred years from this end of English literature and ignoring the history of the English people, social, economic and intellectual ... is a pretty arbitrary selection to begin with.' But Lewis was polemically and rhetorically trailing his coat in this essay.

His real importance and interest lie elsewhere. For a long time he was regarded as a reactionary and archaic defender of the academic *status quo*, which is what Knights called him at the end of his review; no doubt, Lewis would have happily accepted that description. Notwithstanding the insistent rhetorical flourishes, what emerges from Lewis's theoretical reflections is a deep scepticism about the habitual assumptions concerning literary study, particularly the Arnold–Newbolt–Cambridge approach and its cultural underpinnings. Now that approach is increasingly under attack by radical critics, Lewis's opposition to it acquires a new interest. The Christian Lewis and the latter-day Marxists both refuse to see literature as a self-sufficient source of immanent values. The Marxist–feminist–poststructuralist theorist Catherine Belsey was herself trained at Oxford, and her attack on Leavisism echoes old Oxford arguments as well as invoking the new radicalism:

Once upon a time, and a much simpler time it was, there were four great English novelists and D. H. Lawrence. All five of them were in favour of life, and in the course of their careers they were to varying degrees mature. Their maturity and their greatness could be demonstrated by longish quotations from their works which revealed plainly (that is, without the need to argue the case) whatever it was they were adduced in support of.

This was fine as long as you were clear that the main purpose of reading was to arrive at a judgment of an author's worth, as long as you could see what was so plainly evident in the quotes and, above all, as long as you were yourself mature and for life. When any of this was not the case, however, it came out as a tiny bit authoritarian. And when it also led in higher education to the training of generations of nineteen-year-olds to dismiss as immature substantial areas even of the work of the famous five, it began to seem more than a little absurd.

That, at least, is how it looked to those of us who went straight from C. S. Lewis to Roland Barthes, and always tended in consequence to see literary studies as a particularly pleasurable form of cultural history rather than as a secular religion, complete with moral teaching, mystical experiences and access to the continuity of felt life which linked the chosen of the modern world through the pre-eminent few to the prelapsarian organic community before the Civil War.

Belsey's vigorous, coarse-grained polemic not only recalls Lewis's attacks in *An Experiment in Criticism* on the 'Vigilant' school of critics; it echoes Gordon's condemnation of the religiosity of the Newbolt Report, sixty years earlier. Leavisism is now, I believe, part of history; it achieved a great deal, but saving civilization by the power of literary criticism was beyond it. In my reading, admittedly too neat and schematic, Leavis and Lewis were the dominant figures in literary study in the middle decades of this century. In the present cultural context, it is Lewis's arguments and assumptions that seem to me the more challenging, and to have something to contribute to contemporary debates, notwithstanding their antique accent and idiom.

5. BURSTING CANON

By the 1950s English was well established in British universities. The dreams of the nineteenth-century pioneers of democratic mass education, in which the study of vernacular literature would take the place formerly held by classics, seemed to have been fulfilled. The conviction of some early professors of the subject, like Sir Walter Raleigh, that English was suitable only for a small and appropriately equipped minority—echoed in our own day by the late Paul de Man—had not withstood the march of events and the pressure of demand. Though opposition persisted between scholars and critics, traditionalists and Leavisites, it was contained. C. S. Lewis's departure from Oxford in 1954 to a chair at Cambridge, where he was on good personal terms with F. R. Leavis, had a symbolic significance. Whatever disputes existed between factions, the establishment itself seemed stable, like a parliamentary system.

The expansion of academic English gave a fresh role to the critic, and after the Second World War a new generation of university-based critics appeared, rather belatedly, following their wartime service. John Bayley, Donald Davie, Richard Hoggart, Frank Kermode, and Raymond Williams, all published their first books in the fifties. Apart from Williams, whose death in 1988 was a bitter loss to British intellectual life, they are still active. Davie is also a distinguished poet, and Bayley and Williams published novels. Although academics, these critics were still in many respects men of letters, and were treated as such. Their books ranged widely, containing literary history and social criticism, as well as more conventional criticism of fiction and poetry, and they were discussed in the journals where such books were traditionally reviewed. At that time, criticism was still part of general intellectual discourse; thirty years later it has become a form of academic professionalism. In America professionalism was already well advanced; the establishment of English in universities had happened sooner and on a larger scale than in

Britain, and the New Critics were ascendant; Randall Jarrell wrote a famous complaining essay called 'The Age of Criticism'. In Britain the critical bridgehead was more modest, but offered grounds for confident expectations. For a time a Leavisite conviction about the social centrality of criticism reinforced a belief that the critic still had something to say to the wider culture. In 1953 an editorial in the little magazine *Mandrake*—founded by John Wain at Oxford in 1945—went so far as to claim that

as the inventor of the most complete terminology of the creative process, the critic, borrowing his methods from the logician as well as from the psychologist, has replaced the metaphysician since his findings show with a greater exactitude the nature of what we are.

Such confidence could not endure. To invoke lines by Louis MacNeice, 'This poise is perfect but maintained / For one day only.' What looked like the triumphant establishment of English contained the elements of its later instability; these elements were both intrinsic, in what I have described as the synthetic nature of the discipline, and extrinsic, in changing historical circumstance.

The cultural-nationalist strand had been vulnerable from the beginning, presupposing as it did the sacred union of language, literature, and nation. That union was still assumed in the anachronistic pieties of the Newbolt Report, but it was potentially called into question by the existence of a substantial body of literature that was written in English but made no claim to English identity. The canonical texts of what D. H. Lawrence was to call 'Classic American Literature' were all written well before the end of the nineteenth century. It is true that the Americans had been slow to recognize that there was such a canon, and its ultimate emergence no doubt had much to do with the development of a self-confident American cultural nationalism. By now, American Literature is widely accepted, all over the world, as a quite separate canon from English, and is often studied and taught in separate institutional structures. As so often, questions of cultural development cannot be easily separated from questions about institutions. A familiar figure in Continental universities is the academic who is a specialist in American

Literature, as opposed to English Literature, because of the funded opportunities it provides to pursue research and attend conferences in the United States.

In the light of these later developments, there is ironic interest and enlightenment in some words that Matthew Arnold published a century ago. They show Arnold in his wilfully supercilious vein—almost to the point of self-parody—and were all the more provocative in that they were addressed to American readers:

I see advertised *The Primer of American Literature.* Imagine the face of Philip or Alexander at hearing of a Primer of Macedonian Literature! Are we to have a primer of Canadian Literature, too, and a Primer of Australian? We are all contributories to one great literature—English Literature. The contribution of Scotland to this literature is far more serious and important than that of America has so far had time to be; yet a 'Primer of Scotch Literature' would be an absurdity. And these things are not only absurd; they are also retarding.

Some of Arnold's rhetorical questions can be given direct answers; there are, if not 'primers', certainly histories of Canadian and Australian literature, and, indeed, of Scottish literature too. Australia has produced a Nobel prize-winner in Patrick White, and Margaret Atwood and Robertson Davies are Canadian novelists with world-wide reputations. A strong sense of national identity inevitably implies a national literature; this is true, in varying degrees, of all the newer English-speaking nations. The concept of a national literature presupposes cultural nationalism, and vice-versa. In calling for a global English Literature which transcended individual nations Arnold was flying in the face of history. Nevertheless, his patronizing rhetoric was informed by assumptions which, for their time, were reasonable and still have something to be said for them. A substantial literature already existed in the United States, but was invisible to Arnold, just as it was still invisible to the writers of the Newbolt Report over thirty years later. When he wrote, Britain and the United States still seemed to be a unified cultural as well as linguistic area. Americans famously waited on the quayside for the arrival of the ship bringing the next instalment of a serialized Dickens novel; but the traffic was not all one way. Henry Wadsworth Longfellow was a prodigiously popular poet in Britain as well as in America (his present total occlusion is a remarkable indication of the power of established canons to exclude as well as to include). My mother was given a copy of Longfellow's poems as a school prize in 1912 and she knew some of them by heart. She enjoyed, too, the children's stories of Louisa M. Alcott. I read them myself in childhood and was puzzled by the elements of unfamiliarity in settings and attitudes.

In claiming that all literature in English was part of a larger English Literature Arnold was invoking an idea of some splendour that exists as a ghostly opposite to the mutual involvement of vernacular and nationalism: *Weltliteratur*. If English is a global language, as was already becoming apparent in the 1880s, why should it not produce a global literature? It might have done so, in an age without emerging nationalism, just as, in the days of Imperial Rome, men of different races and regions contributed to Latin literature. In the modernism of the early twentieth century the idea of World Literature revived, though generally as polyglottal discourse rather than as universal English. It was advocated by Eugene Jolas, editor of *transition*, the avant-garde Paris review that serialized Joyce's 'Work in Progress', later *Finnegans Wake*, which went some way to inventing a world language based on English. A form of *Weltliteratur* was invoked by Pound in the *Cantos*, and by Hugh MacDiarmid in his late long poems. But Arnold had in mind something closer to the model of Latin, an international and imperial language. The ideal remains unrealizable, for political and cultural as well as linguistic reasons. Imperialism is unacceptable, whereas nationalism continues to be a potent force in the world. There is what looks like a precise answer to Arnold's claim in Colin MacCabe's inaugural lecture at the University of Strathclyde, where he became a Professor of English Studies after the turbulencies at Cambridge in 1981. MacCabe wrote:

'English Literature is dead—long live writing in English'. The multiplication of Englishes throughout the world and their attendant literatures, the impossibility of holding literary development within any one centrally agreed form, it is this explosion of writing in English which reflects back on the past to fissure the monument that is English literature into a plurality of writings.

If Arnold's model is imperialism, MacCabe's is decolonization, and fundamental to it is the assumption that every anglophone country has a different English and a different literature. MacCabe's illustrative tropes, of an explosion and a fissured monument, are very much in my mind in the present work.

I have been pressing rather hard on the element of cultural nationalism that is involved in the study of English (or any other vernacular) literature. This should certainly not be taken as implying that all writers in a given language are inevitably nationalistic. Writers can be, and often are, radical, internationalist, pacifist, and deliberately unpatriotic. We are familiar, too, with those writers who adopt a different language from the one with which they grew up: Conrad or Nabokov in English or Julian Green in French. Again there are the painfully difficult choices facing writers in an ex-colonial situation: whether to write in a vernacular, which will reach only a comparatively small audience, or the former imperial language, which might reach a very large one. Nearer home there is the bilingualism, in English and Gaelic, or English and Welsh, that we find in some writers from the smaller constituent nations of the North-Western Archipelago. There is, too, the bilingualism of cosmopolitan expatriates, such as Samuel Beckett or Joseph Brodsky. My argument, in fact, does not apply to individual writers at all, but to 'literature' as an institutionalized concept. Literature in this sense is, in Roland Barthes's phrase, what gets taught rather than what gets written. Even within a national literary canon there may be a tension or conflict between national and international ways of conceiving literature. The division in American literature between Palefaces and Redskins is one instance, and another lay in the disagreements between the nationalistic Hugh MacDiarmid and the cosmopolitan Edwin Muir about the nature of Scottish literature.

The rise of literary nationalism has resulted in a conceptually untidy situation. American literature has a separate identity from English, but there are figures who belong to both: James, Eliot, Auden, Sylvia Plath. Malcolm Lowry was born and died in England, but he lived much of his life in Canada and wrote his major works there, so in that country he is regarded as part of the national literature. The self-confident emergence of American literature has imposed on

the makers of anthologies and textbooks the need to establish
a separate category of 'British Literature', which develops in
parallel with American Literature, though the further back
one gets in time the more the older concept of English
Literature seems appropriate. Thus, Shakespeare and Milton
certainly belong to English Literature, and Dickens and
Tennyson probably do, while Philip Larkin and William
Golding form part of 'British Literature'. And in such contexts
'British' is in any case of uncertain application; broadly
speaking it refers to writing produced in the British Isles,
except that Irish writers reasonably object to the classification, as Seamus Heaney did, when he was included in the
Penguin Book of Contemporary British Poetry (though he was born
in Northern Ireland, and has British citizenship); another
recent anthology was more accommodatingly called *Some
Contemporary Poets of Britain and Ireland*. Nationalism makes
definition difficult. In practice, one could argue, 'British
literature' is what gets published by British—usually English—publishing houses and periodicals, regardless of prov-
enance within the British Isles. It would also include the work
of the talented expatriates who have greatly added to the
vigour of the British novel in recent years, like Salman
Rushdie, Timothy Mo, and Kazuo Ishiguro, as well as writers
from an older generation, such as Dan Jacobson from South
Africa, Doris Lessing, who was born in what was then Persia
and grew up in what was then Rhodesia, and V. S. Naipaul
from Trinidad.

A rational model of the situation would be unusably
complex. It would begin with the fact that English is now a
global language but was once restricted to the British Isles.
When it was so restricted and for some subsequent centuries,
'English Literature' was what was written, in English, in
those islands, though never just in England; it might include
writing from other parts of the world, like the beginnings of
literary expression in colonial America. But when other
anglophone literatures, first in the United States and then
elsewhere, begin to develop, the concept of English Literature
has to be replaced by 'Literature in English'. This would
cover many constituent literatures, of which British would be
only one, first among equals, perhaps, because of its venerable

origins and illustrious practitioners, but with no further claim to supremacy. And if one interprets 'British' simply to mean work from the British Isles, then it would need several subsets: English, Scottish, Welsh, Irish, and, perhaps, Ulster. So, indeed, might a category like West Indian Literature; how large a constituent literature, or a subset of it, has to be to warrant separate recognition could be a contentious matter, depending on whether one used a defining discourse that was primarily nationalist or primarily literary. Academic organization, with its outriders in publishing, still tends to recognize only three main areas: 'English' literature (i.e. of the British Isles), 'American', and 'Commonwealth', which takes under its wing everything not included in the first two, and is now a manifestly inadequate category.

These speculations and definitions have probably become tedious, but I have pursued them to show just how much confusion and contradiction is concealed when the seemingly innocuous term 'English Literature' is invoked. My personal inclination would be to get back to something like Arnold's capacious understanding of the term, so that all literature written in English would somehow belong to it. But that is no longer feasible; it would invite a charge of imperialism, and it overlooks the degree of cultural specificity implied by the idea of a national literature. There is the related consideration that the cherished literature of new nations often consists of young and tender shoots which might not survive if assessed by the highest standards of critical rigour.

The internationalizing of literature in English has been parallelled by the internationalizing of its study. Every self-respecting university, not only in the English-speaking world, but practically everywhere else, has an entity called an English Department. (I am told that the University of Montreal is an exception, for local political reasons.) As I have remarked, all kinds of activities go on in such places, but it is likely that a lot of time will be devoted to studying and teaching the traditional canon of English Literature, which was largely coextensive with Literature in English; that is to say, from medieval times, or earlier, to the nineteenth century. This internationalizing was not a situation envisaged by the writers of the Newbolt Report. For them, a young student of the English language and its literature was acquiring a great national heritage. The assumption is succinctly summed up in the title of a book by George Sampson, one of the Report's contributors: *English for the English*. In the *Scrutiny* era it was continued when writers were praised for their essential Englishness, a phrase which is not likely to mean much in other parts of the world. Within this mental framework, English was indeed for the English; dubiously so, perhaps, for Americans, who spoke the same language and in some lights could seem like a peculiar version of the English; and not at all for Poles or Japanese. In an earlier draft of this Chapter I wrote, 'An Englishman reading Chaucer or Dickens will, however vaguely and unconsciously, feel himself the heir of traditions which they expressed and developed.' That now looks overstated; the idea of being the unconscious heir to anything provokes a certain scepticism. Many modern students of English seem to have no sense of the past at all. But it may develop in later life; as evidence, one can point to the immense interest in contemporary Britain in museums, which have become a growth industry, and in visiting country houses. The idea of a national heritage is alive; often in factitious, tourist-orientated forms, but taking other and more authentic forms, too, in an interest in vanished ways of popular living, and the early development of industrialism. I shall amend my earlier statement, to the effect that an Englishman (or a British person) reading earlier literature, may if properly responsive to it, find a sense of continuities in mores and customs and attitudes, as well as in nature and landscape and climate. Sometimes these can be very material: the street names and plans of parts of London still link us not only to Dickens but to Ben Jonson. These continuities have been imaginatively exploited by Peter Ackroyd in his novels. Potentially but not certainly, the British reader has a more intimate contact with earlier literature and its cultural contexts than a reader in another country.

This has long been an issue for Americans, who inherited the language, and some of the traditions—legal and parliamentary in particular—whilst firmly rejecting others. They saw themselves, too, as heirs of the literature, though with some diffidences. Shakespeare was part of American literary

culture, but American actors felt they couldn't act Shakespeare. For a long time WASP anglophilia and pieties about
Our Old Home masked the growing cultural division, but in
the end it became inescapable. Reading the canon of English
Literature was still central in American education, but with
little sense of context or matrix. What could a Hispanic
student in New Mexico, or a black in New Jersey, make of
Wordsworth? Quite a lot perhaps, but in different ways from
the British, who are likely to have daffodils in the garden
every spring and the Lake District within visitable distance.
American education responded to the need for forms of
reading independent of cultural and historical context with
the triumphant advance of the New Criticism, which concentrated on the 'words on the page' and their internal structures,
following the publication in 1938 of *Understanding Poetry* by
Cleanth Brooks and Robert Penn Warren. Over a generation
later the vogue in American English departments of deconstruction, which practised a more radical form of context-less
reading, met the same basic need.

The American experience has had visible effects on the
teaching of English in England. The existence of a substantial
American canon, which is read and studied not only in the
United States but throughout the world, has relativized the
traditional English canon. Americans may sometimes
approach their own literature in a mystique of cultural
nationalism; when they study ours—and it has to be remem-
bered that the American academy is still much more extensively concerned with English literature than with
American—they do so in a spirit of brisk professionalism that
is not interested in 'essential Englishness' or the biography of
a nation. Inevitably these attitudes reflect back into the
British situation. It is also significant that much of the current
interest in literary theory has American origins. Current
French theorists are usually translated, and mediated in
others ways, by Americans.

If the potential subject-matter of English study has
extended spatially, into separate literatures across the globe,
it also expands temporally and inexorably at the rate of many
hundreds of volumes a year, since new books are continually
appearing and are rapidly assimilated into the canon. This is

to offer a somewhat simplified account of a complex process. In the early years there was much resistance to the idea of studying recent work in literature courses, though with occasional exceptions; Gerald Graff records that William Lyon Phelps was lecturing on the modern novel at Yale in the 1890s. And in the halcyon days of Cambridge English in the 1920s the links with literary modernism were close: Richards lectured on Eliot and Leavis on Joyce. Oxford, where the undergraduate syllabus used to end in 1830, was more characteristic. When I was engaged in literary research there in the 1950s it was a rule that living authors were not to be studied. When J. I. M. Stewart was commissioned to write the final volume in the *Oxford History of English Literature* his brief was to exclude the living. As a result the book has no account of T. S. Eliot, who died soon after it was published. Even those quite long dead but still 'modern' were regarded with suspicion in some quarters. Anthony Burgess has recalled of his own student days at Manchester University: 'My own professor of English regarded, in 1937, the poems of Gerard Manley Hopkins (died 1889, first published 1918) as too dangerously contemporary even for a session of practical criticism.' Eliot himself did not much approve of English as a university subject and was positively opposed to the study of contemporary writing; he must have been disconcerted at the extent to which his own work had become the object of a critical industry in his own lifetime. C. S. Lewis expressed his thoughts on the matter with characteristic pungency: 'There is an inherent absurdity in making current literature a subject of academic study, and the student who wants a tutor's assistance in reading the works of his own contemporaries might as well ask for a nurse's assistance in blowing his own nose.'

Lewis's remark has interesting implications. It presupposes that the task of the teacher lies in removing contextual difficulty—historical, cultural, linguistic—and that a contemporary text will not present any such difficulty, so there is nothing for the teacher to do. Such texts should be instantly transparent and accessible to the reader. At a time when the difficult masterpieces of modernist literature were still appearing it was, to say the least, an anachronistic attitude. It points to Lewis's lack of interest in systematic interpretation and evaluation, though he was quite capable of engaging in them when his interest was aroused; see, for instance, his admirable discussion of Rider Haggard's *She*. Against Lewis one can set a remark by Allen Tate, that the critic who tells us he understands Dryden but cannot understand Hopkins is telling us he does not understand Dryden. Tate presupposed an ideal of absolute literary competence needed to read any poetry, of any age, that would inevitably involve interpretation and judgement and which found its greatest challenge in contemporary work, where there were no historical dimensions interposed between reader and text. Tate's observation refers to the competence of the teacher, without implying that universities should necessarily offer courses in modern literature. In recent years, however, the battle to exclude it has been definitively lost, largely as a result of student (or consumer) pressure, even in the Oxford English Faculty.

The arguments for exclusion nevertheless remain plausible even if inutile. Anthony Burgess is one distinguished living writer—himself now the object of academic study and 'research'—who accepts them. After the sentence quoted above about his professor's resistance to Hopkins, Burgess continues:

He was probably right. If a writer ceased writing sixty years ago we are conceivably in a position to judge his worth. I have enough of the aborted scholar in me to express doubts about the advisability of studying Iris Murdoch or William Golding or Philip Larkin or Seamus Heaney [*or presumably Anthony Burgess*] in a university course. By about 2030 AD we shall know how we stand with regard to these writers.

By then, of course, many of us will be dead, and today's students will be elderly. They do not wish to wait so long. Again, the underlying assumption of Burgess's comment is worth making explicit. It is that only the worthy, who form part of a timeless order of excellence, or a Great Tradition, are fit for academic study; and that worthiness takes a long time to establish, being indicated by what Johnson called the long continuance of esteem. In fact, texts get into literary syllabuses, particularly from more remote periods, not because they are conspicuously excellent, but simply because they are there, having survived when much else has perished.

Courses on recent literature may, indeed, risk spending time on writing that will not endure. It is a risk that students are quite happy to take, since their fundamental concern is not aesthetic but cultural. Contemporary literature is a focus of interest because it *is* contemporary; it offers, with the refractions and intensities of art, a fresh sense of the Way We Live Now, not necessarily in simple mimetic terms. Or that, at least, is the aspiration. Allowing for differences in disciplines and their constituencies, the interest in contemporary literature is not vastly different from that of students of politics or sociology in contemporary society and culture. Indeed, courses in these subjects sometimes use literary texts as illustrative material. This use, and the general interest in literary works as cultural texts rather than as aesthetic entities, is likely to be disturbing to some teachers of literature. The attempt of the cultural to displace the aesthetic, and the tension between them, is an important element in present difficulties.

I have over the years taught courses in modern, and sometimes in contemporary, literature in British and American universities, and have generally enjoyed the experience, partly because of the student interest and enthusiasm such courses can arouse. Intellectually, though, I have a suspicion that the conservative arguments of Lewis or Burgess may be right. If one has a sense of actual literary value, and of even a residual canon, it is hard to disagree with Burgess's claim that time spent in the 1970s studying Kesey or Brautigan was time wasted: 'the time better spent on a book of *Paradise Lost* or *The Rape of the Lock* was now past and irrecoverable.' It is possible, though, to move, in the study of recent texts, from cultural questions to literary ones, and then to matters of interpretation and value. These, in turn, can point towards the study of older literature. A further consideration is that the demand for ever more contemporary literature as a field of study springs from the determinism of the academy. It is felt that the only way to read anything at all is in an institutional context, by institutional methods. Teaching literature has thus been too successful for its own good; to return to Lewis's derisive image people believe that the only proper, professional way to blow one's nose is the way one's nurse teaches.

Taken together, the spatial and the temporal expansion amount to an explosion, which it would take a three-dimensional model to illustrate adequately. Not only are more and more interesting, even meritorious poems and plays and novels steadily accreting to the canons of British or American literature, there are the other healthily developing anglophone literatures. Proponents of the latter tend to adopt a censorious tone in their claims; it is, we are urged, a scandal and a disgrace that more attention is not given to Nigerian or Indian or New Zealand or other literatures, whether in universities or by private readers in Britain or the United States. National literatures still demand an international readership. And each of them generates an extensive secondary literature: biographies and critical studies, and the primers of Australian or Canadian literature that Matthew Arnold found such an absurd idea.

No one, of course, can read everything, though university teachers do not find it easy to admit that there is any book in their 'field' that they have not read. Fond memories persist of the easier times that existed until about a generation ago, when it was possible for a determined reader to 'keep up' with scholarly work in English as well as to 'keep abreast' of new writing by living writers. That is no longer feasible, least of all for young aspiring academics, whose domestic conditions often seem to make sustained intellectual work all but impossible. Similar situations pertain in other areas of knowledge, *a fortiori* the physical sciences. But there the response is frank professionalism and specialization. Indeed, there are some scientific researchers whose work can be properly understood and assessed by only two or three other scholars in the world, which can cause difficulty in promotion procedures. The humanities, and literary study in particular, are reluctant to accept specialization so openly, though the Americans do so in practice. Specialization is the sensible way forward in professional terms, but it is alien to the spirit which brought vernacular literature into education. The pioneers had no conception of the problems brought by an exploding canon. Believing that English Literature could replace Classics as a humane force in popular education, they no doubt envisaged a corpus approximately as fixed as the corpus of Classical literature, where the same great or major texts could go on being studied indefinitely. Oxford English succeeded for a long time in fixing a curricular *terminus ad quem* in the early nineteenth century, but eventually had to give way. Some of these issues are, in more than one sense, academic. Teachers may feel under pressure, but they muddle through as best they can; notionally upholding the idea of literary study as a broad and still undivided subject, but in practice reconciling themselves to teaching it in a fragmentary fashion. Where the problems become both material and painfully demanding is in the matter of syllabus reform. Discussions of this subject can generate much heat and anguish, since that is where irreconcilable positions are made public, involving a clash not only of conceptual models but of forms of life. Where reform is concerned most participants in discussion are likely to be very fertile in suggesting additions—Women's Writing, Black Writing, History of Ideas, Critical Theory, Creative Writing, Scholarly Method, Classics in Translation, etc.—but are extremely reluctant to give up any of their own courses (though ready to suggest that their colleagues might) to make room for these new areas. But quarts are not to be forced into pint pots, the British undergraduate degree takes only three years, and students' attention spans and capacity to read for very long at a time remain strictly limited. The question of canons, how they are drawn up, preserved, and transmitted, has become prominent and vexatious in the 1980s. In addition to the global expansion and the steady advance into the present and future which I have described, there are ideological pressures for a backward revision of the canon, uncovering neglected texts of the past by women and working-class writers. Questions about canonicity are prominent among those raised by the academic institutionalizing of literary study.

6. BEYOND BELIEF AND BEAUTY

We have seen how the global expansion of writing in English weakened the cultural–nationalist strand in the institution of 'English Literature'. I shall now attempt to show how the religious, ethical, and aesthetic constituents have also become weakened. I previously outlined, perhaps too schematically, the opposition between the 'Oxford' and 'Cambridge' approaches to the subject. One was historical, or at least chronological, combining supposedly objective scholarship and private appreciation. The other was orientated towards criticism, social as well as literary, and regarded the study of literature as extending to 'life and thought', with a direct concern for the preservation of civilization. By the 1950s this opposition was becoming less absolute; to enlarge on an image I have already used, the Labour and Conservative parties may attack each violently in parliament and in the country at large, but will join forces to defend the parliament-ary system from the extremes of left or right (or, indeed, in resisting constitutional innovations such as proportional rep-resentation). Brian Doyle, in a valuable unpublished thesis surveying the cultural history of English studies in British higher education, has shown that by the 1950s the Oxford-based *Review of English Studies* was coming closer to Leavis's approach, moving beyond its previous narrow professionalism to take in larger cultural questions, and to accept literary criticism as a discipline. In the 1960s, the Scrutineer L. C. Knights was Edward VII Professor at Cambridge, and the traditionalist Helen Gardner was Merton Professor at Oxford: both were to write in passionate defence of the imagination. A little later 'humanist' became a term of abuse among Althusserian Marxists and Foucauldians (as it had once been among reactionary Catholics). It is sometimes convenient to accept our enemies' definitions of us, and I shall locate both the Oxford and Cambridge traditions, as they began to draw closer together in the face of alien threats, in the venerable category of humanist.

A prominent feature of literary humanism, in its Cambridge division, was the sense that in some sense literature, or criticism, could fill the space once occupied by religion. This belief rested on a number of assumptions, first made explicit by Richards: that organized religion was giving way before science and secularism; that religion had a necessary part to play in social and individual integration; that, as Arnold had argued, the essential element in religion was not doctrine but emotion, or 'poetry'; and that the latter might be preserved when dogma had disappeared before the forces of history. A deeper general assumption was that 'something' was needed to take the place of religion; this attitude characterized an advancing secularism still illuminated by the afterglow of a declining faith. Eliot once remarked, 'Nothing in this world is a substitute for anything else', and as secularism became total (if in fact it has, which is a matter for debate among sociologists of religion; I am assuming the point now for the sake of the argument), it appeared that not only would religion have to go, but so too would surrogate religions. So we find Catherine Belsey mocking Leavisism as a secular religion. Paul de Man called for

a change in the rationale for the teaching of literature, away from standards of cultural excellence that, in the last analysis, are always based on some form of religious faith, to a principle of disbelief that is not so much scientific as critical, in the full philosophical sense of the term.

In his influential essay, 'The Rhetoric of Temporality', de Man denied validity to 'symbol', which has been a central concept in literary discourse since the Romantics, and which particularly appealed to Christians, such as David Jones and some of the New Critics, because of its analogical resemblance to the idea of sacrament. De Man argued that 'symbol' always collapses into allegory, where the relation between word and experience is entirely arbitrary.

De Man breathed the bleak, bracing air of the systematic atheist. A related development in the fashion among critics and theorists of calling themselves 'materialist', though without the qualifying epithets once customary among Marxists (a reversal of evaluative significance, from negative to positive, as striking as the reversal, in the opposite direction, of the implications of 'humanist'). This evinces a desire to distance themselves, not just from religion, but from the philosophical idealism that might seem to be associated with it, notwithstanding the problems of deducing values from a materialistic world-view. It may also be relevant that a leading contemporary critical theorist, Jonathan Culler, is fanatically antiChristian (as was William Empson in an earlier generation). The reverent agnosticism of eminent Victorians is no longer part of the landscape, and the use of quasi-religious language to defend the value of literature seems less and less plausible.

The use of literature as valuable exempla for right action, in other words, the ethical dimension, long antedates the use of literature as religion. It was an ideal of the Renaissance, coexisting with Christianity, rooted in the humanism of the classics. The Horatian prescription *dulce et utile* summarized its application: edifying truths and models presented in a pleasing form. The practitioners of Oxford English, whose formal study was based on Literae Humaniores, were inheritors of this tradition; in practice it valued great literature for what it revealed of the personal qualities of the great men who produced it; biography was thus almost as valuable as literature itself. This was Tillyard's position; C. S. Lewis showed his independence from Oxford English, which encouraged biographical scholarship, as well as from Cambridge, by rejecting it. Lewis, in fact, had a marked distaste for Renaissance humanism, as Helen Gardner ruefully acknowledged in her British Academy memorial lecture. The humanistic ideal, whether derived from classics or from English, has not worn well. The models of human excellence it presented, far from being universal and timeless, were all too obviously part of a specific culture, noble though its antecedents undoubtedly were. There were many people for whom they had little value or attraction, particularly women, who from the beginning had formed a major constituency in the study of vernacular literature. But the main charge against classical humanism is that it did not work. George Steiner has dwelt with pain and eloquence on the failure of European humanism to avert the emergence of Nazism, the Holocaust, and the descent of a continent into mass barbarism. Men of the finest classical

culture were among the worst of the barbarians. The Second
World War made the once-confident claims for the ethical
value of a literary education seem peculiarly hollow. In
retrospect it seems naïve to have believed them. If Christianity, a religion of peace and love, but armed with supernatural
sanctions, has proved itself unable through history to prevent
its adherents from engaging in atrocity and massacre, why
should we have expected so much from a merely ethical code?

I turn now to the aesthetic strand, which is the hardest to
discuss coherently, or even to keep steadily in view. The very
word 'aesthetic' remains alien and imperfectly assimilated
into English. The *OED* records how it arrived from Germany
in the early decades of the nineteenth century, and though it
was employed by Coleridge and Carlyle among others, they
did so reluctantly, protesting at a barbarous neologism which
nevertheless seemed necessary in defining an emerging field
of philosophical study. The word carries two principal areas
of meaning. The first, looking back to the original Greek
sense, pertains to sensuous perception; the second, and more
common, invokes the idea of the beautiful. 'Aesthetics' has
now become an established if lowly branch of academic
philosophy. In the terminology of literary criticism, 'aesthetic'
tends to have unfavourable resonances, calling up stock
responses about Wildean epigrams, art for art's sake, and
poets in ivory towers. In Kantian terms, aesthetic activity
was contemplative, 'purposiveness without purpose', not concerned with practical behaviour or ends beyond itself (though
Kant believed that beauty was the symbol of the morally
good). Schiller, in the letters on aesthetic education, made a
significant development of the aesthetic, equating it with the
concept of play: an activity that can be truly active and
absorbing, yet autotelic and disinterested (an ideal easily
perverted, however, as when sports are made the focus of
local or national passions). Schiller left a quasi-political
legacy, the left-Romantic tradition, in which aesthetic play is
seen as offering images of liberation and utopian possibility.
Herbert Marcuse continued this tradition in the 1960s, but it
has made little impact on the generally anhedonic participants in recent British critical debate.

The rationales for the institutional study of literature have not often been avowedly and overtly aesthetic, any more than they have been overtly religious; both were largely implicit, to be traced in terminology and forms of argument. The aesthetic sometimes tended to pull towards the religious, as in the *fin de siècle* Religion of Beauty, which attracted the young Stephen Dedalus; T. S. Eliot condemned Arnold's ideal of sentiment-based religion as no more than a version of aestheticism. Combinations of the aesthetic and the nationalist proved popular in the past, in such compilations as *The Golden Treasury*, and, as Paul Fussell has shown, in the cultic value of *The Oxford Book of English Verse* among British front-line soldiers in the First World War. They persist in this day in such cultural manifestations as coffee-table books illustrating the beauties of the English countryside, or the advertisements of the British Tourist Board, where 'England' is an entirely aesthetic entity.

Though anglophone critics find the aesthetic a troublesome concept, its presence may be inferred when the end of literary study is said to be 'appreciation', 'pleasure', or 'enjoyment'. These words were common among the luminaries of Oxford English, from Walter Raleigh and George Gordon, to C. S. Lewis, David Cecil, and Helen Gardner. The last-named has offered a formulation which adds a Platonic and Christian bias to the Kantian concept of aesthetic response as 'disinterested satisfaction': 'Those who hold seriously to enjoyment as the true end of reading speak from within the Greek tradition which rates the life of contemplation above the life of action and holds that man's destiny is to enjoy the vision of truth, beauty and goodness.' Such a formulation would not be acceptable to Leavisites, who have never been happy with enjoyment; nor to Marxists, who believe that the task of literature, like that of philosophy, is not to contemplate the world but to change it. A more pragmatic objection to uses of 'enjoyment' like Gardner's is that the term is so loose it can apply equally to the contemplation and reception of the Beatific Vision, a Chinese vase, or a good dinner.

If 'enjoyment' is an intractable term, 'beauty' is far more so. It is a major Platonic idea and the heart of the discipline of aesthetics. But, 'Beauty is difficult'; the phrase, attributed to Aubrey Beardsley, recurs in Pound's *Pisan Cantos*. Modern criticism has wished to be rid of it. For I. A. Richards, writing in 1924, 'That paralysing apparition, Beauty, the ineffable, ultimate, unanalysable, simple Idea, has at least been dismissed' by recent developments in aesthetics. Benedetto Croce, in his influential *Aesthetic*, first published in English in 1909, attempted to avoid the words 'beauty' and 'beautiful' because of their unruly multiple associations, but decided in the tenth chapter of his book that beauty was an unavoidable concept and acceptable when defined in his terms as the expression of emotion in art. Croce's English follower R. G. Collingwood changed his mind about beauty, eventually claiming that it had nothing to do with the aesthetic, since the word applied to anything that was exceptionally fine of its kind: a beautifully cooked dinner as much as a rose or a picture. Peter Jones, in an outline of Collingwood's philosophy of art, has commented,

> In the early work, beauty, defined as imaginative coherence, was the aim of art and posed the central problem for the philosophy of art . . . later, however, the term merely denoted an attitude of admiration . . . which suggests that perhaps Collingwood had taken more notice of I. A. Richards than he was wont to admit.

Certainly, it has been a long time since 'beauty' played much part in the language of criticism. Wittgenstein remarked in his lectures on aesthetics that we are better off with a terminology that effectively combines evaluation and description. If, for instance, we are pleased with a suit that has been made for us, we approve of the specific qualities, the quality of the material, the styling, the skill of the cut, and so forth. (Though we may still want to call the whole thing a beautiful suit.) This is approximately equivalent to the procedure of the practical critic of a literary text; aesthetic satisfaction is implied in the analysis rather than specifically stated.

Yet the affective response which promotes the idea of beauty and the beautiful is not easily suppressed and assumes many disguises. Indeed, Richards, in a dismissive footnote on Croce, quotes Giovanni Papini's gibe, 'that the entire aesthetic system of Croce amounts merely to a hunt for pseudonyms of the word "art", and may indeed be stated briefly and accurately in this formula: art = intuition = expression =

feeling = imagination = fancy = lyricism = beauty.' A recent sympathetic commentator on Croce acknowledges that he saw 'art', 'lyricality', and 'beauty' as synonyms. The search for synonyms may be defensible as a series of repeated shots at pinning down the ineffable. Furthermore, latter-day linguistics insists that, strictly, there are no synonyms.

If 'beauty' is no longer available, other words in Papini's list remain current critical language, such as 'expression', 'feeling', 'imagination', and, perhaps, 'intuition'. Critics and teachers of literature do not now often speak of poets pursuing beauty, but they may well praise them for their power of imagination and capacity for the precise expression of feeling. The neo-idealist aesthetics of Croce and Collingwood seems very remote from the current climate in critical theory; yet Crocean ideas were widely diffused in the early twentieth century and, I believe, have had a more persistent influence than is generally assumed. They tended to reinforce and direct traditional High Romantic concepts, such as the unity and indivisibility of the literary work, the act of reading as an immediate intuitive apprehension of the poet's expression, and the irrelevance of historical, philosophical, generic, and rhetorical considerations. The well-known opening of D. H. Lawrence's polemical essay on Galsworthy offers a possible instance:

Literary criticism can be no more than a reasoned account of the feeling produced upon the critic by the book he is criticising. Criticism can never be a science; it is, in the first place, much too personal, and in the second, it is concerned with values that science ignores. The touchstone is emotion, not reason. We judge a work of art by its effect on our sincere and vital emotion, and nothing else. All the critical twiddle-twaddle about style and form, all the pseudo-scientific classifying of books in an imitation-botanical fashion is mere impertinence and mostly dull jargon.

One is reminded of basic Romantic formulations, such as Keats's opposition between 'the false beauty proceeding from art' and 'the true voice of feeling'. But the sentiment is also Crocean, in the emphasis on emotion as the touchstone, and particularly in the impatience with pseudo-scientific classifying. I have found no evidence that Lawrence read Croce; but the ideas were in the air. Collingwood's denunciation, in *The Principles of Art*, of bad art as a form of corrupt consciousness

has a Leavisite fervour. Indeed, René Wellek has detected a
Crocean aspect to Leavis: 'he quickly leaves the verbal surface
in order to define the particular emotion or sentiment which
an author conveys. Like Croce, he is primarily interested in
"sentiment" . . .'. Discussing a very different critical tradition,
that of the Russian Formalists, who were among the ancestors
of structuralism, Krystyna Pomorska has observed that
although the original Formalists were not overtly concerned
with evaluation, 'they seem to accept silently the principle
enounced by Croce: that our evaluation of art is always and
necessarily intuitive.'

Crocean aesthetics, resisting the traditional idea of genres
and kinds, turns the whole of literature into a single genre, in
which each individual work is judged in terms of its own
unique expression of emotion. E. D. Hirsch has called this the
'Broad Genre' theory of evaluation. On the whole, philosophical aesthetics seems to work better with musical, pictorial,
and plastic arts than with literature, which has to use words
when it talks to us. And words, notoriously, are rendered
aesthetically impure by carrying meanings. This remains true,
despite Pater's dictum that 'all art inspires to the condition of
music', and such twentieth-century formulations as Archibald
MacLeish's neo-symbolist claim that 'A poem must not mean
but be' or Samuel Beckett's insistence that Joyce's *Finnegans
Wake* was not about a reality, but was that reality itself.

Hirsch has addressed the problem that literature cannot be
satisfactorily and completely identified with art in the Crocean sense (nor with expression, intuition, feeling, and so
forth). He argues, conclusively, I think, that literature is not
an intrinsic concept, though it may present aesthetically
rewarding qualities when, so to speak, it is regarded through
aesthetic spectacles. He gives principled grounds for dealing
with a familiar stumbling-block for students and teachers of
literature, which is that many canonical texts have little
aesthetic value. They may be in the canon by the accident of
survival from a remote epoch; by their historical, cultural, or
intellectual interest; or because they form part of the œuvre
of a writer whose greatest works do meet the claims of art. In
the last case the implied justification is not aesthetic, but

reflects the conviction—which has both Romantic and clas-sical-humanist antecedents—that a great writer is a great man, and that everything he writes is therefore of interest. It is a view that Lewis argued against vehemently in *The Personal Heresy* and which was given a philosophical rationale in the phenomenological criticism of the Geneva School (most acces-sible in English in Hillis Miller's early work). Helen Gardner found the justification of literary study in an unproblematical combination of the affective response and the veneration of greater mortals: 'the critic of literature, like all students of the fine arts, has a special kind of pleasure in his work. He is continually in the company of his intellectual and spiritual betters.' The last casual assumption is remarkable; the decent, God-fearing reader of seventeenth-century poetry might will-ingly grant that George Herbert was his spiritual better, but deny that Lord Rochester was, whilst accepting him as a splendid poet.

Hirsch's position has two implications. On the one hand, not everything conventionally regarded as literature has aes-thetic merit; on the other hand, such merit may well be found in genres not now usually treated as literature. It is a recognizable fact of literary experience that such modes of writing as sermons, oratory, essays, historiography, can offer, in their style and strategy, distinct aesthetic satisfactions, and so might be included in the canon of literature (where, indeed, it used to be taken for granted they belonged). As Lewis has pointed out, much in the current canonical genres originated in such non-aesthetic activities as entertainment, devotion, or instruction.

Accepting that in an academic context aesthetic or affective readings are desirable, though not inevitable or mandatory, one encounters a particular dilemma. In the aesthetic tradi-tion as it emerged from eighteenth-century Germany, contem-plation does not issue in action. Artistic form implies, in Kant's phrase, 'Purposiveness without purpose'. Yet modern students of literature are, on the one hand, invited to respond with contemplative enjoyment to the texts they are studying, and, on the other, to turn their response into action, by making intelligent remarks in tutorials or seminars, writing

essays and answering examination questions. There is necessarily a gap between these institutional discourses and the
individual, unique, possibly ineffable response which is called
for, with Crocean overtones, whether in the context of Leavisism or Oxonian quasi-aestheticism. Some people are more
adroit at leaping it than others. Unease at this dilemma,
which is structural to 'English' as a discipline, is quite
widespread in the academy but not, in my experience, much
discussed.

In these two Chapters I have tried to show that four
constituent strands—nationalistic, religious, ethical, aesthetic—of the nineteenth-century synthesis of 'English' have
become weakened, and why. (The fifth strand, rhetorical
analysis, is technical and instrumental, unaffected by ideological considerations, and looks in good shape, having been
reinforced by semiotics.) They have certainly not weakened
to breaking-point, and woven together in the institutional
synthesis they have, so far, maintained a degree of strength,
despite the dramas and collisions previously discussed. On
the larger social and educational scene, the discipline looms
impressively large, with high student demand and substantial
'performance-indicators' in research. Indeed, some complacent academics think that the subject is in as good heart as
ever, and that there is nothing to worry about. But uncertainty and anxiety are common, for the reasons I have
outlined. What was taken for granted is now widely ques-
tioned. And where questions are raised, theory enters.

7. THEORY AMONG THE ENGLISH

> Theory is what is generated when some aspect of literature, its nature, its history, its place in society, its conditions of production and reception, its meaning in general, or the meanings of particular works, ceases to be given and becomes a question to be argued in a generalized way. Theory is what inevitably arises when literary conventions and critical definitions once taken for granted have become objects of generalized discussion and dispute.
>
> GERALD GRAFF

The related themes I am pursuing are difficult to keep apart, and really require a contrapuntal or fugal exposition. But that would not make for easy writing, still less reading. In practice one can only talk about one thing at a time, and in this Chapter I shall risk a distorting simplicity by looking at questions of theory largely in isolation from institutional matrices and situations, and concentrating on British activities to the exclusion of the American ones that accompanied or preceded them. I defer those contexts to later Chapters.

The word 'theory' has always aroused suspicion amongst the English, who see themselves as practical people and sound empiricists. Indeed, it is often assumed by Continental and North American commentators that there has never been any significant literary theory in England. This ignores I. A. Richards, a pioneer modern theorist, who was very much an Englishman. Michael Edwards, taking a paradoxical approach, has argued that the English have always been strong on literary theory, instancing a distinguished succession of poet-critics: Sidney, Dryden, Johnson, Wordsworth, Coleridge, Shelley, Arnold, Eliot. Most of their important critical texts, Edwards remarks, are theoretical, in that they prompt fundamental reflections about the basic nature of writing, even if, 'One notices about such writing that it does not necessarily offer itself as theory, that it is directed towards what we now call literature and not towards something else.'

Edward's comment is clearly correct, and could be extended: Hopkins's letters and notebooks, for instance, contain a weight of original theorizing that is more substantial and more interesting than much recent writing. But present-day theorists are likely to be dismissive of what has been called 'writers' speculation about their art', finding it impressionistic and unsystematic. 'Theory', to be intellectually respectable, has to be presented as such, and to be a product of the academy, not of the amorphous institution of literature.

In the early 1970s, academic literary theory established bridgeheads in Britain, entering at first directly from France, and then via American translation and intermediaries. When conservative academics eventually became aware of the supposed invasion, they viewed it with alarm, as a threat to their, and their students', proper activity of reading, studying, and enjoying literature. Increasing resistance to the alien forces led to the clashes and controversies described in an earlier Chapter. In my judgement, the advent of theory was not a cause of disruption, but a symptom of it, for reasons suggested in the above quotation from Gerald Graff. For as long as the 'English' synthesis was adequately functioning there was no need or place for theory. Once the consensus began to fragment, theoretical challenges found room to enter. There is an approximate parallel in the history of religion: precise theological definitions of doctrine are called for only when doubters and heretics enter the picture. Until then, shared traditions of worship and devotion are sufficient to unite the believers. It is often argued, as Graff does in the final chapter of *Professing Literature*, that all literary activity is really if implicitly theoretical, and that a self-respecting critic will be specific about theory sooner rather than later. This was René Wellek's position in his debate with Leavis in 1937. But there are other ways of looking at the question. Christopher Ricks, trailing his coat in the wake of the MacCabe Affair, claimed that the critic should have 'principles' rather than 'theory', while Stanley Fish has made a comparable distinction between 'theory' and 'belief': 'A theory is a special achievement of consciousness; a belief is a prerequisite for being conscious at all. Beliefs are not what you think *about* but what you think *with* . . .'. Theory emerges as and when texts or issues are theorized, usually by academics who are dissatisfied with the *status quo*. The idea of 'theory' has now become so pervasive, so much a part of the terms of current debate, and so visibly incorporated into institutions, that I shall not resist using it. There has, indeed, been a change from traditional, empirical, English ways. Nevertheless, the idea of theory may itself need to be theorized and regarded with a measure of scepticism, like other honorific terms in contemporary discourse, such as 'politics' and 'history'. My present use of the word can be understood as being, in Derridean terms, lightly *sous rature*.

What Stanley Fish calls 'belief' is close to what Wittgenstein denotes by a 'form of life', where practice and guiding assumption form a seamless unity. In the recent history of British culture the study of English Literature in secondary and tertiary education comprised a recognizable form of life, principled but not theoretical. In institutional practice, 'English' in public schools tended to be marginal and somewhat disregarded, but became central in the culture of the grammar schools, in ways adumbrated and advocated in the Newbolt Report. That culture presupposed a high degree of what E. D. Hirsch calls 'cultural literacy', particularly in respect of English history and the Christian and classical heritages, requiring competence in Latin and at least one modern language, as well as wide reading in English Literature over and above the demands of the curriculum. This form of life was shared by the sixth forms of grammar schools and the universities to which their students proceeded, and it did not greatly differ whether the frame of reference was 'Cambridge' or 'Oxford', or to import an Arnoldian variation on this model, Hebraic or Hellenic, directed towards 'criticism' or 'appreciation'. (Leavis, a forceful opponent of traditional literary education, indicated in *Education and the University*, just how much cultural competence he took for granted in the student.) Judith Grossman's novel, *Her Own Terms*, published in 1988, looks back at a working-class scholarship-girl in the 1950s, who goes to Oxford from a South London Grammar school; Grossman shows in passing how formidably well-read and linguistically equipped her heroine was. The basic assumption of this form of life, extending from school to university, was that imaginative literature was inherently valuable, and that it was valuable because it pleasurably conveyed emotion and profound insights into the life of things. True to the Romantic tradition from which this belief sprang, the imagination was valued more than the analytical intelligence, the specific more than the general, experience more than discourse, *connaître* more than *savoir*. If ideas as such were discounted, it was because imaginative literature, in its richness and blend of diversity and harmony, had other things to offer.

It is arguable that the disappearance of grammar schools was a further factor in the weakening of the English synthesis, in addition to those I have discussed. At all events, when the innovative literary theory derived from structuralism began to arrive about twenty years ago it found actual or potential fissures in the form of life and it sought to enlarge and penetrate them. An adversarial stance appeared in literary study. It is evident in a curious book, edited by Stephen Heath, Colin MacCabe, and Christopher Prendergast and published in Cambridge in the early 1970s: *Signs of the Times: Introductory Readings in Textual Semiotics*. It was a collection of essays designed to introduce *la nouvelle critique* to ignorant English readers: apart from the editors, the contributors included Julia Kristeva and Philippe Sollers, and there was an interview with Roland Barthes. A polemical note is sounded in the unsigned preface. It acknowledges that the following texts and their arguments are difficult, but

the difficulty is not to be hidden—we ourselves have no right to hide it. Nor, however, is it to be submitted to the terrorism of plain language, that mythical weapon of those who prefer the comforting repetition of the ideological caress; who do not want to READ.

Or, in the slogan of American aerobics teachers, 'No Pain, No Gain'. It was a note often sounded in battles to come.

MacCabe and Heath had studied in Paris, and *Signs of the Times* has its niche in postwar cultural history, marking the first major re-entry of French intellectual influences since Eliot's adherence to Remy de Gourmont and the French neoclassicists, half a century earlier. For the sake of convenience I shall apply the term *la nouvelle critique* to the complex of ideas emerging from the Paris of the 1960s, including many diverse strands: the 'classical' structuralism of the early Barthes, the poststructuralism of his later work, the deconstructionism of Derrida, and whatever name one gives to the work of Foucault and Lacan, in taxonomic historiography and dissident psychoanalysis respectively. Frank Kermode was the first senior academic in English studies to take a sympathetic interest in *la nouvelle critique*, particularly its analysis of narrative. For some years before his move to Cambridge he chaired a seminar at University College London, which discussed the literary implications of structuralism, semiotics, and emergent poststructuralism. He has remarked, 'No other phase of my academic life has given me so much pleasure and instruction.' Kermode's seminar established a useful informal link with the work going on at Cambridge, and the participants included Stephen Heath, Jonathan Culler, who was at that time teaching at Cambridge, and Culler's then wife, Veronica Forrest-Thomson. Other literary theorists who attended were Christine Brooke-Rose, Christopher Norris, and Shlomith Rimmon, and the novelist, B. S. Johnson. Once, Roland Barthes himself came. Kermode recalls the seminars as occasions of good humour and tolerance, despite sharp intellectual disagreements, and he laments that their humane spirit did not survive later events.

By the late seventies some British academics were displaying a wary but sympathetic interest in early or classical structuralism, particularly as it was expounded in Culler's widely read *Structuralist Poetics*, a lucid, urbane work which suggested that structuralism might, without too much difficulty, be adopted to existing academic practice. I was partly convinced by Culler's power of persuasion, and for some time thought that the kinds of analysis he described could be assimilated to practical criticism and the English synthesis. Eventually I decided that assimilation was not possible, given Culler's lack of interest in the interpretation of particular texts and his commitment to the uncovering of the generalized principles of literariness. In *Structuralist Poetics* Culler took an unenthusiastic view of deconstructionism, but he shortly

returned to the United States and succumbed to the deconstructive wave that swept through the American academy in
the late seventies, and into which I did not feel inclined to
plunge. David Lodge was another established British academic and writer who took an early interest in formalist and
structuralist methods and principles. In 1977 he published
The Modes of Modern Writing, an illuminating and original
application of Roman Jakobson's distinction between 'metaphor' and 'metonymy' to the criticism and history of twentieth-century literature. My main reservation about the book,
which is more evident to me now than when it first appeared,
is that Lodge has too direct and univocal an understanding of
the elusive concept of 'literature'. His book showed that new
ideas were in the air, and senior academics began to drop
passing references to Barthes or Derrida, not always
accurately.

Others, more inward with *la nouvelle critique*, adopted a
polemical rhetoric. Veronica Forrest-Thomson—a brilliant
though unstable poet and critic, who died tragically young in
1975—referred in a review to the work of Barthes, Foucault,
and Derrida 'which has led to a literary revolution in France
and will lead—at last—to revolution in our theory and
practice of literature in this country.' The breathless phrase,
'at last', is revealingly placed. The idea of 'revolution' can set
the pulses racing, for a time at least, and in 1980 it was
invoked by Catherine Belsey: 'Only by closing the doors of
the English department against theoretical challenges from
outside can we continue to ignore the "Copernican" revolution which is currently taking place, and which is radically
undermining traditional ways of perceiving both the world
and the text.' Belsey's *Critical Practice*, like MacCabe's study
of Joyce, is fairly aggressive in its tone. I would agree that the
doors of the English department should not remain closed to
theoretical challenges, and in this book I am trying to respond
to them. But applying a mildly deconstructive reading to her
words, it is worth remarking that 'revolution' is an ambivalent
trope. On the one hand, it denotes an absolute, once-and-for-
all change: the Copernican revolution, or the French or
Russian Revolutions. On the other hand, if we think of a
wheel or turntable, 'revolution' implies a mere turning,

continual movement without progress. Nearly ten years after Belsey's book appeared, there has been no revolution in the first sense, and it does not look as if there will be.

Critical Practice was one of the early titles in the 'New Accents' series published by Methuen, under the general editorship of Belsey's colleague at Cardiff, Terence Hawkes. The series aimed to introduce to English readers *la nouvelle critique* and literary theory, along with associated areas such as linguistics, translation, and the study of mass culture. It was from the beginning very successful, which I take to be evidence of the growing sense that the established English synthesis was weakening, with a corresponding desire among students and teachers for new orientations. The series did not have a uniform intellectual line and many varieties of opinion could be found in the contributors. But it appeared at precisely the right moment to catch the poststructuralist tide associated with Derrida and the later Barthes, and several of the most influential titles brought together, rather uneasily, poststructuralism and Marxism. This is true of Belsey's book, of Hawkes's own *Structuralism and Semiotics*, of Tony Bennett's *Marxism and Formalism*, of many of the contributions in Peter Widdowson's *Re-Reading English*, and of Anthony Easthope's *Poetry as Discourse*. These texts share a fighting tone and a conviction that established forms of literary study, and in some cases even the concept of literature itself, have to be overthrown. There is a great readiness to invoke the French, and a conviction, drawn from Saussure and classical structuralism, that language has no necessary connection with reality. In a poststructuralist development of the idea, it is claimed that the most literary texts can offer is the endless 'free play of signifiers'. In the late seventies some people in the mainstream of literary study were inclined to believe, or half-believe, these ideas, or to try them on for size. David Lodge was one; in his inaugural lecture as Professor of Modern English Literature at Birmingham in 1976 he slid from the supposed arbitrariness of language as defined by Saussure to the way in which the masterpieces of modernist literature emphasized form rather than content. This is at best a corrective belief, for whatever else *Ulysses* or *The Waste Land* are doing, they are also invoking for us the Dublin of 1904 or the London of 1921. Lodge himself, in his own admirable novels, has never been hampered by any lack of conviction that the language he employs is really about the social realities that he wittily records. Frank Kermode in *The Genesis of Secrecy* seemed to be engaging in a severance of world and word, and was called to account by Helen Gardner for doing so. It is significant that neither Kermode nor Lodge have inclined towards the more radical deconstructionist road. Kermode has set out his reasons for refusing it in *Essays on Fiction*, and Lodge has remarked, 'To open a book or article by . . . Derrida or one of his disciples is to feel that the mystification and intimidation of the reader is the ultimate aim of the enterprise.'

There was less caution in the 'New Accents' camp where the incapacity of language to convey anything about the 'real' world was eagerly asserted. Belsey wrote:

From this post-Saussurean perspective it is clear that the theory of literature as expressive realism is no longer tenable. . . . If discourses articulate concepts through a system of signs which signify by means of their relationship to each other rather than to entities in the world, and if literature is a signifying practice, all it can reflect is the order inscribed in particular discourses, not the nature of the world.

No more seeing into the life of things, in short. Belsey attempts to unite the poststructuralist and the Marxist parts of her mind by invoking Lacan, Althusser, and Macherey, but signs of strain or outright contradiction are not hard to find. One can compare the passage just quoted, which insists on the unknowability of the real world, with some of her subsequent remarks; as, for instance, when she refers to her argument 'that literature represents the myths and imaginary versions of *real* social relationships', and claims that 'a form of criticism' which refuses to reproduce the pseudo-knowledge offered by the text provides a *real* knowledge of the work of literature', or says that 'the task of criticism, then, is . . . to produce a *real* knowledge of history.' My italics: some reality, at least, is knowable, it seems. The contradictions in Belsey's text have been examined sharply and at some length by Patrick Parrinder.

One notes in passing that the passages just quoted from Belsey contain abstract nouns, 'literature' and 'criticism', which take active verbs, 'represent' and 'refuse' and 'provide'. This is a common rhetorical device in contemporary theoretical writing, and has been usefully analysed—and condemned—by Roger Poole as 'Hegelian grammar', which is 'the use of verbs of decision, movement, or responsibility which are illegitimately coupled to grammatical subjects which are neither animate nor conscious.' In fact, it is a latter-day version of the figure known in classical rhetoric as prosopopoeia. The observant reader may have noticed that I used this construction myself above on p. 98; this was done consciously. I have sometimes whiled away idle moments in speculating how far one could elaborate this figure before the reader became suspicious. Consider, for instance, the following string, and see where implausibility enters: 'the text makes no response . . . the text evades the reader's interrogation . . . the text is frequently silent . . . the text is idle and will not get up in the morning.' Or this: 'At this point ideology makes a forceful intervention . . . the voice of ideology is frequently heard . . . ideology never stops talking.' The effect of the device is to remove or reduce human agency, making events seem the consequence of impersonal forces such as ideology, the unconscious, history, or language itself.

Terence Hawkes's *Structuralism and Semiotics* appeared in 1977 as a timely primer on *la nouvelle critique* and it presents much information in a readable form. It is, however, written in a crusading spirit, without any critical distance, and it is informed, like Belsey's book, by the assumption that language—or literature—can give us no certain knowledge of the world. Hawkes's polemical purpose becomes more and more apparent as the book develops: it is to undermine, not only established literary study, but liberal humanism itself. His arguments are fast-moving but inexact, and he engages in some wild flourishes of Hegelian grammar: 'Writing, in short, does not "reproduce" a reality beyond itself, nor does it "reduce" that reality. In its new freedom, it can be seen to *cause a new reality to come into being*' (Hawkes's italics). Or consider the density of trope and implication in the following: ' "New" New Criticism would thus claim to respond to literature's essential nature in which signifiers are prised utterly free of signifieds, aiming, in its no-holds-barred encounter with the text, for a *coherence* and *validity* of response, not objectivity and truth' (Hawkes's italics). Raymond Tallis has described this passage as being 'of great interest to the pathologist of modern literary theory.'

In certain respects, what Hawkes calls the ' "New" New Criticism' had what looked like connections with the older version. Both were directed towards the formalist reading of literary texts, and some anglophone academics tried to minimize the strangeness of French imports by saying that *la nouvelle critique* was only offering a new version of what had long been familiar in the Anglo-American academy. This assumption ignored great differences in contextual forms of life and conceptual foundation. Nevertheless, Lodge was able to use classical structuralism and aspects of Russian Formalism to refine and extend the existing approaches of formalist criticism. Resemblances were apparent between Northrop Frye's system of archetypes and structuralism; indeed, Hawkes refers, without qualification, to Frye's *Anatomy of Criticism* as a 'classic of North American structuralism'. As I have remarked, Culler's *Structuralist Poetics* encouraged some readers to think in terms of *rapprochement* between the New and the Newer Criticism. Anthony Easthope's *Poetry as Discourse* offers a complex blend of old and new. He takes poststructuralist assumptions about the death of the author and the disappearance of the self-subsistent ego, and applies them to the history of English poetry, in a work which combines ingenious close reading, impressive knowledge of metre, and an overall argument of stratospheric thinness and remoteness. Easthope believes that the modernist concept of 'impersonality', later systematized in the New Criticism, and theorized by Wimsatt and Beardsley in their famous essay 'The Intentional Fallacy', was on the right lines, but did not go far enough, as the author was not really banished. Some of Easthope's approach recalls that of C. S. Lewis in *The Personal Heresy*. He does not mention this book, but he does quote Lewis to the effect that 'nearly all our older poetry was written and read by men to whom the distinction between poetry and rhetoric, in its modern form, would have been meaningless.' In this aspect, at least, there is a traditional slant in Easthope's argument. He sets up poetry, rhetoric, and textuality, as against the myth of presence, the poem as the life-blood of a master spirit, and the Romantic ideal of expressiveness. Thus far Easthope's ideas have affinities both with the New Critical applications of modernism, and Lewis's independent-minded traditionalism. Yet this is only part of his argument. He goes much further, in taking Pound's phrase about the need to break the pentameter, and projects it back over six hundred years of English poetry. Easthope has his own version of the myth of catastrophe that has possessed so many critics and theorists. His villain is the iambic pentameter, often seen as basic to English poetry, but according to Easthope an alien and bourgeois importation, brought in by Chaucer, to the detriment of the truly native measure of the four-beat-line with a varying number of syllables, found in the old alliterative verse. This survived only in an underground way in folk song, nursery rhymes, children's counting verses, and so on. From the Renaissance onwards, metrical repression reigns: 'Once established as national poetic institution pentameter becomes a hegemonic form.' Only in our century has relief come, when modernist poetry, particularly Pound's *Cantos*, breaks away from the pentameter. Easthope's objections are entirely political, focused on the objectionableness of the 'bourgeois', that great unexamined transcendent signified of *marxisant* theoretical writing. In Easthope's hands it becomes a particularly malleable concept. He believes that the bourgeois epoch of history is in its terminal crisis, but concedes that this crisis may have been going on since 1848, which stretches not only 'bourgeois' but 'crisis' to breaking-point.

Easthope acknowledges that the pentameter line had qualities which made it more resourceful than the older accentual metre, since one could achieve a great range of poetic effects by counterpointing intonation against metre, which is what nearly all the major English poets have done, though supposedly imprisoned in this bourgeois strait-jacket. Easthope concedes, 'Spoken performance of pentameter is accordingly open to variation in a way accentual verse is not', and this points to the massive lacuna at the heart of his book. There is no mention at all of Elizabethan poetic drama, where the pentameter line is used with increasingly greater freedom and flexibility. Shakespearan drama is usually thought of as the embodiment of a truly popular art, whatever 'bourgeois' or aristocratic dimensions it also possesses. But Shakespeare remains something of an embarrassment to contemporary theorists of levelling tendency. One contributor to *Re-Reading English* wants to deconstruct Shakespeare and his texts into the socio-economic-cultural-political contexts in which they originated. He writes, 'The notion of the sacrosanct text is alien to the period and yet it is central to the literary criticism of Shakespeare.' In what spirit, then, was the First Folio produced in 1623?

The work of recent British theorists does have lines of connection with older forms of discourse, whether the New Criticism, traditional scholarship, earlier Marxist criticism, or the Cultural Studies approach given a fresh impetus in the 1950s by Richard Hoggart and Raymond Williams. Even Terry Eagleton, the eminent Marxist now installed at Oxford to teach critical theory exclusively, has, as I have elsewhere argued, never completely escaped from the Leavisite Cambridge of the sixties. His most rebarbative work, *Criticism and Ideology*, is an Althusserian rewriting of *The Great Tradition*. As an American commentator has remarked of Eagleton, 'You can take the boy out of Cambridge, but you can't take Cambridge out of the boy.' Yet whatever continuities there are, the general impression, whether pleased or panicky, that recent theoretical work represents something new is broadly correct. The newness is apparent in manner as well as in matter; a rude, derisive tone is noticeable, particularly in the prose of Eagleton and Hawkes. The latter concluded an argument with Graham Hough in the correspondence columns of the *London Review of Books* with the suggestion that Hough should 'piss off'. Some readers may have been shocked that one professor of English should thus refer to another, but these are robust times.

The objects of derision may be placed, in order of increasing generality, in the following list: the institutional study of English Literature in British higher education; English Literature; Englishness; literature; bourgeois society (which includes racism and sexism); late capitalism; Western culture. These items are all connected, and any of them may be used as analogies or homologies for each other. The polemic is supported by an implicit mythology, in which English culture is presented as insular, complacent, empirical, philistine, unreflective, untheoretical, and generally slumped in dogmatic slumbers. Against the dominant dullness and grossness a growing band of lively and intelligent spirits have embarked on a hopeful struggle, calling in aid the power of ideas from other parts of the world, particularly, France.

This looks very like the rerun of a scenario first enacted in the early years of this century, when two unknown expatriate American poets attacked a torpid English literary establishment in the name of nascent modernism, looking to France for their intellectual inspiration and their models of literary achievement. Eliot and Pound did establish a poetic revolution, and in the seventies and early eighties the rhetoric of revolution became attractive to anglophone poststructuralists. But it remained rhetoric, language rather than achievement. The breakdown of English intellectual insularity is welcome in principle, but a few things need to be said about this new turn to France. It has become common form to invoke the magic names of the French theorists, as if the names alone would cause a torpid academic establishment to collapse. The use of names rather than arguments as ammunition has become noticeable in such exercises, on both sides of the Atlantic, as Chris Baldick remarks in a review of Frederick Crews's *Skeptical Engagements*:

One lamentable practice which Crews rightly scorns is the increasingly revived trick of medieval rhetoric in which one attempts to substantiate one's theoretical argument not by anything so vulgarly empirical as a fact or a text but merely by invoking a name from the sacred pantheon. Derrida, Foucault, Kristeva, Lacan, Barthes: just reeling off their names is (as Auden said in a very different context) ever so comfy, since it safely defers the issues at hand to nothing less than a transcendent signified: in short, to a star.

This clinging to authority has, in my experience, become noticeable in graduate students and young academics in the past ten years or so. I take it to be a product of the myth I described above: 'I am fighting against the entrenched forces of insular stupidity, and I call upon the French to aid me!'

Such invocations are, in fact, very vulnerable. French

intellectual debates and revolutions are part of a specific history and culture, expressing their complex dynamics. Thus, classical structuralism, with its cold, formal impersonality, occurs as a reaction to the 1940s existentialist emphasis on the individual ego; and becomes itself overturned or deconstructed by poststructuralist 'playfulness'. Marxists become *nouveaux philosophes*; Julia Kristeva, lecturing at Warwick in 1987, speaks scornfully of the Left . . . English poststructuralists, when wearing their Marxist hats, would undoubtedly want to insist that ideas belong in larger contexts, social, cultural, and political, and cannot easily be abstracted and appropriated to other ends. Terry Eagleton came some way to acknowledging this, in a quasi-refutation of his Althusserian phase, when he included himself among the English Marxist intellectuals who 'managed the difficult dialectical trick of appropriating certain Althusserian concepts in blithe ignorance or disregard of their guilty political context.' This is not to say that the English cannot absorb or debate French or other foreign ideas. This was evidently done in the friendly but sharp exchanges in Kermode's seminar in the early seventies. But it is another matter to use these ideas, or rather the names of their originators, primarily as weapons against an insular establishment. How thoroughly, one wonders, have the ideas been understood? Some English academics are genuinely at home with them, in a way that is directly related to their familiarity with French intellectual culture. Christine Brooke-Rose, for instance, is a bilingual English critic and novelist, who taught in a Paris university for many years. Her substantial and brilliant book *A Rhetoric of the Unreal* uses the work of French intellectual stars in a familiar and matter-of-fact way, without any of the bedazzlement that surrounds them on this side of the Channel. Stephen Heath has some claim to be the only begetter of the English version of *la nouvelle critique*. He studied with Barthes in Paris when Barthes was unknown in England, and later wrote a book on him in French ('Barthesian French' Hough has observed). However much some people at Cambridge disapproved of him, there can be no doubt of Heath's high professional competence in the understanding of structuralism and poststructuralism.

Heath has appended a pertinent note to his translation of Barthes's collection of essays, *Image–Music–Text*, in which he scrupulously discusses the problems in lexis and idiom of translating Barthes. This raises the large question of the role of translation in the transmission of French ideas to English readers. In her book *Beautiful Theories*, the late Elizabeth Bruss made a revealing examination of the way in which Barthes's different translators carried out their task; she shows that whereas Heath did not disguise the difficulty and opacity in Barthes's texts, his American translators turned them into smooth narratives. Other translations from modern French theorists are, one hears, very inadequate. One would not want to suggest that the academics who contribute to the New Accents series (or who write similar texts) cannot read French with ease. Nevertheless, it is noteworthy from the annotation of their books that they use translations wherever possible (as indeed I do myself, life being as short as it is). And, as Marjorie Perloff has remarked, 'in the case of writers like Derrida, Lacan and Barthes, for whom the materiality of the signifier is central, translation is nearly a contradiction in terms.' The use of translation is the most obvious but not the only problem in the transmission of what are cultural as well as intellectual texts. There are French qualities—of irony, wit, cerebral play—that are remarkably difficult to get across, even in a good translation. Nicholas Tredell has said of some New Accents contributors, 'despite their ostensible Gallic sympathies, they crash down on French *jouissance* like a ceiling-full of cold showers.' More importantly, there is the possibility that ideas have been simply misunderstood in their transmission from one cultural context to another. This is the position of Christopher Norris, who modestly but firmly maintains that all anglophone readers except himself have misunderstood Derrida.

I am all too ready to admit that I may have misunderstood what I have read in modern French theory; the problem is in getting any minimal intellectual purchase on it at all. David Lodge, who was prepared to go public as one who 'worked with' structuralism, nevertheless wrote in a newspaper article in 1980:

As an academic critic and university teacher specializing in modern literature and literary theory, I spend much of my time these days reading books and articles that I can barely understand and that cause my wife (a graduate with a good honours degree in English language and literature) to utter loud cries of pain and nausea if her eye happens to fall on them.

Young academics and critics do not seem to have had the same difficulty, or if they do, are not letting on. Indeed, 'lucidity' is liable to be condemned as a form of bourgeois mystification. The struggle to decipher has been presented as a good thing in itself, though construing sentences is not the same thing as achieving intellectual understanding. This, however, raises obscure and vexing questions about the nature of 'textuality'.

There is no thesis without an antithesis, and polemic called forth counter-polemic, and mockery, counter-mockery, in works by conservative academics, such as George Watson's *Modern Literary Thought*, Helen Gardner's *In Defence of the Imagination*, and some of the contributions to *Reconstructing Literature*, a collection of essays edited by Laurence Lerner. More interestingly, theory called forth counter-theory, in the late Geoffrey Thurley's *Counter-Modernism in Current Critical Theory*, A. D. Nuttall's *A New Mimesis*, Patrick Parrinder's *The Failure of Theory*, and Raymond Tallis's *Not Saussure: A Critique of Post-Saussurean Literary Theory*. All of them argue, in different ways and with different emphases, for the realistic and expressive functions of literature; or, in philosophical terms, for the validity of the idea of reference. Agreeing that naïve empiricism is insufficient and that language does not tell us about the world in any simple, unmediated, or transparent way, they still believe that a sense of reality can be conveyed by language (the position derided as mere 'common sense' by the Newest Criticism). Thurley locates *la nouvelle critique* in a particular French intellectual tradition, which makes its uncritical adoption in the anglophone academy peculiarly problematical:

If it is the defining error of empiricism to assume that only statements meant to be checked up on deserve serious attention, it is the defining error of the new French criticism (Foucault, Piaget, Barthes, Derrida and others) to assume that because some statements cannot be verified, no statements can, and hence that all statements fail to refer, leaving us with discourse— language without anchorage in time, psyche or history.

Nuttall makes similar points. The first part of his book is an extended essay in counter-theory, intended as a prolegomenon to the second part, which offers a study of Shakespeare in terms of moral and psychological realism. Hawkes had dismissed the ideas of 'objectivity' and 'truth' in *Structuralism and Semiotics*, but Nuttall insists that such dismissals are pragmatically self-refuting. We may assert that there is no such thing as truth, but we regard that as a true statement. The point has a particular relevance to the work of those who believe, like Foucault, following Nietzsche, that truth is a mere rhetorical device, employed in the interests of oppression, and say so at length. What then is the status of Foucault's saying so? Nevertheless, the very concept of truth seems to be an irritant for some. Nuttall has elsewhere given a mischievous account of an academic occasion in which a speaker insisted on asserting, 'It is a truth that the workers are oppressed.' This, Nuttall remarks, 'acted as a red rag. It was as if the "logical conservatism" of his remark was more significant and more offensive to his (predominantly left-wing) audience than its thoroughly socialist content.'

In *A New Mimesis* Nuttall accused Hawkes of 'collective cultural solipsism'. Hawkes, in turn, gave the book a mockingly dismissive review in the *TLS*, without mentioning Nuttall's accusation against him. Nuttall, like Thurley, writes with a polemical edge, but both of them present their cases in a seriously philosophical fashion. What emerges from recent counter-theory is that French-inspired theory tends to destroy straw men in its attack on reference, insisting that the relation between words and meaning is entirely arbitrary, a matter of difference only. The point has been frequently made that there is no necessary reason why 'dog' should mean the familiar, faithful, barking, domestic quadruped, which in other languages, gets referred to as *chien, Hund, cane*, etc. And within the language-system of English, the sounds and letters of d-o-g are recognizable as such simply because they are not d-i-g, or d-o-n, or l-o-g. Nevertheless, if we say not 'dog' but 'My-dog-Rover-with-the-white-spots-and-the-stumpy-tail', there can be no doubt that we intend not only a specific but a unique reference. There is still a sense in which the relation between words and object can be called 'arbitrary', since we

are not dealing with onomatopeia, but it is quite
unproblematical.

These questions are central to Raymond Tallis's recent
book, *Not Saussure*, which is concerned with the relation
between signs, meaning, and reference in the critical and
intellectual tradition deriving from Saussure. Tallis is a witty
and combative writer, who is opposed to *la nouvelle critique* but
who is prepared to take it seriously and engage with it at
length. He recognizes the mythology of its English adherents,
in which all criticism of their ideas attracts the charge of 'a
characteristically insular suspicion of nasty foreign ideas', but
he is prepared to risk it, continuing:

> Those who feel hostile to much recent literary theory but are unwilling or
> unable to formulate their objections often lazily dismiss it as merely another
> Parisian fashion, citing the rapid displacement of structuralism by post-
> structuralism as evidence that the writings of Barthes, Derrida, Lacan and
> their American epigones constitute a craze rather than a serious intellectual
> movement. There may be some justification for the (insular) suspicion that
> when the Emperor is restocking his wardrobe he usually shops in Paris; but
> the fashionability of ideas does not of itself constitute an honest argument
> against them; indeed, to offer this as one's main response is to betray
> intellectual bankruptcy. It is less easy, but more interesting, to try to
> understand *why* ancient radical doubts about the ability of language to
> express a genuine extra-linguistic reality have been revived in recent
> decades to the point where they seem to have achieved an almost popular
> appeal.

Tallis sets himself the task of showing that much of the
structuralist and poststructuralist enterprise is based on a
misreading of Saussure. Two aspects of Saussure's thought
that have become well established in popular-academic consciousness are the distinctions between (*a*) *langue* and *parole*, a
language-system and its particular manifestations; and (*b*)
'signifier' and 'signified'. It is the latter which, Tallis argues,
has been generally misapplied. In Saussure's original exposition, signifier and signified, though distinct and only arbitrar-
ily related, were supposed to be as indivisible as the two sides
of a piece of paper. We recognize a sign as a set of letters on a
page, or an intelligible series of sounds, or an iconic device,
and in the same perception we grasp what it stands for:
signifier and signified together make up the sign. GDO or
ODG are random collections of letters, not signs (unless we

suspect that they are unfamiliar acronymics, or words in an unknown language), but DOG is the signifier of a sign whose signified is what is elsewhere understood by *chien*, etc. This has nothing to do with reference to any particular dog, or even whether dogs actually exist at all. One could do the same thing with 'unicorn', which has sense but no verifiable reference.

Tallis invokes Frege's distinction between 'The Morning Star' and 'The Evening Star', which are different expressions with different senses or meanings, as would be apparent if we tried to translate them into another language, but they have the same referent (the planet Venus). 'Meaning' is a slippery term, since it can cover both sense and reference. In the poetry of Mallarmé the words 'mean' what a French dictionary tells us they mean, but they also take on the private and idiosyncratic meanings that Mallarmé gives them. Post-structuralism, deriving from Mallarmé as well as Saussure, has developed a heady rhetoric in which signifiers are prised apart from signifieds, in Hawkes's phrase, and then fly away in all directions in their 'free play'. Tallis argues that people talk of 'signifieds', when they should say 'referents'; there is nothing new or unfamiliar in the idea of verbal signs having multiple or even clashing references, and they have long been exploited by poets and punsters, as Tallis does in the title of his book. Interestingly, Anthony Easthope acknowledges the distinction at one point in *Poetry as Discourse*: 'Failure to distinguish clearly between signified and referent, the object it may refer to, has led to serious confusion in some accounts of the ideogram.' Yet it is a confusion he frequently falls into elsewhere, as do other 'New Accents' writers.

Tallis's case is convincing, though he has certainly not said the last word on the matter, and there may well be further arguments from those who are professionally engaged in linguistics. There is interesting supporting material in a book by the American critic Robert Scholes, *Textual Power*, published in 1985 and not consulted by Tallis. In Tallis's reading, Saussure did not move from the sign, which comprised signifier + signified, to reference, because he was not interested in doing so, being concerned only with the internal aspects of a language-system. He did not intend to exclude reality. The error lies with Saussure's expositors. Scholes, however, believes that Saussure is himself inconsistent, and responsible for later confusion, but the thrust of his argument is very close to Tallis's, and both of them are concerned—as were Thurley and Nuttall—to reinstate the validity of reference and to deny that language is a system of 'pure differences', without relation to reality. Scholes provides a useful table, divided into three columns, showing how linguists and philosophers have agreed in making a tripartite division between signifier, signified, and reference, though they present it in a variety of terminologies. For Frege, it was Expression, Sense, Reference (*Ausdruck, Sinn, Bedeutung*). For Carnap, Expression, Intension, Extension. For Ogden and Richards, Symbol, Thought, Referent. For Pierce, Sign, Interpretant, Object. But in Saussure's system there are only the two terms, Signifier and Signified, with nothing in the third column. Scholes comments,

The Saussurean formulation, like many 'linguistic' views of language, eliminates the third term and with this gesture erases the world. For Saussure this was perhaps mainly a methodological convenience, a way of concentrating on the aspects of language that interested him. For deconstruction, however, this erasure of the world is crucial.

Scholes's case is the more telling in that he is far from being a conservative opponent of all recent developments in theory; he has written favourably of structuralism, and unsympathetically about fictional realism (for which, indeed, he has been attacked by Tallis), and elsewhere in *Textual Power* he finds deconstructive reading—as opposed to the theory underlying it—a useful critical method.

The arguments of Tallis and Scholes against a major aspect of poststructuralist theory and practice should be attended to on the level at which they are advanced. But one rather doubts if they will be. Those who are addicted to the vertiginous rhetoric where language tells us nothing about reality, merely about other language, and where signifiers float in endless unattached free play, are apt to be contemptuous of demonstration and logic, seeing them as forms of bourgeois intellectual oppression. Dropping reference is not a matter of tentative acceptance of an unlikely position, but of doctrinal insistence. A. D. Nuttall recalls an occasion when 'an authoritative figure in the world of critical theory announced to a submissive informal circle of coffee-drinkers: "Reference is *out.*" I thought at the time: "Is *Sinn* really conceivable with no *Bedeutung* at all?" But I said nothing.' The connection between poststructuralist conviction and political radicalism is both arbitrary and tenuous, but it is insisted on by some contemporary theorists, with their readiness to invoke analogies between cultural processes, however disparate. Thus, a critical theory seminar engaged in the deconstructive analysis of a poem (or, more likely, of another theoretical text) is seen, in some muffled way, to be striking a blow against Thatcherism. Patrick Parrinder has looked sardonically at this comforting but self-deceiving state of mind. In the Preface to *The Failure of Theory*, he observes, 'To judge by a good deal of recent writing, the following resolutions would attract majority support at a conference of devotees of literary theory.' Among the resolutions are these: 'The theorist is no longer a servant of the literary critic. Theory and criticism should not take second place to imaginative writing' . . . 'All utterances are implicitly theoretical. All theory is political. The task of the theorist is to uncover, and where necessary to denounce, the theoretical-political implications of all discourse whatever' . . . 'The enemies of theory are politically conservative. Theory is radical, and so are its advocates. Pragmatists are not to be trusted.'

Parrinder's attacks are justified. The insistence on the supremacy of the political has become a cliché of recent thinking. But if *everything* is political, as is often proclaimed, then nothing is; one can invoke Saussure in the assertion that meaning is a matter of differentiation. 'Red' is only meaningful in a world where other colours exist. Admittedly, the politically radical implication of poststructuralist and deconstructive theory is a highly problematic idea, and has been resisted by some on the Left such as Terry Eagleton and Frank Lentricchia, and the contributors to a largely Marxist collection of essays, *The Theory of Reading*. Most recently, the discovery that the late Paul de Man, the doyen of American deconstructionists, had been a young collaborationist journalist in Nazi-occupied Belgium has made the issue painfully

acute in the United States. Given the sources of deconstructionism in Nietzsche among others, it is just as likely to have
a nihilist-reactionary dimension as a progressive one. In
practice, left-wing theorists tend to form part of a rainbow
coalition where poststructuralist or deconstructionist positions exist alongside Marxist, Freudian, and feminist ones.
Such disparate allegiances are more likely to agree on what
they oppose than in what they support. The different colours
of the rainbow of theory are evident in 'New Accents' titles,
and in the various journals devoted to theoretical discourse.
Some of this writing is acute and interesting, the product of
lively minds with genuine insights into the state of contemporary culture. I would often rather read it than more conventional forms of literary scholarship. Yet it is frequently open
to pragmatic self-refutation: it argues against reason by the
processes of reason, and a political cause, however radical,
cannot be advanced without the traditional processes of
argument and attending to evidence. There is admittedly the
playfulness of some versions of deconstructionist rhetoric,
which read like prose-poetry. But such texts are subject to the
limitations of purely aesthetic discourse, with no through road
to action, and must become politically suspect. In fact, one
does not have to be a committed deconstructionist to find a
split between meaning and rhetoric in the work of recent
theorists. The rhetoric may point to extreme scepticism or
Pyrrhonism but its users, if pressed, are likely to retreat to
positions which are no more than a modified version of
traditional ones. As Nuttall has remarked, they claim that,

> the dissolution of truth does not mean that no statements are true but only
> that there is no stable, unchanging absolute truth, and that certainty is
> persistently elusive. And the embarrassed questioner retreats, apologizing
> profusely, wondering why he ever fell into such absurd anxiety about this
> luminously sensible body of doctrine . . .

In that case, where is the theoretical revolution? Patrick
Parrinder, focusing on such contradictions and inconsisten-
cies, has concluded that theory is a failure. My own position
is rather different. Believing that the recent emergence of
theory in literary education is a symptom of disorder, I find
the contradictions as symptomatic as the coherences. A high

temperature and a rash may be signs of a failure in the functioning of the organism, but cannot themselves be termed a 'failure'.

Of the elements composing the rainbow coalition, Marxism is the most prominent and intellectually respectable. It has been a major political and cultural force for a hundred years. A large part of the world is notionally governed according to Marxist principles. Yet the people in those countries show little sign of believing in Marxism in the way that some Western intellectuals do. Globally, Marxism has run out of steam, persisting merely as sentiment and tradition, despite its conspicuous presence in parts of the Anglo-American academy. The dominance of right-wing ideas has done little to avert the decline; to invoke Marxism against Thatcherism is to employ an obsolete weapon. The present generation of British and American literary Marxists remind me of the small boy in Joyce's story, 'Araby', who got to the bazaar just as it was closing. After a century of immensely influential life, Marxism is becoming a dying culture, to adapt the phrase of an earlier Marxist thinker, Christopher Caudwell. Things looked different about a generation ago, when the New Left was still new and the texts of the young Marx were in fashion. Then Marxism did seem to represent a serious and dynamic challenge to liberal assumptions. French intellectual life, largely *marxisant* if not wholly Marxist, provided a substantial and supportive hinterland to the New Left. That has now disappeared, and anglophone Marxists are subject to a disabling isolation, despite their energetic activity in the realm of literary theory. They need their allies in the rainbow coalition, it seems.

In a longer perspective, the contribution of Marxists to literary criticism is considerable. It is sufficient to invoke the names of Lukács, Benjamin, Goldmann, and, with reservations, Raymond Williams. Throughout his career Williams had an uncertain relation to Marxism, sometimes adversarial, sometimes allied, and was uncomfortably conscious of paradoxes and difficulties in his establishment position as a professor at Cambridge and a leading British intellectual. On balance, Williams probably gained more than he lost from his attempt to bring—and keep—together the separate traditions of Marxism and British cultural criticism, though as Parrinder has shown in a sensitive discussion of Williams, he made needless difficulties for himself by abandoning the concept of literature. Without doubt, a Marxist approach can be very illuminating when directed at particular cultural and intellectual phenomena. Francis Mulhern's study of *Scrutiny* is a case in point. In fairness, too, one has to admit that Marxism is not monolithic, and that in literary and cultural criticism it provides many possible positions. Terry Eagleton, the leading Marxist critic in England, has occupied most of them in his time. Recently, Eagleton, in denying the total centrality of the class struggle, reached a point that some might claim was no longer compatible with Marxism. Eagleton's Althusserian phase of the mid-1970s was strongly attacked by a Marxist academic, Kiernan Ryan, who has since taken issue with another Marxist, Alan Sinfield, on the extent to which the great literary works of the past can transcend the reactionary ideologies that produced them. Sinfield believed that they were often irredeemably tainted by ideology, at best to be read only in historical terms, or subject to symptomatic readings, seeking the fractures and fissures in the mystified surface of the text that showed the 'true' ideological conditions in which it was produced. Against this, Ryan advanced the humanistic belief that the major canonical texts are not inherently reactionary, and that they contain implicit images and models of human freedom which transcend their immediate historical context and which later readers can respond to. This is an interestingly eclectic argument which recalls Gadamer on the 'fusion of horizons' (the reader's and the text's), Marcuse on the utopian possibilities of high culture, and Sartre on the necessarily progressive implications of major literature. Ryan represents a kind of Marxism that non-Marxists might do business with, in the sense that one can make a rational engagement with it. This is not always the case. Marxists have the dogmatic assurance that comes from possessing a world-view that offers total explanations of social and cultural processes, and which is mysteriously immune to the ideological determinism and deformation that they diagnose in others. It is not easy to engage in discussion with someone who regards other opinions as no more than symptomatic of the way a bourgeois intellectual thinks under late capitalism.

Ryan is representative of that traditional kind of Marxism, variously represented by Trotsky or Lukács, that regards the great literature and art of the past as a common human inheritance, which should be wrested from the exploiting classes and made available to the whole of humanity. Set against it is the Marxist-structuralist position, that finds the concepts of art and literature inherently oppressive. Here, 'symptomatic' reading is central: the literary text does not offer aesthetic or moral value, but is to be interrogated for its ideological implications. In some respects, this is a return to a very traditional kind of cognitive reading, in which the literary work is not read for its 'beauties' but its message, though the 'message' is now likely to be diagnostic rather than uplifting. In the spectrum of contemporary theory, Marxist symptomatic reading has something in common with the deconstructive reading which discovers in the end, not harmony and organic unity, but contradiction and *aporia*. Deconstructionists, though, tend to make the triumphant exposure of *aporia* a goal in itself, whereas Marxists incorporate their findings into a political and ideological system. Nevertheless, this apparent similarity of method has been used as the basis for attempts, tentative and unlikely as they are, to find a *rapprochement* between Marxism and deconstruction. But it is with psychoanalysis that the more obvious affinities of symptomatic reading lie. The Marxist critic reading a text for the ideological traces that it attempts to conceal—'Hegelian grammar' is inescapable in such contexts—by its evasive gaps and silences, has an obvious resemblance to the Freudian analyst examining the manifest content of a patient's dream for the repressed realities that are concealed within it.

Moving on to psychoanalytic, by which I understand Freudian, criticism, I am in a difficulty. Though neither a Marxist nor a Freudian, I find Marxist criticism deeply interesting, but not the Freudian equivalent. The revival of psychoanalytic criticism, usually in its Lacanian version, has been a disconcerting surprise to someone who came to intellectual maturity in the 1950s, when Freud seemed a figure of increasing remoteness. I have no difficulty in accepting certain supposedly key Freudian notions, such as the existence of the unconscious mind and its effect on our daily living, and the self-contradictory and self-defeating quality of much human behaviour, but these are far from being original discoveries. Freud himself said that the poets, not he, discovered the unconscious. Beyond this, I do not accept much of the Freudian mythological apparatus, though *Civilization and its Discontents* has always seemed to me a penetrating if deeply pessimistic work of cultural analysis. Sometimes psychoanalysis claims to be a genuinely scientific activity, in contrast to, say, Jungian mystagogy; at other times, when confronting the proponents of a hard scientific approach to psychology, like behaviourism, psychoanalysis presents itself much more in terms of myth and metaphor and explanatory fictions. It is never very apparent what Freudian claims are based on, though they are widely accepted in our culture. My scepticism has been reinforced by the recent work of Frederick Crews, who for many years was a leading psychoanalytic critic in America. During the 1970s he began to lose faith in the whole Freudian programme, and in his recent book, *Skeptical Engagements*, he provides detailed and substantially supported arguments for abandoning it. Freud is not, however, likely to be generally rejected, since he is so much part of the valued cultural furniture of the West. Furthermore, attacks such as Crews's are, as he acknowledges, not taken seriously and replied to in their own terms, but treated as symptoms of repressed disturbance. Freudians, like Marxists, cannot step outside their own forms of thought to admit that they might be wrong (unless, like Crews, they undergo a deconversion).

The recent revival of interest in psychoanalysis among literary theorists has come from France, and in particular from the work of Jacques Lacan, who brought together Freud and Saussure and produced the slogan, 'the unconscious is structured like a language'. Lacan has been very influential, although he is an almost impenetrably obscure writer. The obscurity is not incidental, a product of carelessness or incompetence in writing, but a deliberate attempt to enact

the wayward processes of the unconscious. As his admirer
Malcolm Bowie acknowledges, Lacan's style is marked by,

disturbances of conventional word order, literal and metaphorical senses
interwoven, periphrasis, ellipsis, leading notions alluded to rather than
declared, abstractions personified, persons becoming abstractions, widely
different words becoming synonyms, synonyms being given widely different
meanings . . .

This is a literary use of language rather than an expository
one, though poststructuralists frequently try to blur the
distinction. Indeed, Lacan was much influenced by surreal-
ism, and Bowie compares his writing to *Finnegans Wake*. Lacan
is a revisionist Freudian, whose effect is to dissolve terms and
concepts that Freud, with his positivistic formation, kept clear
and distinct. Lacan's work is not subject to empirical verification, and indeed is not meant to be. Nevertheless, Raymond
Tallis, whose own training is in medicine, has shown to what
extent one of Lacan's key concepts, the importance of the
'mirror stage' in the development of the infant's sense of self,
has no base in clinical experience. As far as Tallis is concerned, Lacan is a charlatan, the L. Ron Hubbard of psychoanalysis. Yet his system, like others on the contemporary
scene, is constructed so as to repel argument or contrary
evidence. Bowie, whose admiration is tinged with honest
caution, has summed up the Lacanian system in these words:

Just as you can gain access to the cave of the unconscious only by being
inside already, he seems to be saying, so you can gradually reach towards
an understanding of my work only by understanding it in advance. Lacan
offers us a new conception both of science and of truth, and asks us to
abandon many of the procedures for verification or falsification on which
the credibility of scientific enquiry traditionally rests.

Not everyone wants to enter the cave on such terms.

Lacan wished to get back to the original subversive spirit
of Freud's writings, which had been simplified or distorted by
their vulgar popular currency, and by the professionalism of
psychoanalysis. But a similar vulgarizing process has been
applied to Lacan's own ideas, first in France, and then in the
English-speaking world. In Bowie's words, 'Future sociologists of knowledge will no doubt study the mechanisms
whereby an enfeebled "Lacanism" . . . has come to loom
larger within the intellectual life of a society than the original

ideas and texts.' In England, Lacanian ideas have been linked
with Marxist ones, as in MacCabe's *James Joyce and the
Revolution of the Word*; Catherine Belsey's *Critical Practice*, which
identified Lacan's 'symbolic order' of language, into which
the infant enters, with the Althusserian realm of ideology; and
Anthony Easthope's *Poetry as Discourse* which related Lacan's
dissolution of the ego to New Critical impersonality and
structuralist 'dropping of the author'. One would have
thought that Marxism and Lacanism would inhabit wholly
disparate worlds of thought; the former is rationalistic and
teleological, whereas for Lacan, as Bowie says, 'arguments
directed towards a terminus are falsehoods'. Yet there are
affinities, as Frederick Crews points out:

> In Althusser's and Lacan's hands, then, both Marxism and psychoanalysis
> exchange an adaptive materialism for allegory. There is no point at which
> they unamibiguously intersect experience and therefore no point where one
> of their contentions could be modified by behavioural data. They have
> become, not critiques of inhuman arrangements or guidelines for practical
> interventions, but master transcoding devices which will sort any text or
> problem into sets of formally opposed categories.

Both belong to what Geoffrey Thurley diagnosed as the sealed
world of French rationalism; the difficulty of convincingly
transplanting such forms of intellectual discourse from a
French to an English context remains formidable.

The last component of the rainbow coalition that I want to
refer to is feminism. Here the difficulty I found in talking
about psychoanalytic criticism is compounded, not because I
am an unbeliever, but because anything that the middle-aged
male commentator says about feminism is liable to be wrong:
to be approving may be condemned as patronizing, and to be
critical is to be sexist. Compared to the movements I have
discussed, feminist criticism has little theoretical coherence,
though it draws eclectically on poststructuralism, Marxism,
and psychoanalysis. The lack of a single recognizable
approach has been acknowledged by Kathleen McLuskie:

> Every feminist critic has encountered the archly disingenuous qustion:
> 'What exactly is feminist criticism?' The only effective response is 'I'll send
> you a booklist', for feminist criticism can only be defined by the multiplicity
> of critical practices engaged in by feminists.

An obvious characteristic of feminist practice in the academy, unlike the other approaches I have discussed, is the extent to which it immediately does intersect with experience. Classes or discussion groups on women's writing command an enthusiastic response that is often lacking in mainstream teaching. The enthusiasm has, of course, been exploited, in the opportunistic launching of courses in women's studies, and by the publishing industry which has filled the shelves of bookshops—general as well as academic—with books with 'women' in their titles. One of the most interesting and welcome results of literary feminism has been the reprinting of forgotten texts, usually by women but occasionally by men. In an earlier Chapter I argued that the canon is 'bursting', because of the advent of other anglophone literatures, and the increasing interest in contemporary writing. Undoubtedly, the new availability of earlier texts of feminist interest is helping the explosion. At the same time, at the level of practical pedagogy, there is a counter-tendency in the study of the national canon to concentrate more and more on a small and diminishing number of texts. Anything which attempts to reverse this by bringing in unfamiliar work from the past which students have a positive motive for wanting to read must be a good thing, and strikes a blow against cultural amnesia. At the same time, there is an ambiguity in this backwards opening of the canon. Much of the work that is rediscovered may have the literary qualities that will satisfy readers without particular feminist interests: the poems by women that Roger Lonsdale included in *The New Oxford Book of Eighteenth-Century Verse* are a small-scale, easily accessible instance. Nevertheless, in a feminist academic context writing may well be studied, not primarily for its literary but for its cultural interest. This question provoked arguments in America about the *Norton Anthology of Literature by Women*, some of the contents of which were said to have had little value as literature. A common feminist response is to say that the whole idea of 'literary standards', even 'standards' as such, is a form of male domination. I refer to this significant dispute in passing, without engaging in it, except to say that feminists are divided on whether they want to establish a counter-canon or extend the existing one. But the distinction between literary texts and cultural texts is important, and I shall return to it. A further consideration about feminist criticism, is that it is more practical than theoretical, in a familiar English way, and that unlike other schools in the rainbow coalition, it is actively concerned in producing readings of particular texts. Most of them are produced by women, who provide insights that come from relating female experience to a body of writing; logically, there is no reason why these insights should not be available to male critics with the right sympathies and sensibility, but in practice most of this criticism is by women. Such criticism, it is worth noting, is basically mimetic; literature is assumed to relate to experience. Feminist criticism, like Marxist, is avowedly evaluative, which sharply distinguishes it from the generality of current academic criticism, of whatever school. This is desirable in itself, though I do not warm to the feminist MacCarthyism which subjects texts to a close, hostile interrogation in a search for sexist attitudes.

I have attempted to take a rapid view of developments in critical theory, or criticism with a theoretical consciousness, as they have appeared in British culture in the past twenty years. There is an immediate contrast with the literary criticism and theory of the early twentieth century, in that most recent work begins and ends in the academy, and has little contact with current literary practice. Both the New Criticism and *Scrutiny* were products of the modernist literary revolution, and drew on it for their methods and their assumptions. The American critics were usually poets themselves; Leavis made no attempt to be a creative writer— though he has been claimed as such by Ian Robinson—but his own criticism emerged from the Cambridge milieu of the twenties, where Eliot was a dominant influence. A little earlier there was the remarkable work of Edgell Rickword as poet and critic, and, as editor of *The Calendar of Modern Letters*, a setter of the agenda for modern criticism. Earlier still, in Russia, the Formalists had close connections with the Futurist poets, and attempted to provide a rationale for their revolutionary work. Within the academic theory of the present time, approaches may either begin with literature, or with disciplines external to it. Nicolas Tredell has usefully developed this distinction:

There are, broadly speaking, two kinds of theories which now bear on literary studies. First, there is the kind specifically concerned with literature, or with an aspect of it: for example, the Russian Formalist notion of 'literariness' as linguistic defamiliarization; Bakhtin's view of the novel as 'heteroglossic', a carnival of competing voices; Todorov's poetics of narrative, German and American reader-response theories.

Against such theories, Tredell sets those which emerge from other disciplines, and which have lately been more commanding and influential. Such theories, he remarks, 'are not centrally concerned with literature; indeed, they may marginalize or abandon it as a category', and he instances their source in such fields as philosophy, psychology, sociology, anthropology, linguistics. In literary theory they emerge as Marxism, phenomenology, existentialism, structuralism, poststructuralism, deconstruction.

Tredell's analysis is perhaps too synchronic, suggesting that the various modes of literary theory coexist, whether easily or uneasily. And so they do, on the shelves of libraries, or in the pages of textbooks. In practice, though, in terms of what people are currently interested in, a diachronic model is needed. Consider the implications of successiveness and change in the titles or subtitles of some recent books: *After the New Criticism* by Frank Lentricchia; *On Deconstruction: Theory and Criticism After Structuralism* by Jonathan Culler; *Displacement: Derrida and After*, edited by Mark Krupnick; *Beyond Deconstruction* by Howard Felperin; *The Contest of Faculties: Philosophy and Theory After Deconstruction* by Christopher Norris. Significantly, most of them are by Americans, for it is in the American academy that the pressure for change, for constantly new forms of newness, is greatest. Things move more slowly in Britain, but the same pressures exist among that small but active segment of the academy that is concerned with critical theory. This state of affairs has complicated my present task, since what was current when I began thinking about this book a few years ago, and, indeed, when working on earlier drafts of it, is now ceasing to be so. In the present Chapter I have written of movements in theory in the present tense, whereas what is ideally required is something grammatically subtler—perhaps there are languages where it exists—like a special tense in which the present extends back to include actions or events that are already in the recent past. This would be the appropriate tense for the writing of that paradoxical genre, 'contemporary history'. What I have presented as analysis of current movements may well have acquired a historical flavour by the time these words are read. If so, I am not abashed. Contemporary intellectual history is an element in my present enterprise, though the very recent past is hard to see clearly.

I move towards the conclusion of this Chapter by invoking a further term in the sequence of titles quoted above: a recent paper by David Lodge called 'After Bakhtin'. Bakhtin is a latecomer on the anglophone critical scene. His major work was done in Russia in the 1930s and 1940s, he suffered Stalinist repression, was partly rehabilitated, and died in 1975, at a time when very few people in the West had heard of him. But, as Lodge says, 'he was thinking his way, with the minimum of intellectual and material support, through the questions which preoccupy us, decades before we even thought of them.' Bakhtin is a theorist in Tredell's first category, those whose work originates in literature itself. In contrast to the poststructuralists, whose concern with actual literary texts is perfunctory or marginal, Bakhtin's work is focused on two major European authors, Dostoevsky and Rabelais. Though Russian, Bakhtin wrote in a tradition of Germanic scholarship, and his work, particularly in the collection of theoretical essays, *The Dialogic Imagination*, can be prolix, repetitive, and opaque. But the opacity, unlike the ludic obscurities of French poststructuralists, is not intended to undermine traditional meaning. Bakhtin means to mean something, however difficult the meaning, and reading him is recognizably like reading the great critics of the past. As is becoming well known, Bakhtin's central ideas are basically straightforward, and prominent among them is 'dialogue'. Speech implies other speech, either preceding it, or as an anticipated rejoinder. As Lodge puts it, 'According to Bakhtin, language is essentially social or *dialogic*. The words we use come to us already imprinted with meanings, intentions and accents of others, and any utterance we make is directed towards some real or hypothetical Other.' Bakhtin established the kind of binary opposition that is almost commonplace in modern critical theory; it was between the 'monologic' and the 'dialogic'. The former was dominated by a single mode of utterance, as in the traditional literary genres, the lyric, epic, and tragedy. The 'dialogic', which involves a plurality of voices, was particularly characteristic of the novel. At first Bakhtin found this quality, otherwise 'polyphony' or 'heteroglossia', to be particularly characteristic of Dostoevsky, but he later extended it to typify the novel as a genre. Bakhtin is unusual among literary critics in making the focus of his activity the novel rather than lyric poetry or drama. In practice, binary oppositions are very liable to favour one term at the expense of the other, and there can be no doubt that Bakhtin preferred the dialogic to the monologic (a bias that is evident in everyday English, where to engage in dialogue is good, and to utter a monologue is rather bad). This emphasis made the so-called 'monologic' forms of literature problematical, and Lodge quotes from an interesting late essay by Bakhtin which seems to suggest that *all* literary discourse is to some degree dialogic. To remove the distinction completely would seem to undermine the insights that had given force to Bakhtin's earlier criticism. Lodge suggests that this need not happen, if one sees the monologic and dialogic as dominant tendencies rather than mutually exclusive terms.

'Dialogic criticism' can provide new ways of reading. It is distinct from the methods of the old New Criticism, which though believing that lyric poems were dramatic utterances, still read them as the utterance of a single voice. Even when applied to the novel, as in Leavis's writings on novelists or Lodge's own early critical book, *Language of Fiction*, the New Criticism looked for passages of quasi-authorial description, or the exploration of consciousnesses that seem to carry authorial support. Dialogic reading can also defuse poststructuralist scepticism about the possibility of meaning. To quote Lodge again, 'instead of having desperately to defend the possibility of a fixed or stable meaning in isolated utterances, we can cheerfully accept that meaning exists in the process of intersubjective communication, since no utterance ever is truly isolated.' One has the sense that everyone now thinks well of Bakhtin, whether a Marxist like Terry Eagleton, a historical scholar such as Jerome J. McGann, or a practising novelist and critic of fiction, David Lodge. One must resist seeing Bakhtin as the US Cavalry, riding in to rescue a threatened humanism from howling poststructuralists. Bakhtin was, I think, a humanist, but not in any obvious traditional mould. He remained some kind of Marxist, and his concept of the 'carnivalesque', drawn from Rabelais, was presented as a mode of ideological subversion, a pulling down of the mighty from their seats. It will take time for the implications of his work to be properly assimilated and understood; the process involves transposition from a cultural context that is more remote than the French. But the growing interest in it suggests that it offers both a possible way out of present impasses and a way forward.

8. WHO IS DERRIDA, WHAT IS HE?

During the 1980s the stars of French thought fell from the heavens at a disconcerting rate. Louis Althusser, the severe exponent of anti-humanist Marxism, lapsed into uxoricidal depression and was placed in confinement. Then came the deaths of Barthes, Lacan, Foucault. The currency and power of ideas does not depend on their authors' continued physical presence. Indeed, Bakhtin provides an example of someone whose thought has only become influential in the years following his death. Nevertheless, the versions of structuralism and poststructuralism associated with these French masters have not advanced since they left the scene, and if anything have tended to decline. This may be coincidence, or it may be that the star system in French intellectual culture requires its major performers to be visibly on stage. And what was true of France has also been true, a little later, of the English-speaking world.

The major exception to these considerations is the vigorous Jacques Derrida, an admired figure in both the French and the American academic worlds, and a man whose dominance in contemporary critical theory is inescapable. He deserves separate attention, though I shall not attempt an exposition or interpretation of Derrida's thought, which I am incompetent to undertake. My concern is with the nature of his reputation, and the striking extent to which both his admirers and his detractors are unable to agree on what kind of writer Derrida is, or even what he is actually saying.

The one thing all readers are likely to agree on is that Derrida is a very difficult writer, whether he is read in French or in English translation. This charge might be dismissed, of course, as one more example of Anglo-Saxon empirical ignorance, complacent insularity, intellectual laziness, and so forth. Yet the philosopher John Searle has recorded that Foucault once described Derrida's prose style to him as *'obscurantisme terroriste'*. From such a quarter this is significant testimony (though it prompts in me the reflection that it takes one to know one). Searle glosses Foucault's comment by saying, 'The text is written so obscurely that you can't figure out exactly what the thesis is (hence '*obscurantisme*') and then when one criticizes it, the author says, '*Vous m'avez mal compris; vous êtes idiot*' (hence '*terroriste*'). The counter-move to such complaints is to say that the concept of lucidity is itself repressive, and that unravelling Derrida's meanings is itself a deconstructive act, directed against hegemonic ideological positions. Yet despite the obscurity, Derrida's reputation has spread remarkably. In 1983, visiting a university in provincial Norway, I found students of English grappling perplexedly with Derrida, having been encouraged to do so by their British professor. A year or so before that I was at a conference in America where deconstruction bulked largely on the agenda. Between formal sessions I asked an amiable American academic precisely how he managed to familiarize his students with it, given the difficulty. He admitted that it was not easy, and said that, in effect, that what one did was to get them to read the first chapter of any book by Derrida. In such ways, fashion and triviality can go hand in hand.

It is noticeable that though Derrida is a philosopher, albeit one interested in literature, and has always worked in an academic-philosophical context, even if on the margins of the subject, his major impact in North America has been in literature departments. Though some of his followers have philosophical training and interests, and are acquainted with the matrices of Derrida's thought in Hegel, Husserl, and Heidegger, his transmission in literary and cultural contexts has meant that his ideas have become simplified, his paradoxes and contradictions tamed and diminished. One writer, whose interest in poststructuralism is primarily philosophical, has commented:

the reception of Derrida's work, perhaps more than that of any other recent French thinker, has been marked by an astonishingly casual and unquestioning acceptance of certain extremely condensed—not to say sloganistic— characterisations of the history of Western thought, as if this history could be dismissed through its reduction to a set of perfunctory dualisms.

People in literature departments are not used to handling ideas, it not being their *métier*, and traditionally they were not

required to, beyond such elementary tokens as the Elizabeth-
ian World Picture or the Death of God. So it is not surprising
that deconstruction was reduced to what could be easily
handled and passed on.

Why Derrida has had such a vogue in America is indeed a
puzzle, as Searle and others have acknowledged. His name
has been moderately conjured with by British academics, but
there have been few attempts to systematize his work for the
classroom, as has happened in the United States. One obvious
explanation is that deconstruction provided a convenient
successor to the New Criticism in mass higher education,
providing a form of detailed close analysis of texts which does
not require much in the way of contextual cultural literacy.
But Norris has given a further and suggestive explanation:
'The possession of a *written* Constitution whose principles are
yet open to all manner of far-reaching judicial review . . .
gives a political edge to questions of textual and interpretative
theory that they do not have in the British cultural context.'
It is true that deconstructive approaches have emerged in
American law schools as well as in literature departments.

The more simplistic versions of Derrida are common both
to those who admire him and those who detest him. In
admiring expositions revolutionary rhetoric is apparent: Derrida is said to have subverted Western thought, and called in
question the customary concepts of philosophy, literature,
and criticism. A key text is his early essay, 'Structure, Sign
and Play in the Discourse of the Human Sciences', which
concludes that there are two possible interpretations of
interpretation: 'The one seeks to decipher, dreams of
deciphering a truth or an origin which escapes play and the
order of the sign, and which lives the necessity of interpretation as an exile. The other, which is no longer turned toward
the origin, affirms play and tries to pass beyond man and
humanism . . .'. Derrida says that these two interpretations are
absolutely irreconcilable, even though, he adds in his gnomic
fashion, 'we reconcile them in an obscure economy'. It is his
second interpretation, deriving substantially from Nietzsche,
that has become dominant in deconstruction as popularly
understood, where all meaning is turned into 'play'. And it is
this approach which leads to denunciation of Derrida as a

nihilist; in Frederick Crews's words, 'an intellectual nihilist, though a learned and exuberant one'. Raymond Tallis expands the charge, towards the end of his long negative analysis of Derrida's thought:

His is in some ways a tragic case: a man of immense talent and massive erudition, gifted with profound insights, who could not say the things he most wanted to say but who, nevertheless, has gone on to say them. The publicity his ideas have attracted has only deepened the tragedy: the bad influence of those he has himself influenced has added frivolity to the obscurity . . .

Derrida's admirers, and perhaps some disinterested observers, would reject such charges as based on misunderstandings of his work. This, indeed, is the most common defence of Derrida, whether advanced by himself or by his disciples. And yet what does it mean to understand the formulations of someone for whom, on the face of it, final understanding is impossible, or never to be fully achieved? It is this built-in contradiction and barrier to explication that leads to so much discussion of what Derrida really means by those riddling notions that have become slogans: such as, there is no such thing as perception; writing is prior to speech; there is nothing outside the text. These phrases, and others like them, have been debated and pondered, interpreted and reinterpreted, as though they were the formulations of the great philosophers of the past, like Plato or Kant, rather than the work of a living thinker in mid-career. There is a sense in which interpretation without conclusion is a mode of 'play'; deconstruction insists that philosophical texts must be read as though they were literary texts, with full attention to their ambiguities and irresolutions. In this light, arguments about Derrida's 'meaning' have the fascination and intractability of arguments about the interpretation of, say, Eliot's poetry. Indeed, it is a central assumption of deconstruction that the distinction between literature and philosophy is exaggerated, or arbitrary, or even meaningless. Certainly, some of Derrida's later work, such as *The Post Card*, looks more like 'experimental' literature than philosophy in the normal sense. But provisionally granting the premiss that philosophical texts should be interpreted like literature, with careful attention to their textuality, then the question of language intervenes. Arguments in anglophone circles about Derrida's possible meanings are usually based on translations, without reference to the French originals.

Perhaps Derrida's most famous slogan, from *Of Grammatology*, is '*il n'y a pas de hors-texte*'. This can be, and has been, taken in all sorts of ways. At one extreme, it is regarded as self-evidently nihilistic, a dissolution of reality into textuality. At the opposite extreme, an English philosopher has tamed it to a position of common-sense moderation:

> If meaning is brought to birth within the text, the text itself is the bearer of all the Reality that inheres in meaning; and that, when one thinks about it, is, while by no means all the Reality there is, quite a good portion of that part of Reality which matters to us.

Allan Megill has pointed out that an alternative 'meaning' of the phrase is, 'there is no inserted plate' (a French dictionary defines 'hors-texte' as 'Gravure, planche tirée à part et intercalée dans un livre').

Those who take Derrida seriously fall broadly into two camps. There are those who accept him as a subverter of meanings, including his own, an anti-philosopher, a disconcerting jester, gleefully overturning accepted habits of thought. In the second camp are those who regard him as a true philosopher, however provocative his manner, who is restating traditional philosophical problems in a new way. This position is evident among English writers such as Bernard Harrison, Peter Dews, and Christopher Norris. The first approach is more common in the United States. It was brashly exemplified by Geoffrey Hartman, in his tediously playful book, *Saving the Text: Literature/Derrida/Philosophy*. Hartman presents himself in a complicated relationship with Derrida: engaging with him, succumbing to him, imitating him, and trying to resist him. In the last of these veins, Harman acknowledges, 'The problem, on the surface at least, is the persistence, the seriousness, with which an intelligence of this order employs devices that seem to be at best witty and at worst trivial.' Here Hartman is also covertly speaking of himself, for his puns and wordplay and his jokey chapter headings are seldom far from the trivial. Hartman is in the forefront of those deconstructionists who want to abolish the distinctions between philosophy, literature, and criticism, reducing them all to a rich textual stew. In so far as Hartman's book wants to be read as a form of fiction, one can make the adverse literary-critical point that the prose is dense and cloyingly arch, with a crooning, caressing quality about it, suggesting the tone of a man talking quietly and earnestly to himself rather than trying to communicate anything to others. Hostile critics have given Hartman a hard time. Crews has referred to 'a self-congratulatory hermeticism whose purpose seems to lie somewhere between the dropping of names, the displaying of tidbits of esoterica, and the muddling of agency', and Tallis has written a cruel parody of Hartman's prose.

There is a more serious account of Derrida as subverter in Allan Megill's elegant and impressive book, *Prophets of Extremity: Nietzsche, Heidegger, Foucault, Derrida.* Megill writes not as a literary critic but as a philosophically trained historian of ideas. He regards Derrida as an 'artist-philosopher', owing much to Nietzsche, who saw the world as a work of art. Megill discusses Derrida's early interest in French imaginative writers—Mallarmé, Bataille, Sollers, Ponge, Blanchot— whose work was directed to calling the idea of literature in question. He points to Derrida's fascination with fourfold elements, evident in his deconstruction of the Hegelian triad—thesis, antithesis, synthesis—to add a fourth element, which is deconstruction itself. Beyond this specific instance, fourfoldness has a life of its own in his thought; it appears in card-games— 'le jeu des cartes' relates to 'le jeu Descartes'— where there are four suits, plus a joker, whom Megill identifies with Derrida himself. Derrida as joker undermines all practices and ideas, including his own. Megill stresses Derrida's debt to Mallarmé and Nietzsche, two strange masters from the last *fin de siècle* who are exercising such an influence in our own. Nietzsche is Megill's first and greatest example of the 'artist-philosopher', who has been followed by other 'prophets of extremity'. By the time one gets to Derrida, the latest and youngest of the sequence, Nietzsche's myth of art has itself been dissolved by Derrida's pervasive irony: 'If Nietzsche is an ironic mythmaker, Derrida seems only ironic: the radicality of his irony undermines any pretension to myth. Thus instead of articulating a justificatory art, he chooses to question the myth of art itself.' And yet what Derrida writes is as much art as philosophy; Megill compares his *Glas* to *Finnegans Wake*. He remarks, 'the movement of a text by Derrida is directed less by the logic of an argument than by word play, free association, and an almost obsessive recurrence of a limited number of motifs.' Megill himself, in his discussion of Derrida, as in the whole of his book, combines detailed knowledge of the texts, sympathetic treatment of his subject, and an ultimate detachment from it, so that it is not easy to discern his own attitudes. Indeed, he brings his own delicately poised irony to bear at the end of his book when he writes,

If, upon hearing of the manifest truth of the work of art or of the textual, fictional character of the world, the reader will let a knowing smile play upon his face where previously he maintained an attitude of high seriousness, then the aim of this book will have been in part achieved.

Finally, for Megill, the artist-philosophers are more concerned with interpreting reality as an aesthetic phenomenon than with traditional truth-telling. Their value for the reader lies in enlarging or changing our perceptions, in helping us to break out from a deadening routine; in short, the carnivalesque: 'The prophets of extremity put up a distorting mirror against our world—but one which properly attended to, can tell us something about that world, and about the possibilities of changing it, or changing ourselves.' This hortatory and vaguely uplifting conclusion is out of key with the body of Megill's book, which is distinguished by the penetrating quality of its readings, and which, among much else, offers a very persuasive presentation of Derrida as joker.

It is, however, the philosopher rather than the joker who is in evidence in Imre Salusinsky's interview with Derrida, conducted in 1985. It is straightforward and lucid, in great contrast to Derrida's impenetrable interviews with French interlocutors in the late 1960s and early 1970s which are collected in *Positions*. Derrida comes across as seriously concerned with philosophy and the problems of teaching it; and he is non-committal in his response to a question about the possibility of introducing deconstruction into high schools. At one interesting moment he reflects on his responsibilities as a teacher in a very serious-minded way:

I wouldn't advocate a university that would be cut off from society. We know that we have to train people towards a profession. I'm against some sorts of professionalization, but it would be silly to think that the university should have nothing to do with any profession. You have to train people to become doctors or engineers or professors, and at the same time to train them in questioning all that—not only in a critical way, but I would say in a deconstructive way. This is a double responsibility: two responsibilities which sometimes are not compatible. In my own teaching, in my own responsibilities, I think I have to make two gestures simultaneously: to train people, to teach them, to give them a content, to be a good pedagogue, to train teachers, to give them a profession; and at the same time to make them as conscious as possible of the problems of professionalization.

These admirable sentiments are certainly not those of a nihilist. Elsewhere in the interview Derrida invokes his key word 'play' in much the same sense in which Arnold employed it in the 'free play of mind'.

Those who take Derrida seriously as a philosopher can either agree or disagree with him. John Searle is one of the latter. In the late 1970s he clashed with Derrida in the pages of the poststructuralist yearbook, *Glyph*, where Searle made some sharp remarks, such as that Derrida 'has a distressing penchant for saying things that are obviously false.' Derrida's reply did not take the form of a reasoned rebuttal but of ninety pages of verbal clowning, which put Searle in his place by referring to him throughout as 'Sarl', an acronym for 'Societé à responsabilité limitée', which means a limited company. Derrida thus turned his opponent from a person into an institution, and his piece was called 'Limited Inc abc'. Searle returned to the attack in 1983, in a review of Jonathan Culler's *On Deconstruction*. He claimed that Derrida was in error in his claim that throughout the history of Western philosophy speech had been privileged above writing. He further argues that Derrida's fundamental claim that speech is really writing, and that writing is prior to speech, is based on a redefinition of terms, and that by such methods one could prove anything, that the rich are really poor, that the true is really false, and so on. Searle characterizes Derrida as a genuine philosopher, who, because modern philosophy had undermined the transcendental grounding for reality offered by traditional metaphysics, concludes that there is nothing left but the free play of signifiers. Searle finds this an unwarranted conclusion.

Christopher Norris also reads Derrida in philosophical terms, even though professionally he teaches English in the University of Wales. Unlike Searle he admires Derrida, and believes that he is genuinely concerned with major philosophical questions. Indeed, Norris looks for a possible *rapprochement* between deconstruction and the Anglo-American philosophical tradition exemplified by Searle, though he finds that Derrida has more possible affinities with Searle's master, Austin. Norris is at some pains to extricate Derrida's meanings from the American literary critics whom he believes have misappropriated them. An unfamiliar Derrida emerges from Norris's book on him, not a nihilist, an artist-philosopher or a joker, but a profound thinker who does not uphold the positions that are popularly ascribed to him: irrationalism; interpretation as an unending free-for-all; meaning disappearing in a cloud of dispersing signifiers; the abandonment of reference and the disappearance (or death) of the author. Norris writes:

Certainly it has been a main object of Derrida's texts to show how philosophers, from Plato to Husserl, have striven and failed to suppress the signs of rhetorical disruption in the discourse of philosophic reason. But he has also been careful to repudiate that facile misreading of deconstruction— prevalent among literary critics—which thinks to turn the tables on philosophy by proclaiming that 'all concepts are metaphors', or that philosophic truth-claims are really metaphorical through and through.

Such readings or misreadings tend to originate in Nietzsche. For Norris, and, as he claims, for Derrida, deconstruction is

a rigorous attempt to *think the limits* of that principle of reason which has shaped the emergence of Western philosophy, science and technology at large . . . the activity of deconstruction is strictly inconceivable outside the tradition of enlightened rational critique whose classic formulations are still to be found in Kant (Norris's italics).

Norris's book is, in its own terms, persuasive and carefully argued. He shows himself to be here, as he did in his earlier *Deconstruction: Theory and Practice*, an admirably lucid and urbane expositor of difficult ideas. Anyone who can say so clearly just what Derrida is saying, or doing, immediately puts the reader in his debt. Yet the clarity and rigour may in themselves be problematical. This was the position argued some years ago by practitioners of *la nouvelle critique*, who believed that clarity in argument was a form of ideological mystification, reinforcing the *status quo*. Put in such extreme terms, the position is clearly absurd and self-defeating. But, for Derrida, whose fusion—or (con)fusion—of obscurity and playfulness is an essential element in his textuality, Norris's exposition may represent a process of intellectual tidying up which leaves out something important. Working hard against the prevalent impression of Derrida as some kind of irresponsible comedian, Norris continually insists on his 'rigorous' and 'scrupulous' reading of philosophical and literary texts. One takes the point, whilst insisting that scrupulosity and rigour are matters of means not ends. A generation or so ago, New Critics and Scrutineers did assume that scrupulosity and rigour were self-justifying ends in criticism. Since then much theoretical work has been directed at this short-sighted empiricism, uncovering the pattern of cultural or ideological assumptions that supported it. Norris falls short of isolating or defining the actual end to which Derrida's scrupulous and rigorous readings are directed. This is perhaps inevitable since deconstruction resists teleology, and it is this resistance that has enabled its enemies to call it nihilist. Leaving intellectual content aside, there is an obvious contrast between Norris's manner, which is in the best English academic tradition, clear, cautious, attentive to evidence, moving from one conclusion to the next, and Derrida's exuberant obfuscation. In his introduction Norris acknowledges the difficulty of writing about him at all in such a context:

That he should now figure as an addition to the Modern Masters series is yet another irony of Derrida's ascent to intellectual stardom. No philosopher has done more to disown the idea that his writings embody some kind of masterly or authoritative wisdom. And the irony is compounded by the fact that Derrida goes out of his way to resist any kind of adequate treatment in a book like this.

Norris's book is, in fact, more than adequate as a title in a series on Modern Masters. Yet it is likely that he has imposed a colour-filter on Derrida, which lets through the rational elements and occludes the irrational ones. Norris virtually admits as much from time to time. Discussing *Of Grammatology*, he says he will treat it as a book with a theme, even though Derrida wants to discourage such an approach to it.

Derrida's famous paper 'Structure, Sign and Play' aroused much excitement when it was delivered at a conference on structuralism at Johns Hopkins in 1966, and has since acquired a mythological significance as the fountainhead of American deconstruction. In so far as that essay gives some warrant to the idea of free-for-all hermeneutics, then, concedes Norris, ' "Structure, Sign and Play" is a text which, at least in its closing paragraphs, falls below the highest standards of Derridean argumentative rigour.'

Despite these occasional reservations, Norris writes as a disciple, who believes that other disciples, as well as Derrida's enemies, have got him wrong. Arguing for what he believes to be the right way of reading Derrida, Norris makes what is essentially a forensic case. What does emerge from it is that Norris's way of reading Derrida is likely to make considerable demands on the reader. The texts are to be read and reread, with all the scrupulosity and rigour that Norris attributes to Derrida, and if not wholly in French, at least with frequent references to the original. For Norris the provocative sloganistic phrases by which Derrida is best known will make true sense only when restored to the contexts from which they have been taken. Norris may well be right that Derrida deserves such attention, but he is not often likely to receive it in the conditions of actual pedagogy, or in the random public exchanges of higher cultural life, which put a premium on the simplifying and the reductive.

It is, nevertheless, interesting that Norris should say, in passing, of Nietzsche; 'there are many competing versions of Nietzsche, none possessing any absolute claim to articulate the "truth" of his text, but *all* of them—and this is Derrida's point—made possible by something in the logic, the syntax or the structural resources of his writing.' What is true of Nietzsche is surely true of Derrida, of whom there are many competing versions; Norris presumably believes that his contains the truth, without distancing quotation marks. But the other versions, admiring ones like Hartman's or Megill's, and hostile ones like Tallis's, are all based on something in his writing. And it is their Derrida, the nihilist or joker, who has been so influential in literature departments. There are other possible interpretations. Michael Ryan has looked for a

rapprochement between deconstruction and Marxism. Edward
Said discovers a kind of negative theology in Derrida's
writing, and Nicolas Tredell says something similar, 'one
might draw some interesting comparisons between, for
instance, deconstruction and Nagarjunan Buddhism, which
dissolves a metaphysics of presence into a metaphysics of
absence, the Void.'

One may, in Derridean terms, play with these conflicting
versions of 'Derrida', but sooner or later, if one is writing
about him, or teaching him, then one has to choose, since
they are *competing* versions. It may be that to choose is to
distort so protean an entity. If so, this is yet one more of the
paradoxes attending this remarkable figure, who, disavowing
mastery has become a Master, and who undermines his
meanings in advancing them.

9. SPLENDOURS AND MISERIES OF THE ACADEMY

Traditionally, people who wrote criticism often also wrote poetry or novels, and engaged in the discussion of politics and public affairs. Things are now otherwise. As Frank Kermode has put it,

> You won't find it easy to name an important critic who was a critic, and nothing else; that is, until quite recently. The world is now full of literary critics, some held to be important, who do nothing else but write literary criticism, and they all work in universities.

Kermode is referring to the demise of the man of letters, or the 'bookman' as he became known in late-Victorian England, and his replacement by the professionalized university critic. Kermode sees this change—which is at the heart of what I am writing about—as having radical implications for letters, comparable to such things as the advent, first of printing and then of cheap paper; the bourgeoisie's greater leisure for private reading; and the abandonment by circulating libraries of the three-volume novel, which had been the favoured vehicle for fiction during much of the nineteenth century: Kermode exaggerates a little, I think; nothing in the establishment of university English is as important as the innovations in culture and technology which established the book in its modern form. But he is right in seeing the movement of criticism from literature to the academy as having large cultural implications. Kermode thinks that this process, with all that it implies, is a fact of life, which has to be lived with, whatever we think of it. We may have no choice but to do so, though I believe that the change has been more damaging than beneficial. There is the further consideration that universities may not indefinitely be secure havens for literary criticism, in the cold economic climate and rampant anti-intellectualism of Thatcherite Britain, and of many other parts of the world.

When English was established in British universities criticism played at best a minor part in it. There was a 'critical paper' in the Oxford degree, but the emphasis was substantially on scholarship of a tough traditional kind, without much concession to the Arnoldian free play of mind. For a long time Oxford English was directed towards scholarship and was suspicious of criticism, and this attitude was reflected in its house organ, *The Review of English Studies*. Helen Gardner, for many years an Oxford luminary, did not believe that the purpose of 'English' was to turn out critics, any more than it was to produce poets and novelists. The graduate in English was to be to some extent a scholar, in so far as he or she had a sense of the past and the capacity to understand literature in its historical contexts, particularly linguistic; beyond that, what was looked for was wide reading, an appreciation of masterpieces, and a capacity to write well, attend to evidence, and disentangle sense from nonsense in argument. It was not, in fact, a bad educational programme, but it did not have the glamour of Cambridge English, where the idea of criticism was central, as instanced by the great success and influence of Richards's *Practical Criticism*. Gardner, like other Oxford Anglicans, resisted 'the religious and missionary approach to the study of literature evident in the Newbolt report and the Cambridge pioneers. She was not positively hostile to criticism, indeed, she produced a book called *The Business of Criticism*. But her concept of criticism was that it should be elucidatory and illuminating rather than evaluative. Her assumptions are broadly Crocean; value appeared in the individual's response to the particular work, but should not be erected into hierarchies, and the reader should cultivate 'the receptiveness and disinterestedness which are the conditions of aesthetic experience.' Non-evaluative criticism, as propounded by the successive Merton professors, Gardner and Carey, has long been a popular ideal at Oxford. But another Oxford professor, John Bayley, sees things differently. Discussing a book on Dostoevsky, he remarks that while the author has much of interest to say about *The Idiot* 'she does not quite persuade one that it comes off, indeed she does not really try, because like many scholars today she is more concerned with showing how the thing works than with judging if it works well.'

From the beginning academic literary study was divided between those who saw it as inevitably involved with making judgements and those who did not. Cambridge English represented the former: Richards and Leavis wanted an evaluative criticism, because they did not believe that literature was simply a matter of disinterested individual response; it was an index to the condition of civilization, which made judgements imperative. Wherever Leavis exerted an influence, either directly, on his pupils, or via *Scrutiny*, then criticism was emphatically evaluative. In practice this often meant that immature minds would take over Leavis's own evaluations without relating them to their own experience of literature, resulting in the diffusion of callow or inept judgements that has been condemned from the right by C. S. Lewis and from the left by Catherine Belsey. Although the New Criticism in its later American manifestations generally pursued a purely formal and elucidatory analysis, Gerald Graff reminds us that the original New Critics *were* evaluative, since they wrote as conservative Southerners who were much concerned with ideals of cultural health. They were also, for the most part, practising poets and men of letters, who would want to make judgements. Similarly, Cambridge English was originally sustained by the achievements of literary modernism which had a new agenda to write. In later academic criticism, it is only among Marxists and feminists that we find an overt evaluative pressure. Elsewhere the idea of a supposedly non-evaluative criticism has become general. I have remarked on its dominance in Oxford English, and a generation ago it was given magisterial expression in Northrop Frye's *Anatomy of Criticism*, which aspired to a 'scientific' criticism where there would be no place for evaluation, since it is not nobler to study stars than earthworms. In the recent work of the global anglophone academy, evaluative criticism has largely disappeared. In its simpler, popularizing aspects the emphasis is on illumination and elucidation, and in its more advanced interpretative reaches the critic is concerned to trace unnoticed patterns of coherence and unity, or, more probably these days, incoherences and aporias. Yet vestigial gestures towards value persist, usually at the end of an exposition, where the critic in a final flourish claims, or at least hopes, that something valuable has emerged from the analysis; a revelation of the quality of the author's imagination; or of the inevitable tendency of all texts to be about their own processes of composition, or to come apart in the reader's hand; or of the aesthetic fascination of the patterns of imagery that have been revealed; or, at the very least, and least interestingly, that something 'interesting' will have been said.

Most of this academic activity is not, in fact, criticism as traditionally understood but something else, which is fundamentally a form of technical description. Helen Gardner was aware of the problem, observing that the pursuit of image patterns, or of the ideas in a poem, can be useful to the interpreter, but cannot 'be more than auxiliary in leading us to the true "meaning" of the work, which is the meaning which enlarges our own imaginative life.' What Gardner calls 'meaning' is, I take it, the work's unique expression of value, which we grasp intuitively. John Bayley, after the remark quoted above, goes on to complain about 'the almost purely technical nature of this modern criticism, even more unsuited to how we actually respond to Dostoevsky than it is to most authors.' Long ago, in the heyday of Cambridge English, Richards was making a similar distinction between the 'critical' and the 'technical': 'All remarks as to the ways and means by which experiences arise or are brought about are technical, but critical remarks are about the values of experiences and the reasons for regarding them as valuable, or not valuable.' Geoffrey Thurley claimed that much modern criticism, so-called, was mainly concerned with 'scansion', which is the description, often very close and attentive, of the structural, formal, and technical features of a text. Such criticism Thurley argued, very convincingly, never bridges the gap between description and interpretation, which for Thurley involves evaluation. In practice, much academic interpretation—whether New Critical, archetypal, deconstructive, or whatever—is really, in his terms, a more or less refined form of description or 'scansion'. He is very dismissive about the famous reading of a Shakespeare sonnet by Jakobson and Jones, which minutely analyses its linguistic features, and emerges with a banal paraphrase which, Thurley remarks, 'any schoolboy would scorn to produce'. If we take criticism out of its academic context and apply it to more things than literature, it is evident that comparisons of value are fundamental to it. Consider, for instance, informed discussions of sporting events, which are always displays of evaluative analysis: who played well, who disappointingly, and why and how; or whether a team has played better at home or away, this season or last. It is true that in such discussions the judgemental element does not exist in isolation, since it is interwoven with description, technical assessment of moves in play, and so forth, in ways suggested in Wittgenstein's lectures on aesthetics. But to remove this element results in, at best, a decaffeinated criticism.

It has been taken for granted for a long time that criticism and the academy go naturally together, and a large pedagogic and publishing industry has been built on that assumption. Nevertheless, I believe that the marriage, whatever its public appearance, is a difficult one, and results in bad faith and deception. Helen Gardner was not a deep thinker, but she saw certain things more clearly than many sharper minds. She was wrong to think that genuine criticism could be severed from evaluation, but right to think that there was no place for such criticism in the academy. The 'criticism' which is copiously produced and read in literature departments eschews judgement for 'scansion', technical analysis, and elaborate interpretations which nevertheless remain fundamentally descriptive. This state of affairs is not, I think, an aberration, but is inevitable in the structures of higher education.

The example of Leavis and *Scrutiny* may suggest otherwise. Leavis was a major critic and a very influential educator, who was convinced both that criticism was essentially evaluative and that it was at the heart of English studies. Yet Leavis was in many respects not a man of his time; though himself a dedicated university teacher, he was in spirit the last of the Victorian sages, who were men of letters and of affairs, not academics (prescinding from Arnold's and Ruskin's marginal tenure of chairs at Oxford). *Scrutiny* had an enormous influence on English studies, particularly in England, but its immediate model was the non-academic *Calendar of Modern Letters*, and more remotely the great Victorian reviews, whose contents might be described as the higher literary journalism. In its early years *Scrutiny* was a fine embodiment of the spirit of criticism, literary and cultural. Leavis's judgements were very much his own, laboriously arrived at, and presented with subtlety and rigour. But these judgements were then taken over and pre-packaged for pedagogic purposes, so one had the spectacle of the Leavisite schoolmaster or university teacher who presented his students with duplicated copies of, say, sonnets by Hopkins and Rossetti, which they were invited to compare and contrast in evaluative terms. There was no doubt that they were expected to admire the former and scorn the latter; anyone misguided enough to get the preference the wrong way round, would be regarded as at best naïve and misguided, and at worst corrupted in sensibility. Denys Thompson's *Reading and Discrimination* (1934) is a collection of such comparative exercises. Leavisism assumed that its rewriting of the canon had a once-and-for-all quality, so that it was inconceivable that anyone could come to admire Shelley again, though this is precisely what has happened under the influence of Harold Bloom, who is dedicated to overturning the Eliot–Leavis version of poetic history. The attempt to enforce an evaluative criticism in the academy inevitably results in rigidity and dogmatism and, ultimately, a form of brainwashing. Leavisites, of course, claimed that they were committed to discussion, argument, the free play of mind; in so far as they were, it was contained within the enclosing form of life, not directed against it, rather like arguments within Marxist–Leninist ideology. It was this aspect of Leavisism that Oxford English, with its broad though often flaccid eclecticism, was most opposed to.

Venturing to propound a law of intellectual life, I suggest that evaluative criticism enters institutional literary study under the influence of practising writers, or of critics who have a close discipular relation to them, but that in time it is rejected, like an alien organ. Writers, whose criticism arises directly from the problems and possibilities of their art, are inevitably evaluative; Baudelaire showed how being a poet also involves being a critic. Eliot's early and best criticism was what he called 'workshop' criticism, an attempt to realign literary tradition in the interests of the kind of poetry he wanted to write. Leavis, at the beginning of his career a whole-hearted admirer of Eliot, took over Eliot's tentative critical models and systematized them. Later he responded in a similar way to D. H. Lawrence's criticism, as well as to his creative achievement. In America, as I have remarked, the original New Critics were evaluative, in ways closely connected to their own poetic practice. Also in America there is the singular example of Yvor Winters, sometimes seen as an equivalent of Leavis, who was a poet of conservative but original talents, and a fiercely judgemental critic, who weirdly redrew the canons of English and American literature, so that T. Sturge Moore and Elizabeth Daryush emerged as major twentieth-century poets. Unlike Leavis's, Winters's deconstruction of tradition proved too extreme to have even a temporary lodgement in the academy, though his readings of sixteenth-century poetry have had some influence, and a theorist such as Gerald Graff acknowledges a debt to Winters, who was his teacher.

It remains to show why genuine criticism is not at home in the academy; or, more precisely, why it is irreconcilable with pedagogic practice. Criticism, I take it, is an activity that occurs between equals, whatever its object. The critic is an unusually acute and well-informed reader, but there should be equality of esteem between the critic and other readers. What he or she has to say is always open to comment, questioning, refutation. This is apparent in the correspondence columns of those publications where the tradition of public criticism continues, like the *Times Literary Supplement* and the *London Review of Books*. There is, of course, an immense amount to be learned from good critics, but the critic's role and tone are not those of a teacher. Critical seminars within the university may sometimes blur this distinction if they contain elements of genuine intellectual exchange. Leavis defined critical discussion as taking the form, 'This is so, isn't it?' expecting the answer, 'yes, but . . .' (though never, 'I very much doubt it' or 'No, in thunder!'). This formula may characterize the best form of discussion. But it is disingenuous for academics to pretend that they can participate in such discussion on terms of complete equality with their students, for there are questions of power and authority involved; at the end of the day, grades and marks, assessing and examining, come into the picture. Students do not forget these overshadowing realities even if academics, caught up in the euphoria of a 'really lively discussion', sometimes do. The reality is often closer to that memorably described by David Lodge:

occasionally one feels, as a teacher, rather like a soccer referee who, having blown his whistle for the kick-off, finds the players disconcertingly reluctant to make a move and is reduced to dribbling the ball himself furiously from end to end, scoring brilliant goals in undefended nets, while the motionless players look curiously on.

Not only should there be equality of esteem and status between critic and readers, though the former may appear as first among equals, they should all be in possession of the subject of discussion. They should all have read the book, in short. This is why reviewing is not properly speaking criticism, though it calls for critical qualities, and an extended review-article, looking at a whole œuvre, may well be. This is true in all aspects of culture. If we are discussing a football match or a meal in a restaurant, then at the very least we should all have seen the match or eaten the meal. Furthermore, we should have a shared understanding of the rules of discourse about such subjects. A proper discussion of a football match cannot occur if one of the participants is quite ignorant of the rules of the game; and the kind of assessment of a restaurant meal that would involve the possible insertion of the establishment into a good food guide (or perhaps its deletion from it) will not get very far if one of the diners does not care for the meal because his idea of a gastronomic treat is a cheeseburger and french fries (though within the order of the burger discriminations are possible). The critical reader of a poem needs to have some idea of what a poem is, which need not be a theoretically sophisticated idea, and some acquaintance with poetry already.

In this context I want to refer to a brief but highly significant passage in Richards's *Practical Criticism*. In the latter part of the book Richards discusses the reports on the 'protocols', the anonymous reports on the anonymous poems or extracts the respondents had been given to read. He examines their various kinds of failure in reading, arising from the reader's susceptibility to personal fantasy, dominance by dogma, over-literalness, careless construing, and so on. Most of these failures are in the order of mental operation, which is in accordance with Richards's dominantly psychologistic approach. This is still true when he says that some of the respondents lacked the emotional maturity to respond adequately to poetry. But he then goes on to remark that a further cause of inadequate response is the reader's unfamiliarity with poetry: 'A lack of experience with poetry must be placed next to general inexperience of life in this list of deficiencies.' Here Richards switches from a psychological to a cultural factor. The remark has not been much noticed, but its implications must undermine the way in which 'practical criticism' is often employed in literary education. It has long been common practice to give students isolated passages of poetry or prose, often but not always anonymous, to analyse, discuss, and respond to, in the manner of Richards's original undertaking. In this exercise students are urged to clear their minds of presuppositions, to concentrate on 'the words on the page', and then to write down their responses. The reading is deliberately contextless, and the mind is assumed or encouraged to be a *tabula rasa*. (More traditional pedagogy went for appreciation rather than analysis, urging the reader to a direct experience of the poem, perhaps inhaling its beauty like the scent of a flower; but the underlying process was similar.) Such assumptions are quite contrary to what we know of how perception works. The practice of 'practical criticism' in fact unconsciously takes it for granted that the readers already know enough about poetry to have a grasp of rules and conventions sufficient to make adequate sense of the passage. Richards had to acknowledge that what he called 'the relatively cultivated youth of our age' were not very familiar with poetry. If that was true, then, how much more true is it now, given the vast changes in education, society, and culture that have ensued since 1929? I am not now going to engage in lamentations about the ignorance and lack of reading of present-day undergraduates, though I have done so in my time, and could be easily provoked into them again. I merely want to make the limited point that many of these students—who may be highly intelligent—do not have the existing familiarity with poetry, not to mention the general knowledge and cultural literacy, that would enable them to engage as equals in genuinely critical discussion.

Leavis held firm to the idea that any kind of responsible discussion of literature was a critical act, so that the academic was inescapably engaged in criticism when lecturing or conducting a seminar. In reality this is unlikely to be true, as student and teacher do not have an equal possession of the text. In other academic areas it is assumed that the teacher knows more than the student, and is there to convey this knowledge, whether as a corpus or a skill. The conveying need not, indeed should not, be done in an authoritarian way. In seminar teaching it should elicit feedback, questioning, the bringing out of implications or contradictions, and the opening up of fresh aspects of the subject. Nevertheless, teaching implies an imbalance of knowledge, otherwise it would not be necessary. The formal lecture, that archaic but strangely persistent mode, makes this apparent. In literature teaching the emphasis is on shared experience rather than the conveying of information; a lecture is supposed to provide knowledge, elucidation, or interpretation of texts on the assumption that the auditors have already read them. As anyone who has worked in an English department will know, many of those listening to the lecture will not have done the necessary reading, and are so reduced to hearing about and taking notes on something of which they have not had direct literary experience (even passing on their notes to friends who were absent from the lecture). In a Crocean or Leavisite perspective this conveying of knowledge without experience is a useless activity. It is, however, a common one, and a kind of collective bad faith.

Attempts are still made to introduce an element of evaluative criticism into academic teaching, whether from a surviving Leavisism, or under Marxist or feminist auspices. My own efforts to do so have been instructive, but discouraging. Judgements made in the course of a lecture will be taken down in notes as if they were facts, whereas it is in the nature of critical judgements that they cannot be taken over by others; it is on this dilemma, I believe, that Leavisism ultimately foundered. In the habitual contexts of English Literature teaching, students assume that if a work is on a reading list then it must be of approved quality, otherwise why is it there? Attempts to provide adverse judgements on canonical works tend to be resented as 'finding fault with' or 'picking holes in' these works of established merit, the result of a tiresome foible on the part of the teacher, and leading to disorientation if persisted in. In these matters, I think the students may have a more realistic sense of the situation than the teacher. There has been much discussion recently of the nature of literary canons; university teachers of English are seen as both initiators and guardians of the canon (as, for instance, by Kermode in his essay, 'Institutional Control of Interpretation'). The academic institutionalizing of literary study inevitably leads to the establishing of canons (made necessary, among much else, by the logistic requirements of reading lists and bookshop orders), and where there are canons evaluation is, in the context of pedagogy, either impossible or unrewardingly difficult, since canonization implies merit. And what is true of undergraduate teaching in England is equally true, *mutatis mutandis*, of the high-pressure environment of American graduate schools. Furthermore, the great mass of academic critical writing produced in the United States is elucidatory, analytical, descriptive, scansional, not evaluative. What is everywhere assumed, if not always made explicit, is that literary judgement has no place in the academy. This is a correct assumption, since the institutional conditions preclude its effective existence.

Academics can still write evaluative criticism of course, and in so far as they do they are producing the kind of criticism practised by men of letters. John Bayley provides an interesting instance. Remarking that Dostoevsky's *The Idiot* does not altogether 'come off', he is making a coherent and discussable point, whether or not one accepts it. Samuel Johnson might have said something similar, though in a very different idiom, about some accepted masterpiece of European literature. But it is possible that the Dostoevsky scholar whose book prompted Bayley's comment might not have understood it—

how could an acknowledged great novel, worth writing about at length, be said not to 'come off'? Bayley is a senior academic who has kept his distance from institutional pressures and writes in the manner of the traditional man of letters.

The despised belletrist criticism of an earlier day could make radical judgements in an off-hand manner; those articles, for instance, with titles like 'On Rereading Stendhal', which come to the conclusion that Stendhal has been much overrated. An established professor of French Literature might nowadays privately believe as much, but would probably think it unprofessional or damaging to argue the case publicly. Leavis, who notoriously had no hesitation about attacking canonical figures, was closer to this tradition, however much he detested the belletrist spirit, than he was to later developments in academic criticism. His iconoclasm about Milton, for instance, was anticipated by Walter Bagehot. Conversely, men of letters have always been ready for exciting literary discoveries. The young T. S. Eliot, coming across Laforgue as a Harvard undergraduate is a celebrated instance; there is André Gide, well on in middle age, registering his delight and astonishment at James Hogg's *Confessions of a Justified Sinner*.

Donald Davie, in a dispirited essay called 'Criticism and the Academy', ruefully acknowledges that the belletrist criticism of men of letters such as Edmund Wilson and Cyril Connolly (unequal figures, these, one has to remark) might have more to be said for it than he, as a lifelong academic, would be happy to acknowledge:

> Edmund Wilson and Cyril Connolly were as ready to talk of Ovid as of the memoirs of Ulysses S. Grant, and indeed ready to illuminate the one by shafts of light thrown from the other . . . Connolly and Wilson, we may agree, lived dangerously; they took risks, knowing full well that they were not *au fait* with the latest scholarship, had not mastered 'the secondary material'. And we tell our graduate students that they must never take such risks, construing as scruple what in fact is timidity.

Davie himself provides the example of a dedicated university teacher, who is at the same time a fine poet, a practitioner of rigorously evaluative criticism, and a judicious reviewer. He is, in fact, a rare surviving embodiment of those long-vanished ideals of the 1950s, when it briefly seemed that University English might provide a terrain where all these practices could converge.

Morris Dickstein has contributed an excellent essay to the collection in which Davie's piece appears, called 'Journalism and Criticism'. Acknowledging the apparent opposition between these two terms, he goes on to argue, and to show from historical evidence, that throughout the nineteenth century, and into the early twentieth, much of the central function of criticism was carried by literary and cultural journalism, most of it, admittedly, of a more spacious and literate order than is common today. It is to this tradition, I have suggested, that *Scrutiny* was indebted. At the present time, it has become attenuated but not extinct, and it continues in the long review-articles in the *New York Review of Books* and *London Review of Books*, and a few other periodicals. Academics contribute to it, certainly, but writing as critics, not academics, for it involves judgement as much as elucidation. To take a particular instance, Martin Amis's *The Moronic Inferno*, published in 1986, is a collection of reprinted journalistic pieces on life, literature, and culture in contemporary America, a country for which he has mixed feelings of attraction and repulsion. It is the work of a novelist and journalist, not an academic, and notwithstanding the sometimes excessive brightness of the prose and the shortwindedness of the articles it seems to me a brilliant late embodiment of the Anglo-American tradition of literary and social criticism.

A central figure in Dickstein's essay is Henry James, a great critic, who could be subtly descriptive, elucidatory, analytical, and judgemental within the same piece of writing. As Dickstein points out, much of James's critical writing was produced according to the exigencies of journalism and magazine publication; nevertheless, as now brought together in two large and handsome volumes in the Library of America series, it must be the finest body of literary criticism in English from a single author. The whiggish notion that such writing might be somehow improved on or even supplanted by the critical mass-production of the anglophone academy is quite self-delusory.

II

Richards, as we have seen, thought that in order to be a good reader of poetry one must already be a reader of poetry. This is true, to a lesser extent, of all forms of imaginative writing, but poetry is the most obviously governed by convention and genre, and in the eyes of both the Russian Formalists and of non-literary readers the most likely to display linguistic deformation. In many academic disciplines no prior knowledge is required or assumed. It is possible for sixth-form students in British secondary schools to take the Advanced- ('A'-) level examination for school-leavers in such subjects as philosophy or economics or sociology, but it is not at all common, and incoming university students of these subjects usually begin at the beginning, with open minds but with the necessary commitment to learning. In principle it would be quite possible for the study of English poetry to begin in a similar *ab initio* fashion, except that it would be fruitless for someone to embark on it who did not have at least some familiarity with poetry and a wish to read more. This is because the study of poetry *as* poetry—rather than as histori- cal or cultural material—is a matter of intuitive and affective response, not just of willingness to accept an intellectual discipline, as might be the case with philosophy, economics, and so forth. (I grant that the difference is not absolute, and there may be elements of the affective and the intuitive in the pursuit of any intellectual discipline, but they are likely to be marginal.) It could be a rewarding form of teaching to help an uninformed but well-motivated student to come to terms with poetry, but it would involve time and leisure. The student would need to read as widely as possible in different kinds of poetry, to learn something about literary history, genre, and convention, and to acquire the practical-critical skills of close reading. All this might well be accomplished in the comparat- ively open-ended context of adult or continuing education, which is not dominated by the teleology of the examination system. In the high-pressured and directive context of under- graduate teaching it may be desirable, but is not practically possible. Too often, even the desirability is not recognized.

It is my experience that many students of English Literature with good A-level results dislike poetry, or at least feel baffled by it, and can go through a three-year degree course without this attitude being radically changed. There are elements of a vicious version of the hermeneutic circle involved: people don't like poetry because they haven't read enough to come to terms with it, and they haven't read enough because they don't like it. Several factors are involved in this unhappy state of affairs: a general decline in cultural literacy, and in skill and practice in reading. Poetry demands a form of reading that, though rewarding, is unusually intensive, and it is often avoided in sixth-form English teaching. Work for the A-level examination in English Literature means a narrow concentration on a limited number of texts, and curricular pressures do not leave time for the undirected contextual reading that would provide broader literary experience. Furthermore, I suspect that many sixth-form English teachers have acquired an Honours degree in the subject without ever coming to like or appreciate poetry, and they pass on their incapacities. Hence the concentration on plays and novels, often modern ones, which is made increasingly possible with A-level syllabuses governed by the specious lure of relevance. There are, of course, complex social and cultural factors to consider. It is a common leftist belief that poetry is an 'élitist' mode, precisely because of the cultural literacy it presupposes, which gives an unfair advantage to students from middle-class homes with books. The advantage is undeniably there; but what of the ever-increasing number from middle-class homes without books? The grammar schools once provided the necessary culture of learning, as well as specific instruction, for students from under privileged homes, as we see in Judith Grossman's *Her Own Terms*, or Anthony Burgess's autobiographical recollection of reading English at Manchester University in the late thirties (some twenty years before I started teaching there myself). Many things have changed since then. Not only have the grammar schools disappeared, but the number of students going into higher education to read English has greatly increased, the social catchment is wider, and reading has come to seem more difficult.

It was a recurring motif in the Newbolt Report, echoed by Leavis, that English was not just another school or university subject, to be placed alongside geography or geology. There is some truth in this, but not altogether in the sense that was there intended. Unlike other academic disciplines, English in higher education presupposes both an existing knowledge and an existing competence, which in practice is often lacking. As I have suggested, up to a generation ago a common form of life united sixth-form and university English, regardless of whether their orientation was 'Oxford' or 'Cambridge', since the latter made much the same assumptions about literacy and competence as the former. That shared culture has gone, though its traces have persisted for a long time, at least among those unworldly older academics who assume that students of English will have read the whole of Shakespeare in the sixth form, or that they can readily identify classical or biblical references. The belated realization that these things are no longer so leads to the embittered and baffled reaction that they *ought* to be so. However, that is a declining reaction; the experience of regularly interviewing would-be entrants to an English degree course soon induces a sense of realism. In the state of affairs that still obtained when I entered the profession in 1959 the grammar school teacher and the university teacher of English were not radically different kinds of person; indeed, contingent or accidental factors might have determined which career path was followed. Since then there has been a marked divergence between school and university; students have become less well equipped, and academics, particularly young ones, have become more high-powered, ambitious, and professionalized. I am convinced that many students often do not understand what is being said in teaching situations, though they become adept at pretending to, as they do not wish to lose face. There is a further factor that feminists have drawn attention to, which is that the majority of students of English are women, whereas the majority of academics teaching it are male, and that the female students have a built-in deference to male teachers and to the minority of male students. This is broadly true, and has long distorted the group dynamics of seminars, though I have the sense that things are changing as women become more self-confident (the arrival in increasing numbers of female mature students has been helpful). At the same time, I have noticed that women academics can be ruthless bullies of girl students, with the possibly laudable motive of giving them the equivalent of a good shake.

David Lodge, whose experience as novelist, critic, and professor of English has given him many insights into the situation I am describing, provides in his recent novel *Nice Work*, a neat instance of the gap between students and teacher. Dr Robyn Penrose is a recognizable type of advanced young academic, leftist, feminist, poststructuralist:

> She probably knows more about the nineteenth century industrial novel than anyone else in the entire world. How can all that knowledge be condensed into a fifty-minute lecture to students who know almost nothing about it? The interests of scholarship and pedagogy are at odds here. What Robyn likes to do is to deconstruct the texts, to probe the gaps and absences in them, to uncover what they are *not* saying, to expose their ideological bad faith, to cut a cross-section through the twisted strands of their semiotic codes and literary conventions. What the students want her to do is to give them some basic facts that will enable them to read the novels as simple straightforward reflections of 'reality', and to write simple, straightforward, exam-passing essays about them.

In an American context, E. D. Hirsch has remarked on a similar conflict of interest between students who want to know the basic meanings of texts, in their historical contexts, and junior academics who believe there are no basic meanings, only a multiplicity of interpretations. Such divisions are not, so to speak, purely academic. They lead to confusion on the part of students, and it may be too glib to say, as one sometimes hears, that such confusion and disorientation are an inherently desirable part of the educational process. It does not always work like that, for they can lead to real difficulties in study, and sometimes to pastoral problems.

III

One of Lodge's earlier novels, *Changing Places*, hilariously exploits a series of typological oppositions. The fundamental one is between a famous university on the American West Coast, Plotinus, and a more modest but still self-respecting one in the English Midlands, Rummidge. These places are not, as the phrase goes, a million miles away from Berkeley and Birmingham respectively (each of whose campuses is dominated, as it happens, by a tower copied from the Palazzo Publico at Sienna; in the novel these are transformed to upright versions of the Leaning Tower of Pisa). The two central characters are both academic teachers of English: Morris Zapp is one of the biggest guns in the Plotinus faculty, who elects to take a visiting professorship at Rummidge in order to escape from his marital problems; his place is taken by Phillip Swallow, a naïve, amiable, unambitious Rummidge lecturer. As the novel moves, with much formal inventiveness, back and forth between Plotinus and Rummidge, we observe Zapp and Swallow coping with different forms of local culture shock. They go on to exchange roles as well as jobs, and finally, for a time, wives. In sociological terms they are 'ideal types' and the differences between them have all kinds of thematic and representative significance. They enact a polarity between American and British academic life in general, and English studies in particular. Zapp is the supreme professional, who embodies, albeit comically, those ideals of professionalism that have long been dominant in the North American academy and are becoming so in the British. His aim is simple: to write a series of commentaries on the novels of Jane Austen which would say everything that could be said about them, from every conceivable angle:

historical, biographical, rhetorical, mythical, Freudian, Jungian, existentialist, Marxist, structuralist, Christian-allegorical, ethical, exponential, linguistic, phenomenological, archetypal, you name it; so that when each commentary was written there would be simply *nothing further to say* about the novel in question. The object of the exercise . . . was not to enhance others' enjoyment and understanding of Jane Austen, still less to honour the novelist herself, but to put a definitive stop to the production of any further garbage on the subject. The commentaries would not be designed for the general reader but for the specialist, who, looking up Zapp, would find that the book, article or thesis he had been planning had already been anticipated and, more likely than not, invalidated. After Zapp, the rest would be silence.

Zapp is impatient of other academics with tentative minds, who begin articles, 'I want to raise some questions about so-and-so.' 'Any damn fool . . . could think of questions; it was *answers* that separated the men from the boys.' He regards the study of literature as quite separate from life, with evaluation and affective responses rigorously excluded:

> The failure to keep the categories of life and literature distinct led to all kinds of heresy and nonsense: to 'liking' and 'not liking' books for instance, preferring some authors to others and such-like whimsicalities which, he had constantly to remind his students, were of no conceivable interest to anyone except themselves (sometimes he shocked them by declaring that, speaking personally on this low, subjective level, he found Jane Austen a pain in the ass).

Changing Places, published in 1975, is set in 1969; when Zapp reappears in a later novel, *Small World*, set ten years later, he has changed his attitudes, in accordance with major shifts in the *Zeitgeist*. He is now a poststructuralist and has abandoned the great Jane Austen project, as he disbelieves in the possibility of any kind of definite textual meaning or interpretation: 'every decoding is another encoding.' Zapp is simply keeping up with the state of the art; he is more convinced than ever that professionalism is its own justification and reward. When an anguished Phillip Swallow asks him what, in Zapp's scheme of things, is the point of engaging in literary study, he serenely replies, 'The point, of course, is to uphold the institution of academic literary studies. We maintain our position in society by publicly performing a certain ritual, just like any other group of workers in the realm of discourse—lawyers, politicians, journalists.'

In *Changing Places* the Englishman Swallow is Zapp's opposite in all possible respects. If Zapp believes that writing about literature has nothing to do with liking it, Swallow likes it all too much to be able to write about it:

> This undiscriminating enthusiasm ... prevented him from settling on a 'field' to cultivate as his own. He had done his initial research on Jane Austen, but since then had turned his attention to topics as varied as medieval sermons, Elizabethan sonnet sequences, Restoration heroic tragedy, eighteenth-century broadsides, the novels of William Godwin, the poetry of Elizabeth Barrett Browning and premonitions of the Theatre of the Absurd in the plays of George Bernard Shaw. None of these projects had been completed. Seldom, indeed, had he drawn up a preliminary bibliography before his attention was distracted by some new or revived interest in something entirely different. He ran hither and thither between the shelves of Eng. Lit. like a child in a toyshop—so reluctant to choose one item to the exclusion of others that he ended up empty-handed.

Swallow's predicament is a very familiar one in British academics of his generation, as is his non-possession of a Ph.D., that basic certificate of academic professionalism in American eyes (and now in English ones). This is remarked on in an exchange between Zapp and Luke Hogan, chairman of the Plotinus English Department, before Swallow arrives:

'any clown with a Ph.D. should be able to teach English 99.'
'He doesn't have a Ph.D.,' Hogan said.
'*What?*'
'They have a different system in England, Morris. The Ph.D. isn't so important.'
'You mean the jobs are hereditary?'

The Americans are professionals and Swallow is an amateur, which, we recall, has the primary sense of 'lover'. Yet there is one sense in which Swallow has thoroughly assimilated the professionalism of the academy. Though he has difficulty in writing anything for publication, he is a scrupulous and painstaking examiner, and his own examination papers are carefully pondered, finely drafted works of art. He even dreams of publishing a concise, comprehensive survey of English Literature in the form of examination questions: '*Collected Literary Questions*, by Philip Swallow. A book to be compared to Pascal's *Pensées* or Wittgenstein's *Philosophical Investigations* . . .'.

Older academics, of whatever persuasion, were hostile to the idea of overt professionalism in literary study. Their position was not altogether consistent, since they were committed to professional standards of achievement within the discipline, and, as they were paid to engage in it, were themselves professionals. Yet, without doubt, they would have been horrified by Morris Zapp and what he stood for. In Britain university English was developed with undergraduate teaching primarily in mind, in a culture that included the sixth forms of schools. Until recently, graduate teaching was a very marginal activity. In the United States the graduate school is the major arena of pedagogic activity and intellectual life. It is here that research papers are generated and read and discussed, and where the academic superstars go through their paces and inspire their dedicated students. As early as 1921, the Newbolt Report, summarizing the evidence of

Professor Ernest de Sélincourt, expressed deep unease about the American approach to literary research:

> Many of the elaborate theses on English Literature produced by American students for their Doctorate, and afterwards published, were monuments of misdirected effort; in short, a true sense of literature as a living thing was lost, and in its place was substituted an investigation after the worse pattern of German 'research', deadening alike to those who wrote and those who read it.

The anti-Germanism reflects the Report's composition in the aftermath of the First World War; at the same time, this passage looks far ahead, already foreshadowing the opposition between Zapp and Swallow as representative figures.

In 1963, Leavis published an essay called 'Research in English', attacking what he called 'a menacing academicism against which we have to be militantly upon our guard—a form of academicism institutionally established in America, and one the tendency towards which in this country—the developments of civilization favouring it—is much strengthened by American influence . . .'. One particularly undesirable consequence of this tendency was the 'proliferation of the blankly or brutally crass kinds of doctoral manufacture'.

Leavis was suspicious of the PhD, though he acknowledged that good work could, in the right circumstances, be produced in that medium, such as his wife's *Fiction and the Reading Public*. He is insistent that the only students who should work at doctoral level are those of first-class ability, who are independent of mind and inner-directed, so that they can work without much supervision, apart from 'a standing relation with a congenial senior to whom he can go now and then for criticism and advice.' Leavis accepts that this admirable but stern ideal was already under threat:

> the university has a new duty, we are told: there is a besieging host, ever-increasing, of Indians, Africans, Commonwealth people in general, Levantines, who aspire to become university teachers of English literature, and must therefore have a PhD—preferably a Cambridge one (though it is admitted that a large proportion of them couldn't hope to take the English Tripos with much credit—even if they could pass).

As a university teacher of English, one reads this abrasive passage, twenty-five years on, with a painful sense of recognition. There can be no doubt that the PhD, no longer seen as a sign of unusually high scholarly achievement, has become simply a certificate of professional competence, and that intellectual standards have declined accordingly. The decline has been inconspicuous rather than dramatic, and is patchy; the existence in British academic life of external examiners is something of a safeguard (they are unknown in American universities, where quality control is even less secure). Even so, potential examiners are known qualities: some are likely to be severe, some lenient, and the experienced and canny supervisor or head of department is likely to make nominations accordingly. Nevertheless, weak candidates still get failed, which is always a bitter and embarrassing business, negating the value of several years' work, often leading to anger within a department, internal enquiries about the quality of supervision, and even threats of legal action from the disappointed candidate. I have declined to act as external examiner to candidates whose subject or thesis title seemed to be so dubious that a successful treatment of it could only be done by a candidate of exceptional brilliance; in such cases it is likely that the candidate has had inadequate or misguided supervision. In a busy life, it is easier to avoid embarrassment than to have to extricate oneself from it. Much difficulty could be avoided if the only candidates permitted to work for a PhD were those who were virtually certain to obtain it, but that is not a feasible option in the modern university.

Similar considerations make me sometimes decline to examine students from foreign parts. This is not because of xenophobia, still less 'racism'; prudence is the principal consideration. Leavis's tirade against such students was an insensitive treatment of what was already a sensitive topic, and is now far more so. In the 1980s, following on government cuts in finance, British universities have been engaged in a desperate scramble for overseas students and the more-or-less economic fees they are required to pay. It is an undignified business, but survival demands it. Higher degrees in English are an obvious target for foreign students who have been trained in the subject in their own country, and who wish to obtain a doctoral qualification in an anglophone university before themselves becoming teachers. The university welcomes them as a source of income; some students are funded by their own governments to obtain a doctorate and enter public service. There is, in one way, an admirable balance of supply and demand, and some applicants are good by any standards. Nevertheless, this situation presents hard decisions to those responsible for graduate admissions. Should one turn away weaker candidates, and so lose the university income, or admit them, with the possibility of academic, cultural, and pastoral problems ensuing for several years? Furthermore, there can be no absolute certainty that a candidate's thesis will pass in the end, however carefully the examiners are selected. In such cases failure is even more painful than with a home student, and one has heard rumours of failed candidates having to return several years of fees to their government, and suffering even worse penalties. The problems are not universal, one must emphasize. Some students, particularly those from the Indian subcontinent who have been selected for Commonwealth Scholarships, are capable of performing very well at higher degree level, and then returning to an academic career in their own countries. When overseas students do present difficulties—and I am sure many academics will be familiar with distressing or scandalous cases—it is not because they are lacking in industry or intellectual ability. Many of them would do perfectly well in disciplines which are less idiosyncratic than English and have a more obvious international currency, like linguistics or economics or marketing. But in this respect, at least, English in the English academy, as Leavis liked to emphasize, is not just another subject. It expresses a mystique, is to a high degree culture-specific, can seem elusive, and is not easily reduced to the rules and agreed procedures of other disciplines.

It is not just overseas graduate students who have problems. We must all have known home undergraduates who have worked very hard on an English course, who may be ambitious to do well, and who still, to their intense disappointment, end up doing badly. This is not a matter of poor teaching, for such students can be the despair of conscientious teachers. What is involved is an inability to penetrate the culture of the subject and to achieve the appropriate blend of knowledge, analysis, and affective response that is needed to perform well in an English course. Their minds are somehow not right for it; in some other discipline they might have performed quite respectably.

Protests about professionalization also came in the 1960s from the *prominenti* of Oxford English. C. S. Lewis wrote:

> What is . . . surprising and disquieting is the fact that those who might be expected *ex officio* to have a profound and permanent appreciation of literature may in reality have nothing of the sort. They are mere professionals. Perhaps they once had the full response, but the 'hammer, hammer on the hard, high road' has long since dinned it out of them. I am thinking of unfortunate scholars in foreign universities who cannot 'hold down their jobs' unless they repeatedly publish articles each of which must say, or seem to say, something new about some literary work . . .

By foreign universities Lewis presumably meant American ones. A few years later, Helen Gardner, in her inaugural lecture, lamented the 'pressure to publish' on people working in English studies: 'there is something peculiarly distasteful and peculiarly absurd about forced labour in my field. A real deformation of values is suggested by the common use of such terms as "productive scholars" and "scholarly output".' Gardner suggested that there was nothing wrong with apparent idleness, since it could often in the long run prove to be 'the true seed-plot of thought'. Twenty years on, the phrases which she saw as indicating a deformation of values have become commonplace in the Thatcherite academy, where contemplation is regarded as idleness, rather than the other way round, and Leavis's abominated 'technologico-Bentham-ism' is firmly in the saddle. Despite the contempt expressed in the past for the American principle of 'publish or perish', British universities are more and more looking at volume of publication—otherwise, 'performance indicators'—as a sign of virtue. Quantity is easier to consider than quality, of course, and I have found that a promotions committee can be thrown into bemusement and mild disarray by suggesting that many of the publications on a candidate's CV might better have not been published. To express such thoughts is to feel oneself uncomfortably situated between opposed concepts of what a university is.

Leavis, Lewis, and Gardner shared traditional values, even though Cambridge and Oxford spoke with different accents.

Common to the passages quoted above is the assumption that it is possible to denounce 'academicism' or 'professionalism' whilst being a member of the academic profession. That spirit persists, particularly in Oxford; witness John Bayley: 'Most of the theories Eagleton expounds may soon seem outlandish curiosities, cooked up by teachers of literature who need to feel professional, in the sense that philosophers or scientists do, or powerful, like politicians.' As I have remarked, the Warton Professor habitually adopts the attitude of a traditional man of letters rather than a paid academic. It takes enviable *sprezzatura* and self-confidence to perform as a teacher of literature who does *not* need to feel professional. There is, of course, nothing to prevent an academic from criticizing professionalism, which is indeed what I am doing now. But I am conscious of a sense of contradiction that clearly did not afflict those illustrious figures.

When literary criticism moved into the academy, it received obvious privileges and status. Critics and scholars had access to libraries, and the paid leisure to think, read, and write during university vacations, and, sometimes, sabbatical leave. There was the intellectual stimulus to be gained from discussion with colleagues, and the challenge of teaching lively young minds. And for some there were conferences and congresses in glamorous places, the glittering prizes satirically displayed in Lodge's *Small World*. None of this was available to the hard-pressed scholarly hacks in Gissing's *New Grub Street*, or to the real-life Francis Thompson, keeping himself just alive by high-quality literary journalism, which involved working for twelve hours every day and taking no holidays. But, in the words of the old Spanish proverb, 'Take what you want, said God, and pay.' There was a high price to be paid for these amenities and privileges, which was, quite simply, professionalism. This was not the relaxed professionalism of the man of letters, but the stringent new professionalism of the academy. For a time teachers of literature could assume that they were in but not of the academy, and keep a healthy distance from institutional pressures. But universities have changed immensely in recent decades, and because of their close, complex and sometimes difficult relations with the public world, their procedures have become standardized and

uniform, reflecting concern about justification and accountability. In this situation, the teaching of English Literature has
not, on the face of it, done badly. It is a large subject, much
in demand, and is very cheap to teach. Within the modern
academy, English is treated with respect, though those teaching it may feel themselves impaled on the perennial dilemma
of making it appear either a soft option or inhumanely
technical and jargon-ridden. The Newbolt–Leavis claim that
English was not just one more academic subject does not
survive well in this climate. English *is* treated as one subject
among many, albeit an important one, and has to assume
institutional responsibilities as well as accepting privileges.

The task of the academic is to teach and engage in research,
and, if required, to take on administrative duties. Although
there is parity of esteem among academic subjects, and dog is
careful not to eat dog, at least in public, a scientific model of
knowledge has, I believe, come to dominate the modern
academy, and to affect attitudes to and within humanistic
learning. Such knowledge is progressive, rendering earlier
versions of itself obsolete, and it circulates quickly and visibly
through the accepted professional channels, like journals and
conference-papers. It is also subject to quantifiable assessment, in terms of volume of publication, frequency of citation,
amounts of research funding, and the calibre of referees. In
English Studies this is the world of Morris Zapp, not of Phillip
Swallow. It has long been established in American universities; hence the acute consciousness of period, and the rapidity
with which, in the state-of-the-art graduate schools and
research establishments, critical approaches have followed
one another: New Critical, structuralist, poststructuralist,
deconstructionist, feminist, Marxist, New Historicist, dialogic. It is not that academic critics make a conscious effort to
imitate their colleagues in the sciences, it is that they have
come to adopt their concept of knowledge, and its professional
servicing and supportive structures. The path that the young
academic must follow who wants tenure, and still more
advancement and fame, is clearly marked. Morris Zapp had
published four books before he was thirty.

'Research' in English has never been easy to define. There
are still many able academics who see their activity as

research in the traditional sense, by engaging in biographical, historical, or editorial work. But where English departments are concerned 'research' is more usually understood in the broader sense of adding conceptual rather than factual knowledge, which in practice means the proliferation of interpretation. The brighter sort of aspiring academic is more commonly found marking up paperback copies of standard texts in different coloured inks than delving in libraries. Indeed, Terence Hawkes has defined and defended what he calls 'paperback research' as a proper activity for those who lack the scholarly resources of the ancient universities. The advent of poststructuralism has given a great impetus to interpretive productivity, since all the literary texts that were once interpreted to show organic unity and complexity of meaning can now be interpreted to reveal underlying clashes. Research in this sense and teaching can be in conflict, for the reasons suggested by Hirsch. In an article reviewing Culler's *On Deconstruction*, Hirsch flatly rejects the idea that knowledge in English is continually developing. He observes,

'English' in American schools and universities has always been a cultural, not a progressive, intellectual subject. Although 'English' does have connections with the genuine disciplines of history and philosophy it came into being for cultural rather than disciplinary reasons.

English, for Hirsch, is basically to do with educational and cultural values, helping 'to provide the myths and values we live by', rather than generating ever new and more narrowly directed interpretations. Hirsch is here defiantly looking back to something like the spirit which, in England, inspired the Newbolt Report and *Scrutiny* in its heyday, and which no doubt still evokes a sympathetic response in teachers on both sides of the Atlantic. But it is hard to see it making much headway against the ideology that now pervades academic institutions. The fundamental model is the physical sciences, but in the current transactions and debates in and around English, social studies offers a closer and more approachable example. Michael Edwards refers to

the assumption that only enquiry into literature that is founded on the state of the art in sociology or other adjacent disciplines is valid, the rest being impressionist and subjective. I once asked a colleague in linguistics if this meant that the criticism of, oh, Addison, Keats, Hopkins, Forster, was valueless. I thought of the question as rhetorical, but his reply was 'Yes'.

The assumption that the cultural achievements of the past are actually obsolete is more likely to be implied than so explicitly stated, but it is a logical implication of a progressivist concept of knowledge. Less radically, intellectual fashion means that some names are in, and others out. Marjorie Perloff has remarked that young American academics and students have a shared culture based on having read or studied the same books: 'they have, by and large, taken courses that expose them to writers like Freud, Nietzsche, and Marx, whereas the odds are that they have not taken a course in, say, the lyric poetry of Goethe, the fiction of Stendhal, or the theatre of Molière.' In America fashion can actually be enforced. A few years ago, as part of an annual round-up of critical books for *Encounter*, I reviewed an interestingly speculative work on modern fiction by an American academic. My feelings about the book were positive rather the reverse, but I complained in my review that it was studded with references to fashionable French gurus that were purely cosmetic, adding nothing to the author's argument. A year or so later I chanced to meet him and he acknowledged that this was just criticism, but that he had been obliged to insert these names so that his book would look like a truly up-to-date, in-touch work of scholarship. In 1982 at Stanford I heard similar accounts of academic publishers requiring appropriate names and references in books.

Despite the protective embrace of professionalism and the general mutuality of respect and acceptance that pertains between disciplines, the academic teacher of literature is in a peculiar position in relation to his colleagues elsewhere, in ways that have been remarked on by John Bayley and Raymond Williams, and no doubt by others; in certain respects English does remain an essentially different subject. We see history produced in history departments, philosophy in philosophy departments, sociology in sociology departments, and so on, by academics for whom teaching and research are two aspects of a unified activity. This is not true of literature departments; what they produce is criticism and scholarship, not literature, leaving out of account the occasional scholar-poet or writer in residence. This situation has left literature teachers with the sense that compared with their colleagues they are not masters in their own house, since they are dependent for their material on a product manufactured elsewhere by shifty and unreliable suppliers. The attempt to remedy this deficiency and achieve a true professionalism may be one reason for the rapid growth of literary theory in the anglophone academy. If the academy cannot itself produce literature, and if even criticism can be written outside of it by novelists, poets, and literary journalists, then what it, and only it, *can* produce is theory. Here is the authentic product of the English department, parallel to the history and philosophy which are generated down the corridor. It is an error to assume, as I did myself at one time, that theory necessarily exists in an ancillary and elucidatory relationship to criticism, which is in turn at the service of literature. That is a common-sense way of looking at it, but in practice literary and critical theory has become an autonomous subject. Poststructuralists aspire to remove what they regard as the arbitrary distinctions between literature, criticism, theory, and philosophy, and Geoffrey Hartman has made it clear that he believes what he writes to be worthy of the esteem and attention normally given to 'creative' writing. So, looked at in some lights, theory becomes literature. This was the contention of Elizabeth Bruss's perverse but deeply interesting book, *Beautiful Theories*. She writes:

And if the reading public as a whole is shrinking, if literature is increasingly relegated to the schools as something 'to be studied'—if, in a word, the majority of readers now are scholars (whether students or professional academics)—then the claims of literary theory to be our representative literary genre become stronger still. What better inspiration could a literature of theory have than an audience composed of theorists and critics?

This is not, I think, meant to be ironical, and it represents a quite logical development from the premiss that the whole production, definition, and reception of literature has now become intramural to the academy. In this context, what goes on outside, what is actually written by poets and novelists, is of minor interest. Paul de Man is reported to have said that a literary work is merely an event in the history of interpretation. A natural response to this state of affairs would be to say that theory cut off from the writing of literature is no more than a sterile academicism. But that misses the point, if theory can be identified with literature.

These are the symptoms of a triumphant professionalism, which is sustained by the particular conditions of American academic life: the intensely competitive environment of the prestigious graduate schools, the free market in salaries which entices the superstars of the profession from one campus to another, the large funds available for research, journals, and conferences. Admittedly, conditions in the American academy are a little tighter than they once were, but what looks like stringency by American standards is still lavishness by British ones. Britain can never hope to compete with all this. Nevertheless, professionalism on American lines is still the ideal that academic administrators uphold, since it can indicate to sceptical politicians and the public at large that universities are engaged in the visible activity which generates 'performance-indicators'. In this climate, the academic in English and other subjects in the humanities, who is busy, who publishes a lot, who goes to conferences, cannot but be preferred to the quiet scholar, who keeps a low profile, even seems rather idle, but is taking his time over a major piece of scholarly writing that may involve many years' work and which he does not intend to give to the world until he is ready. Such people have in the past been left to go their own way without interference. Nowadays they may be esteemed by their peers who know something of their work, but this esteem has little currency value in the committee-rooms where performance is appraised. These academics may be respected, but they are also regarded as tiresome. The culture of science looks for rapid and visible results, and it is this, despite occasional formal disavowals, that is setting the agenda. Wittgenstein, widely thought of as the greatest philosopher of the twentieth century, published very little in his lifetime, and is unlikely to have got tenure in a modern British university.

To see these activities as representing the apotheosis of Morris Zapp and the eclipse of Phillip Swallow is tempting but too simple. British versions of Zapp are probably now in

America anyway, finding a proper market-based reward for their talents and energy. American professionalism may be the ideal, but differences between the British and American academic systems are noticeable. The greater spread of American higher education means that, proportionate to population, there are far more universities, all with English departments; if they were as proportionately numerous in Britain, we would have about 1,000 universities. Hence the wide and generally understood variations in academic calibre between American universities. Furthermore, the greater commitment to undergraduate teaching gives English studies in Britain a different character. And, least definably, there is the cultural nationalism, the concept of 'Englishness' that, from the beginning, has been a major element in the subject. It produces a mystique which obstructs total professionalism and separates British from American attitudes. Yet despite these differences, English English has gone quite a long way down the road of a more-or-less Americanized professionalism, as identified and rejected in the 1960s by Leavis, Lewis, and Gardner.

From the point of view of those who are currently in charge of higher education, English must be an awkward subject. It is popular, in demand, and cheap. Yet its quasi-mystical elements prevent it from fully using its potential. It is the heir of a nineteenth-century ideology that, though supposedly liberal and contemplative, is also élitist, anti-vocational, anti-market, and indeed downright hostile to the idea that higher education should prepare young people to take their places in a wealth-producing economy. An excessively elevated sense of standards means that there are difficulties about English Departments taking on overseas research students in numbers sufficient to help the university in its financial difficulties. Academics in English are loners reluctant to engage in team projects or pull together in research centres. They can be irritatingly slow to publish, and it is often difficult to know how they spend their time. On the brighter side, there are those younger and more active lecturers who do their duty and generate performance-indicators in the form of books and articles. It is true that in some cases these publications may be of extreme radical tendency, attacking the established practices of academic English teaching, but that is no objection, since it is the fact of publication that counts, not its content. The real problem is that the writers of such texts may make political difficulties within a department, or teach in ways difficult for students to understand. Again, English departments can be unhelpful about participating in schemes for training academics how to teach, claiming that teaching literature is less easily defined and methodologized than teaching engineering or economics. At a time when a good public image is essential for universities, English is unable to explain itself in ways immediately intelligible to the outsider, is notoriously riven with doubts and disagreements that prevent it from having a shared sense of purpose, and may at intervals erupt into crises that attract the wrong sort of publicity. It is time, it is thought, for English to organize itself in ways that make it more like a proper academic discipline, with clear procedures and goals. The adjacent social sciences provide the model for a genuine professionalism and accountability. As long ago as 1969 a small committee asked to report, from outside the Faculty, on the perennially troubled state of Cambridge English concluded,

we believe that undergraduates in English would benefit from more 'systematic' and less 'inspirational' instruction and that this systematic instruction and its associated reading lists should be agreed by the teachers concerned and closely related to the needs of the Tripos course.

I have never heard this case made in anything like the explicit fashion in which I have just outlined it, and I do not think it ever would be publicly made. Yet one picks it up, in hints and implications, in the not-quite-concealed exasperation of polite administrators, in the raised eyebrows and brief knowing smiles of senior academics on committees; indeed, it is as much a matter of what is significantly not said, as of what is said; in poststructuralist terms, of lacunae, *vides*, silences. The people who teach in English Departments are certainly aware of a lurking, inchoate threat to their peace of mind, and there is no successor to Leavis as a force to strengthen morale and defy institutional pressures.

Traditional English teaching is also under attack from the rainbow coalition of the left. There are curious parallels and similarities between bureaucratic calls for *Gleichschaltung* and radical subversions of bourgeois humanism. Both have the effect of weakening still further the synthesis of approaches that have characterized academic English since its inception. We can again turn to Morris Zapp as the embodiment of a thorough-going professionalism. (It may be objected that I am taking far too earnest a view of a wonderfully comic fictional character. But Lodge's sociological understanding is considerable, and Zapp serves very well as an 'ideal type' of a present-day academic. Dempsey in *Changing Places* and *Small World* is an approximate British equivalent.) Zapp wants the subject to be organized, systematic, objective, in a word— though it is not a word he uses—scientific. There is to be no nonsense about value, preferring some books or authors to others, or personal responses, which have a merely anecdotal or autobiographical interest. Working on Jane Austen was not all that different from working on trade cycles, or low-temperature physics; these were the kind of things that went on in the modern university. Admittedly, in his later appearances Zapp has gone poststructuralist, and abandoned system and objectivity; but his commitment to professionalism is greater than ever. Traditionally, the notion of personal response and what the Newbolt Report called 'literature as a living thing' were regarded by all schools as at the heart of English study, but there is no place for them in Zapp's perspective. They would be signs of an unprofessional subjectivism and impressionism; in recent radical discourse they indicate an undesirable mystification.

Alan Sinfield, in a revealing Marxist analysis of the way Shakespeare is treated in public examination papers, remarks that they 'construct Shakespeare and the candidate in terms of individual subjectivity through their stress upon Shakespeare's free-standing genius, their emphasis on characterization and their demand for the candidate's personal response.' Elsewhere, Sinfield makes the cogent point that the idea of a personal judgement that nevertheless has to approximate to an accepted opinion involves the candidate in learning tricks. This is true, and points to one of the central problems in institutionalized literary pedagogy. Nevertheless, it is not clear from current Marxist criticism and theory, which in the rainbow coalition is often buttressed by Lacanian ideas of the decentred self, whether it is prepared to accept *any* form at all of a personal, subjective or affective response, or whether all that must wait until after the revolution. In the latter case, it will meanwhile have the effect of turning literary study into something much closer to the sociology that Marxists have colonized in the modern academy.

I argued in an earlier section of this Chapter that questions of value have always had an uncertain place in institutional literary study, and Catherine Belsey explicitly seeks to banish them. She argues for a study of reading that would work towards political ends and 'replace the mysterious objectives of aesthetic satisfaction and moral enrichment.' In such a perspective, 'literary value becomes irrelevant: political assassination is problematized in Pickering's play, *Horestes* (1567) as well as in *Hamlet.*' Bureaucrat and radical have no time for each other, but they are both undermining traditional humanism.

IV

The so-called New Historicism provides a curious fusion of academicism and radicalism. In 1986, J. Hillis Miller, than whom no one is better placed to judge, told the Modern Language Association of America that by the mid-1980s critical theory had shifted from invoking 'language' as a prime foundational term to a cluster of words which included 'history', 'politics', 'society', and 'culture'. 'History' has been given prominence by the New Historicists, while for some graduate students and younger academics 'politics' has come to seem, as the Goldsmiths Professor at Oxford lately remarked to me, a kind of vital protein, without which a literary work is fatally impoverished. In Britain the other terms referred to by Miller, 'society' and 'culture', have been familiar at least since the 1950s, which saw the early work of Hoggart and Williams and the cultural climate of the New Left, which in turn drew on *Scrutiny* and the Victorian debates on the Condition of England.

At a superficial glance, the New Historicism can seem, especially to an Oxford graduate of my generation, rather like old-style historical scholarship. When Fredric Jameson exhorts the reader, 'Always historicize!' one recalls Helen Gardner's assertion, 'All art, including contemporary art, is historical.' But there are important differences. The older scholarship treated history as the march of events, combining change and continuity, but without a mind or will of its own. The contemporary historicism, fuelled by Marx and Foucault, presents history as a force in its own right, ceaselessly dramatizing clashes of class and power. It has particularly focused on Renaissance literature and the struggles for dominance which are enacted in it, or are assumed to be. The New Historicism refuses to treat the literary works of the past as transcendent entities, removed from social and historical contexts, and embodying supposedly timeless values. Yet it contains a contradiction, since the class-struggle, or more generally the struggle against oppression, is thought of as always visibly at work in history in a clearly timeless way. Freud, in *Civilization and its Discontents*, advanced the profoundly historicist suggestion that we should be cautious about interpreting the miseries of earlier times, since what now looks like unacceptable suffering may have felt less so in a different culture. If one rejects Freud's suggestion—for instance, by quoting contemporary accounts from the victims—then one is inescapably positing a transhistorical human nature. In practice the Marxist practitioners of the New Historicism tend to interpret Shakespeare plays in accordance with the political interests of the late twentieth century. Thus, *The Tempest* is about colonialism; not only *The Taming of the Shrew* but *King Lear* and *Measure for Measure* are a focus for feminist readings; while *Henry V* encodes a contemporary Elizabethan colonialist endeavour, 'the fantasy of a successful Irish campaign'. These readings are intermittently illuminating, if reductive, and basically they are doing what criticism has always done, which is to interpret the works of the past in the terms and concepts of the critic's own age. It is precisely this capacity for renewed interpretation that makes literature of *more* than simply historical interest. Latter-day Marxist interpreters of Shakespeare are doing much the same as the conservative proponents of the Elizabethan World Picture did thirty or forty years ago, though with a different

conceptual model. The contemporary New Historicists, however, are unlike interpreters of the past, in that they are
concerned with exclusively political readings, without any
possibility of aesthetic or affective responses. Shakespeare
provides a particular problem for radical critics who ideologically object to eminence. Sinfield observes that Shakespeare is made 'to speak mainly for the right . . . as the great
National Poet whose plays embody universal truths . . .'. Yet
Shakespeare has more than a merely national reputation,
kept in being by those who manipulate ideological power. He
has, to a remarkable extent, a global reputation. Despite the
barrier of translation, his plays are known and enjoyed and
regularly performed in many countries. This is a phenomenon
which I find impressive and mysterious. It suggests that there
are universal human qualities, and that people can recognize
them in Shakespeare's dramas, over the centuries and through
many cultural mediations. Sinfield, I imagine, would decline
to accept this. The problem about Shakespeare for critics of
his mind-set is that to take him seriously at all is to accept an
alien agenda. A truly revolutionary approach to Shakespeare
would be to dismiss him, on the lines of the Dadaist and
Futurist campaigns against the venerated high art of the past.
But that might be going too far for academic professionals,
however radical their stances. The more feasible alternative
is to dismember his plays between the history of his own day
and the ideologies of ours.

Marxists invoke 'History' as a 'transcendent signified', the
ultimate in terms of which everything else is to be explained;
but there are many histories, not one, and we choose those
which suit us. As Edward Pechter puts it, 'History does not
tell us what the text is, because we decide what history is, and
then put history into the text, rather than the other way
round.' Something similar is true of 'politics', another transcendent signified and argument-stopper. Since politics is
traditionally one of the major defining activities of a rational
humanity, the discussion of literature in political terms is not
only possible but desirable, as the major critics of the past
have shown. But the word 'politics' itself needs to be deconstructed, since politics is to do with our ideals of what human
life should be, about which there has never been agreement;

indeed, it is out of the disagreement that politics arises. In point of fact, when radical theorists invoke 'politics' they mean Marxist politics, in the paradoxically timeless fashion I have just referred to. An awkward truth though is that in the twentieth century some of the most committed political criticism has come from conservatives, like Eliot and the Southern Agrarians. An erudite work by an Oxford New Historicist, David Norbrook's *Poetry and Politics in the English Renaissance*, illustrates the structuralist truism that in a binary grouping one of the two terms tends to assume dominance. Norbrook's interest is clearly far more in politics than in poetry.

The most significant aspect of the New Historicism, political questions apart, is that it represents a move away from the contextless, intensive concentration on particular texts equally characteristic of the New Criticism, classical structuralism, and deconstruction. This has major pedagogic implications, since students can no longer hope to make sense of poems or plays just by reading them carefully, but must spend time in libraries getting up on the historical context. Or, if they do not, they have to take on trust the material that the New Historicist scholar-critic hands them. This seems to me retrogressive, and in some respects a return to the kind of thing I heard in my younger days in Oxford: 'One *cannot* hope to understand A, unless one also knows about B, C, D, etc.' A literary text is, manifestly, the product of a particular historical situation, and may be interpreted in the light of its origins and initial reception, as has been done in the discussions of Romantic literature by Marilyn Butler and Jerome J. McGann, who can be called New Historicists minus the ideological charge. Yet historical interpretation of literature fairly easily loses sight of literary interests; if it goes far enough, the interpreter may assume that the idea of poetry or drama as art can be abandoned, since what counts are cultural traces, of whatever kind, and the ideological impressions they appear to bear. In which case 'history' becomes a force to be resisted by readers who like literature, and who may also like history, but have never thought they were one and the same thing.

V

No discussion of the institutionalizing of literary study in higher education would be complete without a mention of the academic publishing that exists in a close, indeed symbiotic relation with it. 'Publication' is increasingly important, not just to secure advancement in an individual academic's career, but as a sign of an institution's status. I think it true to say that at the present time it is not at all difficult for academics to appear in print. I am not thinking primarily of the well-established learned journals, which have high editorial standards and a long queue of articles waiting to appear. (In the pursuit of performance-indicators, publication in 'refereed journals' counts for much, though I am not sure if I have ever appeared in a refereed journal in my life.) However, new academic journals are regularly launched, devoted to one or other of the many specialisms into which English is fragmenting, and in their earlier issues, at least, are likely to be looking for contributions. It is, however, in the vastly expanded world of academic book publishing that the greatest opportunties lie. I do not claim to understand the economics of this system, which depends on small print-runs and numbingly high prices, and the assumption that institutional libraries will 'want', or need, to buy these books. But it is evident that publishers, to stay in business, need to bring out a large number of titles every year. This is true in other academic areas, of course, but English is one of the largest earners, since books in this area can be hopefully addressed to 'general readers', in a ritual recognition that there is a world elsewhere, as well as to students (though I suspect they are mostly read by teachers). University teachers of English are regular recipients of visitations from hopeful, fresh-faced publishers' editors trawling for new titles. Even PhD students can be approached before they have finished their theses, though the publication of unrevised theses seems to me undesirable, common though it has become: a thesis is written, as a rule, for two examiners, whereas a book, however specialized, should have a rather wider readership in mind.

Certainly, any academic who wants to write a book on a canonical author, topic, or period, is likely to get a contract without very much formality (particularly if it has to do with 'women' or 'theory', or ideally both). This is not the case, though, if the proposed subject is outside the catchment area of school and university examinations, as Terry Lovell discovered when she offered to write a book on Gissing for a left-wing series, which had asked for one on Jane Austen. There is, I have found, some gentle entertainment to be had in discussion with publishers' representatives, observing the wide-eyed eagerness with which they greet potentially saleable ideas, and their clenched, wary, glazed-eyes response to proposals they feel negative about, or perhaps do not understand. The discussion may be restricted to impeccably intellectual topics, but the play of market forces is going on all the time just below the surface. In one sense, everyone benefits from the buoyancy of academic book publishing. The academic gets the publication record that leads to tenure or advancement, and his or her name becomes known in the profession; the institution gains performance-indicators; and the publisher keeps a full and interesting list. It is hard to speak against a situation that makes everyone happy, but one has to say it represents a form of intellectual inflation that is just as pernicious in its way as monetary inflation. Far too many inferior or unnecessary academic books are published each year. Some publishers maintain traditionally stringent standards, but others, in a competitive market, are relaxed about quality control. It is far from unknown for an expert reader who provides an unfavourable report on a book in manuscript to find it nevertheless being published a year or so later.

The book from its invention has been a commodity, dependent on patronage or the market for its circulation, and this is a fact of history that there is little point in complaining about. But in the present economic state of academic publishing the encounter between market forces and intellectual value tends to subordinate the latter to the former. This situation is common in many academic areas, as I have discovered talking to colleagues, and it may be that this state of inflation and over-production is economically unavoidable, that many inferior books have to be published in order to let the good ones appear. But what is unavoidable may still be

undesirable, and one might as well say so. Where literary
criticism is concerned, we are faced with the depressing reality
that this is now just one more academic specialism, a large
specialism, admittedly, produced by and consumed within
the academy. The price of books of academic criticism
indicates that they are not aimed at the educated general
reader (once they cost about the same as a bottle of whisky;
now they cost three to four times as much). So many books,
to pick up a point once made by Malcolm Bradbury, are
published primarily to be stored, moving smoothly from
publishers' warehouse to library stacks without arousing
much disturbance on the way, and are discussed, if at all,
only in scholarly journals. I have already remarked on the
different situation thirty years ago, when criticism still occupied a traditional place as part of public discourse, and the
first books of a distinguished generation of British critics—
Bayley, Davie, Hoggart, Kermode, Wain, Williams—were
reviewed in the daily and weekly press.

At the present time interpretation, often of a narrow and
unrewarding kind, flourishes, usually though falsely claimed
on publishers' blurbs to be saying something completely new
and important. Many interesting works of English Literature
of the past remain unedited and unavailable, and it is a pity
that the ingenuity and assiduity that goes into the labour, or
play, of interpretation could not be directed to the truly useful
work of editing these texts. Meanwhile the publishers' cata-
logues arrive regularly, with their copious listings not just of
new titles, but of new series, aimed to appeal to the collecting
instinct. I dutifully read through them with sinking feelings
and, sometimes, a touch of nausea. I do not seem to be alone
in this response. The writer of an admirable article on
research in the humanities published in the *TLS* in 1987
wrote, 'I believe passionately in the value of those activities
we call "the Humanities", yet when I see a compilation like
the British Library's *Current Research in Britain (1986): The
Humanities* . . . I feel sick.'

10. CULTURAL STUDY, POETIC ART

I

Consensus is too much to expect in the present state of
English Studies, but I detect a convergence of ideas among
those whose starting-points and ideological assumptions are
very different. There is an emerging belief that the study of
'literature as literature' needs to be replaced by, or incorporated into, a form of cultural studies. On the Left it was
advanced by Raymond Williams; Dollimore and Sinfield, in
their introduction to *Political Shakespeare*, argue for 'cultural
materialism', which brings together historical context, theoretical method, political commitment, and textual analysis in
an effort to overturn established readings of Shakespeare. In
America, there are similar moves from Marxists, but also
from those who are in cultural terms centrists or moderate
conservatives. As we have noted, literary study in the United
States involves a large quantitative spread of the subject,
intensive professionalism, and a virtual absence of the
national mystique that characterizes English English. There
is a variety of approaches in graduate schools and change is
more easily envisaged. Robert Scholes writes in *Textual Power*:

> interpretation is not a pure skill but a discipline deeply dependent on
> knowledge. It is not as much a matter of generating meanings out of a text
> as it is a matter of making connections between a particular verbal text and
> a larger cultural text, which is the matrix or master code that the literary
> text both depends upon and modifies. In order to teach the interpretation
> of a literary text, we must be prepared to teach the cultural text as well.

Such an approach is, of course, counter to the contextless
concentration on the single text that characterized the New
Criticism, and which served American literary education for
many years. Nevertheless, Scholes is right to say that
'interpretation is not a pure skill but a discipline deeply
dependent on knowledge'; as much was conceded by Richards
in *Practical Criticism*, a fundamental text of the New Criticism,
when he acknowledged that those who had not already read

enough poetry would read poems badly. Scholes makes useful and practical suggestions for helping students to read better in this situation. Like the English Marxists, though for more pragmatic reasons, he wants to demystify literary study, and to substitute 'textual study' for it. This would not abolish literature but would remove its exclusivity as a category; the task of the English Department is to be redefined as 'studying texts' rather than 'teaching literature'. Gerald Graff, in *Professing Literature*, is sympathetic to Scholes's approach, quoting him to the effect that what we call skill in reading involves 'a knowledge of the codes that were operative in the composition of any given text and the historical situation in which it was composed.' Graff also invokes the Bakhtinian concept of dialogue, where every utterance implies another utterance, which it answers, attacks, continues, or relates to in some way. Such contextualizing tends to do away with the modernist and New Critical elevation of the Poem in Itself, the verbal icon, the well-wrought urn, the jar upon a hill in Tennessee. In a return to the Latin origin of the word, 'textuality' weaves everything together. When Scholes proposes 'studying texts' he invokes the terminology of semiotics, but he is, in effect, working in a tradition of rhetorical analysis that has always been an element in institutional English study, and which in the 1930s resulted in the work of Leavis and Thompson and other Scrutineers on contemporary culture and its artefacts.

Scholes's proposal to teach the 'cultural text' as well as the 'literary text' makes good sense; but, for the best of motives, he tends to a brisk simplification in his approach. In truth, there is not one cultural text, but a multiplicity of them, both concentric and overlapping. As Henry James so memorably put it in his great essay, 'The Art of Fiction', 'Experience is never limited, and it is never complete . . .'. If we assume— and it is probably the right assumption—that students can no longer easily read isolated literary texts, but need to make sense of them in a variety of contexts, much power is given to the teacher who decides which are the relevant cultural codes to be invoked and expounded; Marxists, at least, are specific on the matter. Graff acknowledges the problem and proposes an openly dialectical and adversarial form of teaching. Literary theory, he says, should not just be one more academic subject, to be taught by a 'theory-specialist', but should inform the way in which an English Department organizes itself. It should acknowledge that there are conflicts between critical approaches, and should make the students' confrontation of them part of the pedagogic process. As an example, Graff raises the relation of a feminist literary canon to more familiar ones. Such a canon has been attacked for proposing 'political' rather than 'literary' values as its foundation. Graff suggests that students should be familiarized with the conflict by being asked to compare *The Norton Anthology of Literature by Women* with a traditional anthology and come to their own conclusions. He makes the reasonable point that the upholders of traditional positions might achieve a new plausibility if they could be seen actually arguing for them, rather than merely asserting them.

I like Graff's proposals, but they seem to me utopian. They might work in the graduate school of a good American university, where a variety of methods already abounds. I cannot see how they could be established in British literary education, where there are no graduate schools as such, and the narrow, uphill tunnel of A-level work leads on to the rocky, cloudy uplands of the undergraduate degree, with its confused mixture of practical criticism and thematic study, analysis and literary history, coverage and special subjects. Undergraduates of moderate ability do not much like being asked to choose between differing judgements on the same text; I can imagine them becoming confused and resentful if they were asked to choose between different critical approaches and all their attendant ideological baggage. Certainly, I have known some undergraduates who would rise brilliantly to such a challenge; but they are an exception, and one cannot base a course on what would suit the exceptional student, much as one would like to. Indeed, 'mixed ability teaching' is a major if not often acknowledged problem in higher education, particularly in English, where the extent of prior knowledge is so variable. Graff's proposals for a structured pluralism are admirable in theory, but in practice they would, I fear, merely increase the demoralization of students and teachers.

E. D. Hirsch, in his recent book, *Cultural Literacy*, has

moved far beyond the problems of literary study to provide an agenda for American society itself. He raises large issues: how much does one need to know to understand and engage in the dialogues within society, and between past and present, on the simplest level of knowing what is being talked about? Even casual acquaintance is better than total ignorance, and 'it's acceptable to take one's entire knowledge of *Romeo and Juliet* from *Cliff Notes*. That is because cultural literacy is a canon of information not texts.' Hirsch is trailing his coat, but he is concerned with what takes place in society at large, not in college courses. Yet within the context of organized literary study, it is true that much of the difficulty students have in making sense of texts comes from a lack of information, or to use the older term, a deficiency in general knowledge. As a scholar and theorist, Hirsch is known, apart from his unfashionable but vigorously argued advocacy of intentionalism, for his conviction that literature is not a coherent concept, and has no definable essence, and that by extension 'English' as a discipline has no absolute method. He believes that literary study has a cultural and humane rather than an intellectual value; and the implication of his recent work is that there are other ways of attaining cultural value. This has some affinity with the Marxist position. In a published argument between Scholes and Hirsch, the former made the following statement, on the assumption that the conservative Hirsch would disagree with it:

At the heart of my belief . . . is the conviction that *no text* is so trivial as to be outside the bounds of humanistic study. The meanest graffito, if fully understood, can be a treasure of human expressiveness . . . The best texts for this purpose should be determined locally, by local conditions, limited and facilitated by local wisdom. Above all, they should not be imposed and regulated by a central power.

Nevertheless, Hirsch responded that (apart from a phrase which I have elided), 'There is not a single one of these platitudes that I don't subscribe to wholeheartedly . . .'.

There are continuities between the positions I have so far outlined, despite their differing ideological biases. Scholes is not a Marxist, but his American cultural populism has affinities with recent Marxist writing; at the same time, Hirsch and Scholes find themselves in unexpected agreement.

One might reach out to other affinities. When Scholes writes that '*no text* is so trivial as to be outside the bounds of humanistic study', I am reminded of C. S. Lewis's argument that any piece of writing has a claim to being literary if someone can read it in a 'literary'—i.e. an absorbed, attentive, loving—fashion. The effect of all these approaches is to remove 'literature', as conventionally defined, canonized, institutionalized, and taught, from the exclusive and isolated position which it has long occupied in the anglophone academy. Even the modest proposal that literature should be read in its cultural context has large implications. I am very sympathetic to it, and have tried to put it into effect in some of my own writing, but there is an accompanying danger that literature becomes absorbed by culture, and that literary values are superseded by cultural ones. This may seem innocuous and acceptable, but the implications should be understood. The kind of poem that a literary critic would regard as banal, ill-written, shallow in feeling, and platitudinous in sentiment, might have major human interest for the cultural historian. Granted that there is an absolute need for humanistic values to prevail in a neo-utilitarian and materialistic age, one is faced with a significant divergence in the nature of these values. The experience of reading major works of literature can have an overpowering effect on the responsive reader (usually, but by no means invariably, the young reader). Kafka wrote that a book should be an axe to shatter the frozen sea within us; Eliot said that we should properly 'find *Othello* or *Lear* frightful'. The right sort of literary experience can be like a nuclear explosion, whereas the 'human expressiveness' that Scholes detects in the humblest graffito is more like the low-level radioactivity that is always present in the natural environment.

There is, in fact, a good case for resisting the takeover of literature by culture, though it is not as strong as I once thought it was. My doubts have grown during the years I have been thinking about and then writing this book, but for the moment I will concede that for many scholars and teachers a clarion-call to defend 'literature as literature' would prove rousing and timely. It was sounded a few years ago by Helen Gardner in *In Defence of the Imagination*, by the contributors to Laurence Lerner's *Reconstructing Literature*, and in America by Gerald Graff's *Literature Against Itself* (Graff's position has shifted somewhat in his more recent *Professing Literature*). It was heard loud and clear in the unedifying battles of the early eighties. And turning away from calls to battle and the accompanying rise in blood pressure, it seems reasonable for teachers of literature to go on teaching what they have been trained to teach, and what they like, understand, and are familiar with, without also having to take on many varieties of history—intellectual, cultural, political, social, economic, artistic, and musical—not to mention sociology, the study of popular culture, including the merest graffito, and, inevitably, literary theory. The contextualizing of even the simplest poem has no obvious point to end at, once begun. And the process by which the contextualizing is carried out would itself invite interrogation and theorization; Marxists committed to 'cultural materialism' would be impatient of a form of contextualizing founded in the history of ideas. Similarly, to look at our activity in the self-reflective consciousness provided by 'theory' can be salutary; it is a good thing to know what we are doing, and, if possible, why. But as Morris Zapp puts it in his poststructuralist phase, 'every decoding is another encoding.' When we have given, or been given, a seemingly adequate theoretical account of our processes, then that account may itself need to be understood and analysed in a further, meta-theoretical discourse, and so on. Why stop?

Although literature is increasingly explained by 'culture', in an instance of the principle that one of the terms in binary opposition always becomes dominant, the process might be reversed. A thoroughgoing deconstructive analysis would show culture being absorbed into literature, or at least into textuality and verbal play. It is for this reason that deconstruction remains a fundamental threat to Marxism, and by implication to other culturalist and contextualizing approaches. Experienced teachers ought to be able to deflect the naïve foundationalism that insists that literary works 'can only be understood' in such-and-such a cultural, social, or ideological context, by contextualizing the proponent's own discourse. One can invoke, too, Ricks's insistence that the language of the agenda sets the terms of the debate: to speak of 'principles' and 'faith' is to offer an alternative discourse to the invocation of 'theory' and 'ideology'.

To speak personally, I might have found life easier, though possibly less interesting, if the English synthesis had continued to exist in approximately the same state as when I became a university teacher at the end of the 1950s: a genuine humane discipline, self-respecting, enjoyable, expanding, with methods that were established and familiar, if subject to variation between the different emphases associated with Oxford and Cambridge. As we know, this agreeable stasis did not continue; the synthesis started to come apart for reasons which I have tried to explain. A further disrupting factor was the academy's assumption that knowledge did not stand still but was advancing and progressive; if English accepted the security and opportunities of academic institutionalization, then it had to accept its concept of knowledge, and generate appropriate forms and volume of research. If this meant there were potential conflicts between research and pedagogy, that was a price that had to be paid. With the passing of time, the subject expanded further, institutional pressures became greater, and a gap widened between the professionals who taught literature and the poets, novelists, and dramatists, somewhere out in society, who wrote it, notwithstanding the increasing presence of contemporary literature as a university subject. In this last respect, American experience is significantly different; writers-in-residence are common on campuses as teachers of creative writing, though literary theorists show little interest in what is being written.

Donald Davie has suggested that one reason for the explosion of theory is that it provides 'a stamping ground for the innumerable people in departments of English (also of French, of German, of Classics) who have energy and intelligence but no literary sensibility.' Davie's provocative point is well taken. 'Literary sensibility' is easier to recognize than to define, but it is analogous to having an unusually good ear for music, and has something in common with the creative faculty, even when the critic who possesses it is not an imaginative writer. It has never been *de rigueur* for academics who rise to high places in English departments, and, conversely, students who possess it may not do well in formal examinations. The idea of literary sensibility would probably be dismissed by the culturalists of the Left as a piece of mystification, and certainly few of them have shown signs of possessing it, on either side of the Atlantic. It implies that capacity for personal affective response that is dismissed by those who wish to transform literature into a purely cognitive discourse. The most visible and vocal theorists have high energy and intelligence; they also seem to find imaginative writing rather boring before it is processed into theory.

The drift of my rhetoric might seem to be taking me towards a traditional defence of literature, of the imagination, of creativity, of humane values in general. I believe profoundly in all these things, it goes without saying; my difficulty lies in knowing how defensible they are in the form in which they are visibly institutionalized in the anglophone academy. My reflections are not encouraging, though they are not altogether negative. The first line of defence of established literary study against culturalist pressures is to emphasize 'literature as literature' rather than as a version of philosophy, history, sociology, and so forth. Hirsch has rejected this phrase as delusive and logically meaningless, and this rejection might itself be rejected as an instance of the rat-trap logic to which he is inclined, an improper attempt to define a subject in more rigorous terms than the subject requires. Utterances about literature make sense, and are generally understood, within the form of life in which they are habitually made. Nevertheless, long before Hirsch, C. S. Lewis wrote that many discussions about 'literature' are discussions of a nonentity; for Lewis, literature was about as non-specific a term as 'talking' or 'utterance'. It was what was said that was important. If we look at what is located at present under the general heading of 'literature' we find an extraordinary variety of texts, with only very tenuous family resemblances between them. How far, for instance, do *Middlemarch* and an imagist haiku resemble each other? Very little, I would have thought, though the student of nineteenth- and twentieth-century literature' is likely to encounter both of them. The idea of literature that currently informs English teaching makes arbitrary associations and exclusions. Novels, for instance, have less in common with lyric poetry than with other forms of extended narrative, such as historiography, biography, autobiography—a genre of which there have been some interesting studies lately—or even some kinds of essay. Conversely, poetry is in many ways closer to music than to the more extended and discursive literary forms. The canon of literature as currently studied has, in some respects, expanded enormously, by the introduction of contemporary literature, of American and other anglophone literatures, and of work by marginalized social groups. But in other ways the core canon has shrunk, by being limited to the obviously fictive genres, poetry, drama, and the novel. This represents a much narrower view of the subject than was common in the early days of institutional literary study, when works of history, biography, philosophy, and divinity were part of the canon. Today, even the most traditional courses in English Literature do not, as a rule, include the English Bible, reasonably thought to be one of the masterpieces of our literature.

Underlying the restriction of the canon are a number of interrelated factors, unified by the institutional need to give the subject a proper identity. In a view of the subject radically different from Hirsch's or Lewis's, 'literariness' emerges as an essential concept, akin to 'philosophy' or 'history'. A text of the past may be of interest to a critic, a philosopher, and a historian, and each would discover his appropriate interest within it. 'Literariness' is to be found as a basic principle in the work of the Russian Formalists and the New Critics, and, elaborately formulated, in Frye's *Anatomy of Criticism*. It inevitably presents itself in formalistic terms, and sometimes in overtly aesthetic ones. The latter presentation is not so common, because of the generally unfavourable associations of 'aesthetic' in our culture, though it is implied whenever students are asked to approach a poem as a work of art, rather than as an historical document or a philosophical argument. Indeed, a diluted Croceanism underlies much of our critical and pedagogic discourse, with its references to 'expression', 'feelings', 'intuitions', and 'unique personal responses'. Poems are more plausibly referred to as works of art than novels; the latter may have obviously aesthetic qualities, but have many other things in them as well. Some of the greatest novels ever written, James's 'great fluid puddings', are hard to make much of in purely aesthetic or formalistic terms. Nevertheless, the ultimate defence of literature against the culturalist or contextualizing pressures which want to turn it into something else is usually along aesthetic lines.

At this point I shall return to Hirsch, who argues that there can be no intrinsic understanding of literature, only a variety of understandings: 'Aesthetic categories are intrinsic to aesthetic *inquiries*, but not to the nature of literary work. Exactly the same can be said of ethical and psychological categories, or any critical categories whatever.' This points the way to the culturalist approach to which Hirsch has elsewhere shown himself sympathetic. Music, I take it, could be defended in essentialist and aesthetic terms, but not literature; this point, also, was made by Lewis in *The Personal Heresy*. Hirsch's formulation does not exclude the possibility of understanding literature in aesthetic terms, it merely prohibits us from claiming that this is how literature is, essentially, to be comprehended. In practice, it weakens the claim of literary study to be a coherent and self-sufficient discipline. One may choose to adopt a broadly aesthetic approach to texts, as is often done, perfectly appropriately, but one then encounters what seems to me a potentially disabling contradiction. In practical pedagogy the student is encouraged to read, carefully, attentively, sensitively, a particular text. As we have seen, there may be cultural barriers to such reading, but leaving aside that potential difficulty, we invite the student to make a unique, personal response to the text, to tune in to the true voice of feeling, to participate in its expressiveness; in short, to have an aesthetic experience. This is true even of the seemingly tougher-minded Cambridge approach. Williams has referred to 'a conception of literature as a series of authors to whom there must, *must* be "personal evaluative response" or its available facsimile.' In Romantic-Crocean terms, the experience is assumed to be both unique and ineffable, to be undergone in a form of negative capability, without, in Keats's words, any irritable reaching after fact and reason. Croce, in the ninth chapter of *Aesthetic*, attacks the idea of applying rhetorical or critical terms to the unique act of aesthetic expression. Nevertheless, this, in one way or another, is what we then require the student to do; the ineffable is to be transformed into efficient communication, whether in seminar discussion, an essay, or an examination answer. Fact and reason are to be reached after. The contradiction has long been lived with in practice, and students become adept in faking responses. Nevertheless, it points to a flaw in the aesthetic defence of literary education, and one which implicitly encourages culturalist claims to take it over. I should add that my own understanding of literature is largely in aesthetic terms; at least, of poetry; where fiction and drama are concerned, aesthetic approaches can, at best, only be partial. The idea of aesthetic education, as formulated by Schiller, seems an entirely noble one; the difficulty is in accommodating it to contemporary pedagogy. This dilemma has been present since the beginnings of institutionalized literary study. It was nicely illustrated in F. H. Townsend's satirical addition to Wordsworth's address to the cuckoo:

> O Cuckoo! shall I call thee Bird,
> Or but a wandering Voice?
> State the alternative preferred
> With reasons for your choice.

It largely disappears when literary texts are treated as cultural traces in a cognitive rather than an affective reading.

I am conscious that to question publicly the established methods of English study is to lay oneself open to the charge of giving aid and comfort to the philistines and utilitarians who want to remake higher education according to their own ideals, if that is the word for them. My position is, I hope, straightforward. I am a firm believer in extending higher education and in preserving the humanities, by all possible means, against technologico–Benthamite attacks. But the humanities comprise a number of disciplines and subjects, of which English is only one; the Leavisite attempt to turn it into the Queen of the Sciences never looked like succeeding. To identify English as peculiarly problematical should not weaken the general defence of humane values in education, and may in the longer run help to strengthen them. A successful military campaign may require giving up some

tactically untenable territory. Having taught English Literature for a long time in universities, on both sides of the
Atlantic, and having spent some years pondering the questions raised in this book, I have come to some very tentative
conclusions about what might be done; they are not, I might
add, of the kind I thought I would come to when I began
working on it.

In the wake of the MacCabe affair in 1981, an editorial in
the *Times Higher Education Supplement* said that a fissiparous
discipline such as English had a number of hard choices in
front of it: it could become even more pluralistic and diffuse,
with accompanying pedagogic problems; it could repressively
impose one favoured approach; or it could split. Raymond
Williams came to think that a splitting of the discipline was
increasingly likely, since cultural materialism and radical
semiotics were not compatible with the dominant paradigm
of literary study: 'For these necessarily include the paradigm
itself as a matter for analysis, rather than as a governing
definition of the object of knowledge.' In this situation, the
question had to be raised:

can a radically different work still be carried on under a single heading or
department when there is not just diversity of approach but more serious
and fundamental differences about the object of knowledge (despite overlapping of the actual material of study)?

For reasons which are much more pragmatic than ideological, I have come to think that a separation of Cultural
Studies from English, though not easy, would be the least
damaging way forward for both parties. It would represent a
realignment within the humanities, not a diminution of them.
Cultural Studies would be visibly plural and fragmented,
involving the study of literary texts, alongside others in
history, philosophy, politics, sociology, film, and other disciplines. Students' expectations would be shaped accordingly,
and they would be spared the struggle to grasp the elusive
'point' of the subject which is a feature of life in English
Departments. There are quite good educational reasons for
believing that a diverse spread of subjects is more suitable for
the late twentieth-century academy than the traditional
single-honours degree, as is suggested by experience in America, and in Britain in polytechnics and colleges of higher

education. (Not to mention PPE, otherwise Modern Greats, at Oxford.) In so far as literature would inevitably play a substantial part in any such course, the students reading it would learn the appropriate cultural codes rather than being expected to know them already. They would also be spared the fall-out from damaging academic debates about the nature of the canon, and the virtues of coverage versus concentration. There would be no fixed canon, and no coverage. Such a degree course would not suit everyone, but it might well be attractive to the late entrants and mature students who are increasingly common participants in higher education, particularly in the humanities, and who bring valuable experience of life and work to their study, but may have rather little formal preparation. It would also be more appropriate for the unambitious students of moderate talents who currently apply for an English degree, but would be more at home in a less intensive programme of liberal study. Cultural Studies would provide a more productive environment for the radical academics and rainbow coalitionists at present functioning in English Departments, who have conspicuous energy and intelligence, but little literary sensibility or aesthetic interests. Literature, when taught in such a context, would, no doubt, be given a culturalist and contextualist treatment, and I believe that there is nothing inherently objectionable about this. But I am also attracted by Graff's suggestion that those who favoured a 'literary', aesthetic, affective way of reading would then experience the satisfaction of working against the prevailing grain. Once established, 'Cultural Studies' might show structural affinities with Social Studies and move closer to that area. It might also become dominated by Marxists and cultural materialists, but not inevitably so; academic sociology offers points of comparison here. And in any case, Marxism looks like a declining force. My proposal will, I know, appear as selling the pass, to traditionalist teachers of English Literature, and perhaps upset them, which I am sorry for. I will point out, though, that it is in some ways a very conservative proposal, inviting a return to origins. When 'English' first came on the scene in the nineteenth century, it was precisely as a form of Cultural Studies, involving not only language and literature, but history, geography, philosophy, and so on, requiring the first professors of the subject to be polymaths. It was only later that the aesthetic dimension of literary study became emphasized, with an accompanying concentration on the fictional genres.

The other part of my proposal will probably prove annoying to radicals, thereby ensuring a proper balance. If Cultural Studies goes its own way, what happens to what is left? I would certainly not favour a rump version of one of the current forms of English degree, with their recurring arguments about canons and coverage, the definition of literature, and the place of theory. Instead, I propose taking the logic of generic concentration as far as it can go, with a degree which would study, in detail, a single genre, poetry. There are certain academic precedents, particularly the uncontroversial establishment in a number of universities of degrees in drama, which do work previously thought of as belonging to an English degree. The other model I have in mind is the degree in music, which is intensive, technical, and demanding, and attracts a small number of well-qualified entrants. A degree of a comparable kind, directed at poetry, is, I think, feasible, and would be more coherent and rewarding than existing degrees in English Literature. It would attract the automatic charge of 'élitist', but so, potentially, do many worthwhile kinds of intellectual activity. The reason for concentrating on poetry is that it is the most visibly 'literary', formal, and conventional of the major genres, and would provide the best scope for study within an aesthetic frame of reference. 'Poetry' is itself a very flexible term, extending from Elizabethan lyrics to *Don Juan*, and from *Paradise Lost* to imagist epiphanies. In my suggested scheme it would certainly include Elizabethan and Jacobean poetic drama. By dropping the novel and other kinds of drama, more time would be provided for the extensive reading of poetry which is so essential if one is to make sense of any one poem. There might be regrets over giving up the novel, but after having been deeply interested in that form for many years (even to the extent of writing one) and often teaching courses on the novel, I have come to the conclusion that the pedagogic difficulties involved are extreme. Percy Lubbock, at the end of *The Craft of Fiction*, acknowledged that as soon as we have finished reading a novel we begin to forget it, and what is left to talk about is a vague cloud of fading impressions: 'the book vanishes as we lay hands on it.' In the face of this central problem, the valuable work that has gone on in recent years in narratology, and other aspects of fictional form, is curiously difficult to apply in practice. Teaching often involves looking in detail at particular passages, in the hope that the part will relate coherently to the whole, but the doctrine of the hermeneutic circle reminds us that we cannot understand the parts until we understand the whole (and vice versa). Fredric Jameson has made a vigorous statement of this difficulty:

> Every serious practising critic knows a secret which is less often publicly discussed, namely, that there exists no ready-made corridor between the sealed chambers of stylistic investigation and that equally unventilated space in which the object of study is reconstituted as narrative structure. In practice, whatever the solution adopted there is always an uncomfortable shifting of gears in the movement from one of these perspectives to the other: nor does the assertion of this or that 'homology' between style and narrative do much more than to pronounce resolved in advance the dilemma for which it was supposed to provide a working answer.

If novels are to be studied as part of an exclusive course, they might be better located in Cultural Studies. The teachers on such a programme would have to confront the difficulty I have just raised, as well as questions about the mimetic values of fiction in the face of structuralist and poststructuralist assertions that word and world have no necessary relation.

Something of the problem defined by Jameson would also apply to the reading of longer poems, but I believe it would be more manageable; with poetry, a better case can be made for homologies between style and structure. A course dealing with poetry would certainly raise theoretical problems, whose discussion would be part of the programme. The most demanding would be one I have previously raised: namely, that though the successful encounter with a poem may result in a unique aesthetic experience, academic practice demands that it be turned into non-aesthetic discourse. Furthermore, not everyone who is invited to respond to an admired poem will have any such experience. And although talking about poems 'as poetry' will imply an aesthetic reading rather than a culturalist or historical one, it must be acknowledged that there is inescapable culturalist and historical underpinning of the idea of a canon; not all the poems to be read will have much aesthetic value. What one hopes for is for the student to remain open to the possibility of aesthetic experience, to accept and enjoy it when it occurs, but not to fake responses if it does not. Such a course would be primarily concerned with the formal, technical, and conventional aspects of poetry, considered both synchronically and diachronically; in a word, 'rhetoric'. Its starting-point might be Hopkins's definition of rhetoric as 'the common teachable part of poetry'. Such a statement implies that there are aspects of poetry which may *not* be so easily teachable. Indeed, Hopkins distinguished between 'rhetoric' and 'poetical insight and inspiration'. The model, as I have said, would be a degree in music, and would include history and theory as well as analysis. Most importantly, it would also include exercises in composition, of the kind once common in the study of classics. I prefer not to call this 'creative writing', since the late-Romantic ideological implications of 'creative' are irrelevant, even undesirable. The intention is that students of elaborate structures in language should be able to construct them as well as receive and consume them, if only to achieve a better understanding of how poems are made. Something of the sort has already been introduced into some English degrees, under the aegis of the Verbal Arts Association, who have made a welcome start with such work.

The reading of English poetry would be accompanied by a consideration of historical as well as current theories of poetry. These would include the arguments of the major poet-critics of the past: Sidney, Jonson, Dryden, Johnson, and on to the Romantics, Victorians, and modernists. I cannot see how the canon of poetry could avoid being constructed along historical lines, though the problem and implications of canon-formation should be faced, as part of theoretical study. It could take account of recent attempts to enlarge the canon, particularly by the addition of poetry by women, and other marginalized groups. Indeed, such an academic structure might provide a good opportunity for the exercise suggested by Graff, in which students (many of whom would probably be women) would consider a feminist anthology of women poets of the past, and discuss how far they are admissible into the existing poetic canon, and what theoretical criteria might govern such admission. The canon would be largely English, not for a priori nationalistic reasons, but because it is written in English, and until fairly recently most poetry written in English was also written in England, or at least, in the British Isles. There is no reason why American poetry, or poetry from other anglophone literatures, should not be read, given a minimal amount of culture and contextual instruction (which may also be needed, of course, in the reading of English poems).

To what extent students on such a degree would also need to read poetry in another language is a difficult question. In principle it is extremely desirable, not only because of the basic 'otherness' of foreign poetry, but because such knowledge gives one a better sense of what English poetry can and cannot do. In practice, given the monoglot tendency in secondary education it might be difficult to recruit students with the necessary competence. The University of Warwick has for some time provided the possibility of studying both English and foreign texts in a comparative way at undergraduate level. The lessons have, however, been inconclusive. It is certainly the case that a student with, say, a moderately good pass in A-level French may have little capacity for the responsive reading of French poetry. Within the Warwick structure students have the possibility of learning another language intensively from scratch in the first year, so they can read straightforward literary texts at the end of it. That, at least is the assumption, but there have been disagreements about how well it works. Some years ago the teachers of one language pronounced themselves satisfied that at the end of a year the students of it had the capacity for literary reading; the equally competent and concerned teachers of another language were convinced that their students had achieved no such capacity, and that the process was rather a waste of time. Much, of course, depends on individual motivation and capacity. Many people who are accomplished linguists have no literary sensibility. On the other hand, there are those who have only an imperfect formal competence in a language but

who by a combination of guesswork and intuition can somehow make contact with the aesthetic qualities of a foreign
poem. Impressive translations have been made on such a
basis, though usually by poets. It is not a quality that it is
sensible to expect in the generality of students. For those who
do not have much real competence in other languages, there
is the possibility of coming to terms with poems in the older,
more remote forms of English. Chaucer, I assume, would
form part of such a programme anyway. Langland and the
Gawain poet, read in the original, would extend both poetic
experience and linguistic understanding. Indeed, the historical study of language together with contemporary stylistics,
probably ought to feature in any such course. Personally, I
reject the Oxford claim that English Literature begins with
Anglo-Saxon, and would not make it a required subject. But
an option in it might be provided for those who were curious
about what English poetry was like before, so to speak, it
became English.

I already seem to be overloading a non-existent syllabus.
There is an element of utopianism in drafting such proposals,
though I believe these ideas are worth pursuing. The student
intake would be limited to those who have a genuine literary
sensibility, who are interested in poetry, and are already in
the habit of reading it. This might exclude many students
who are currently enrolled in English degrees, even those with
good A-levels which can now be obtained very largely by
studying drama and fiction. Indeed, I am not sure what the
correlation would be between formal attainments and the
right qualities needed to take a degree in poetry. Some
students entering it could have quite other claims and qualifications than A-level English. It might well appeal to poets
or would-be poets, who, contrary to popular myths about
inspiration, are usually keenly interested in the technical
aspects of composition.

What I have proposed in the foregoing pages is a conscious
surrender to the culturalists of much of the activity that now
goes on in English degrees, in order to retain something more
coherent, defensible, and inherently valuable. Culturalists
will point out—as C. S. Lewis once did—that much poetry
of the past was not written for aesthetic ends, but for religious,

political, or other social purposes. This is true; but such poems have outlived their original purposes and now survive as aesthetic entities. We may, following Hirsch, accept that there is no such thing as a poetic or aesthetic essence; but we can say that such texts are rewarding when approached in aesthetic terms, or, in Lewis's words, are read in literary ways. The parallel with studying music has more than structural significance. Music is the most obviously aesthetic of the arts—to whose condition they all aspire, according to Walter Pater—yet it submits easily to formal and technical analysis. Interestingly, music, though a major cultural form, has not attracted the attention of contemporary culturalists. It may be that there is literally nothing they can say about it in the terms they are accustomed to using. The sociologists of art who discuss music have to restrict themselves to the conditions in which it is performed, produced, or received, rather than the music itself.

The affinities between music and poetry have been familiar since antiquity, though they are largely ignored in the current intellectual climate. Poetry, of course, can never *become* music, despite the dream of nineteenth century symbolists, since, as Eliot's Sweeney put it, 'I gotta use words when I talk to you.' But a restatement of that ancient affinity should strengthen poetry against political and culturalist claims. The academic study of music may be a specialist field, but music, of every kind, is widely diffused and performed; only a small percentage of those attending concerts or recitals will have taken degrees in music. Similarly, one would like to see a state of affairs in which many more people read and enjoyed poetry than had taken a degree in it.

The degree in poetry I have outlined would attempt to be open about its theoretical assumptions. I do not believe there is any absolute virtue in such openness, in fact, I think that education is ideally carried on in a shared form of life where there is agreement about fundamentals and attention can be concentrated on the task in hand. But no such state of affairs exists in our culture, and it is self-delusory and damaging to pretend that it does. The challenge to one's premises and assumptions will be made and has to be faced, though one might prefer to reply in terms of 'principles' rather than of 'theory'. The reply I envisage is likely to prove unsatisfactory to radicals and utilitarians alike, since it would state that poetry is ultimately its own justification, like music or games. One hopes that reading it may have good effects, of the kind described by Wordsworth in the 1800 Preface, or more succinctly summed up by Lewis in the conclusion to *An Experiment in Criticism*, where he says that literature heals the wound without undermining the privilege of individuality. Yet to study literature, or poetry, in the hope of achieving these effects is perverse, like playing a game, not for the pleasure of the game, but simply in order to keep fit. The latter is a desirable by-product, but it is not what the game should be about. The humanizing and moral effects of reading literature must be left to occur as and when they will, which will be different in every individual. They certainly cannot be turned into the stated goal of an academic programme. The attempt to do just this, pursued with inappropriate insistence, ultimately vitiated the Leavisite campaign.

II

I have tried to show in this book that though the academic institutionalizing of vernacular literary study which began about a century ago had good, even inescapable reasons in its origins, its later progress has not had the effects the founders hoped for. This is largely because, once incorporated into the academy, this study had to adopt the values and principles of the academy, and develop as the institution developed. An ideal of professionalism became dominant, and teachers of English did their best to adopt it, producing an ever greater volume of critical and scholarly writing whose motive was as much career development as the expansion of knowledge. And yet, they could never become as truly professional as their colleagues in other disciplines, since 'literature' did not belong in the academy and was not generated there, though criticism and scholarship might be. English, as the Newbolt Report and Leavis had insisted, was not like other academic subjects, though all the pressures of the modern academy, which include both privileges and responsibilities, have tried to make it come in line. The professionalized academic critic wanted to forget that there had been a time when criticism was part of literature; and the belief that criticism or theory could be literature in themselves was perhaps part of the process of exorcizing other values and attitudes. Poets and novelists see the situation differently, and so, indeed, do many students, who tend to want something different from what their ablest teachers wish to give them. The complex of disparate elements comprising academic English was always unstable, though they might have stayed together longer if it had not been for the demands of the academic environment.

In the 1950s, it seemed as if there might be a place for literature in the academy, so that the writing of fiction or poetry, of criticism, and the teaching of literature would become a unified form of life. As we know, it did not happen. Thirty years on, English is a large and entrenched subject, and there is no likelihood of putting the clock back, and starting again in some other way: my proposal for a division between Cultural Studies and a degree in poetry is a pragmatic proposal for a way out of current difficulties. Other factors, like the institutional need to advance knowledge, to publish, to engage in research, and generate performance-indicators, would remain, whatever new academic structures emerged.

There is, however, another way in which a useful advance might be made. Again, one looks back to the nineteenth-century origins of English literary studies, when the first pioneers and missionaries, men such as Morley and Furnivall, travelled all over the country to talk about English literature in adult education classes and working men's clubs. Indeed, it was the pressure from this large and disadvantaged constituency that helped to establish vernacular literary education. There has always been a vigorous tradition of English studies in adult education, and indeed it was through such classes that I was myself able to become a mature student in the early 1950s. In the present situation, there is more and more scope for adult or continuing education, with an older or academically late-developing constituency. In such work there is an opportunity for English to, in a sense, escape from the academy, literally to go extra-mural, and to re-establish those connections with the larger society that were originally part of its *raison d'être*. Literature classes with older people can be rewarding; they bring a longer experience of life to bear on the subject, and often a wide range of reading. They are also exempt from the demands of examination passing, assessment, and certification, that I believe have a more distorting effect in the teaching of literature than in other academic areas. The subject can be pursued for its own satisfaction. However, a difficulty with extra-mural study is that teachers have to work very hard in order to keep classes in being, since there are no external compulsions on students to attend, and their motivation and level of interest are very variable. Malcolm Bradbury's story, 'The Adult Education Class', nicely dramatizes the difficulties and dangers. Adult classes, in fact, require exceptionally good teaching, of a kind that may be remote from the professional ideals of many present-day academics.

At the present time, there is much interest in the English past, evoked in exhibitions commemorating historical events, and evident in the spread of museums and the great popularity of visiting country homes. This interest has several aspects. One of them, as the Left disapprovingly points out, is a mythologized version of past greatness which obfuscates the disagreeable realities of the present. Certainly there are many bogus images of the national past around, culminating in the dream world peddled abroad by the British Tourist Board (though this is, alas, what Americans and others want to visit). But people need myths of one sort or another, and the Left has its own, in memories of Wat Tyler, Cromwell, the Tolpuddle Martyrs, and the heroic industrial struggles of the past. Mythology, however partial, is better than blank amnesia. This current feeling for the past might provide a way in adult classes of shifting the emphasis from popular modern writing to earlier literature. Chaucer looked at in isolation can seem daunting, but Chaucer read in a cultural and historical context, with visual and other aids, could come alive as a great poet, speaking across six centuries, in a Gadamerian fusion of horizons. I am not, though, recommending the ideological antiquarianism of the New Historicism, which has little interest in poetry as such. This is a speculative proposal, merely, and it may fall foul of the fact that in our image-ridden culture reading is difficult, and literary texts still demand to be *read*, rigorously and carefully. In cultural history reading 'about' something may be good enough; in studying literature it is not.

There is a good deal more to say, and to think about, concerning the relations between the intra- and extra-mural teaching of literature. The above considerations are simply meant to signal my conviction that a change of balance is desirable, with a move away from the narrow professionalism of the academy, and a modest return to the original motives of the discipline of English. Something similar is true of literary criticism. At the moment the academy has a near-monopoly of the subject, and I would like to see it broken, in a recognition of the traditional cultural truth that good criticism can be written by poets and novelists, and indeed by people whose professional concern is not with literature at all. Reviewing and criticism are separate activities, but the best literary journalism can provide genuine and valuable criticism, as Morris Dickstein has pointed out. What is needed are more journals that are prepared to publish long, serious, reflective essays or review-articles, as the *London Review of Books* does. Victoria Glendinning, writing as a biographer and literary journalist, has offered some judicious thoughts on the question, which summarize much of my argument:

No one could doubt that the application of the academic mind to literature has been salutary in bringing rigour and discipline into criticism: cleaner texts, scholarly annotations, precise analysis, intelligent—even transforming—interpretations and readings; and an intolerance for woolly emotional responses, vague inflated recommendations, and subjective wallowings of all kinds. But the academic mind, and the exigencies of the academic career, have had the effect of splitting off academic approaches to literature from the 'reading', in that word's widest sense, of ordinary people . . . An ambitious lecturer in an English Department is writing for his peer group, not for the general public.

The tenor of this book has been pessimistic, but not, I hope, despairing. Some readers will find its arguments unconvincing, believing that what I see as problems are not problems at all. I can conceive of such a response coming from two quite different kinds of reader. The first would be moderate conservatives of placid and unreflective temperament who are happily engaged with their research and their teaching, and who believe that the discipline of English is in good heart, with lots of interesting books coming out and buoyant student demand. They support a genial pluralism in English studies, encouraging a hundred flowers to bloom, though putting up a cautious resistance to the extremes of foreign ideology and theory. The other kind would be academics who are committed to a tough professionalism on the American model, who believe that knowledge advances and becomes obsolete, that theory is essential, and that nothing of interest can be said about literature outside an institutional framework. In Lodge's characterology, they are Robyn Penroses aspiring to be Morris Zapps. What I have deplored or been sceptical about they would find admirable. They tend to be young, energetic, and ambitious, but there are by now professors of that outlook. All I can say to the objectors in both categories is that those who do not see a problem do not have a problem, and they can happily ignore what I have written. But other readers will, I imagine, accept the general drift of what I have said, whilst disagreeing on many points of detail.

Not wanting to seem too negative, I have outlined ways in which the discipline of English as currently constituted might divide, to the benefit of both parties. But knowing how the academic mind works, I am not optimistic about change. As Noel Annan wrote in his life of Leslie Stephen: 'The ingenuity in argument, the subtlety in drawing distinctions, the dexterous prevarications, the imperative reasons for procrastination, perpetually bewilder and confound the novice in university administration.' In this respect, at least, little has altered since the nineteenth century. The most likely future is no overt change, with the discipline of English becoming less and less coherent, riven by feuds and revolts, but still presenting the external appearances of a large, well-established and respectable academic subject. It could go on for a long time in this condition, like the Spanish Empire in its centuries of decline.

APPENDIX

The Calendar of Modern Letters[1]

The Calendar of Modern Letters remains an exemplary, even mythological, force in modern literary history, and is generally regarded as one of the outstanding reviews of the twentieth century. In 1933 F. R. Leavis edited a collection of essays reprinted from it called *Towards Standards of Criticism*. The *Calendar's* influence on *Scrutiny* was certainly great, but to regard it primarily as a prolegomenon to the later and longer-lived magazine is to distort its significance. Under the title of *The Calendar of Modern Letters* it was published monthly from March 1925 to February 1926; it then became a quarterly as *The Calendar* and ran from April 1926 to July 1927. It was edited by Edgell Rickword, assisted by Douglas Garman and Bertram Higgins. Rickword (1898–1982), who was described by D. H. Lawrence as 'that *Calendar* young man', was an important if enigmatic figure in the literary world of the 1920s. As a poet he made the transition from traditional to modern idioms in a way that was comparable to though different from Eliot's; like Eliot, Rickword was indebted to the English Metaphysicals and the French Symbolists, but the creative mix was different. His productive career as a poet was largely confined to the 1920s, but his work of that decade shows him to be one of the best poets of his time, who is still not sufficiently appreciated. I would make a similar claim for Rickword as a literary critic; his *Essays and Opinions 1921–1931*, edited by Alan Young (Cheadle, 1974), reveals a critic of formidable intelligence and insight, and forms an indispensable guide to the literary opinion of the decade.

The First World War was a major formative influence on Rickword, reinforcing from personal experience the modernist sense of a decisive break with the past, and prompting him to write a handful of fine war poems that have become anthology pieces, like 'Winter Warfare' and 'Trench Poets'. He joined the army in 1916, served on the Western Front, was twice wounded, and lost the sight of one eye. He went up to Oxford in October 1919 to read French, but soon became dissatisfied with the academic content of the course. He was also hard up and wanted to get married, and he left Oxford after four terms. Oxford at that time was intellectually vigorous because of the many ex-servicemen who had gone up to complete or commence their studies; the idle, glittering world of *Brideshead Revisited* was still a few years in the future. At Oxford Rickword got to know a number of young writers, some of whom later became contributors to the *Calendar*; they included L. P. Hartley, Edmund Blunden, A. E. Coppard,

[1] Reprinted from *The Yearbook of English Studies*, 16 (1986), Literary Periodicals Special Number.

Siegfried Sassoon, W. J. Turner, and Roy Campbell. Bertram Higgins was an undergraduate from Australia, and a little later Rickword met Douglas Garman, a younger Cambridge graduate whose sister Mary had married Roy Campbell. Another Garman sister married Ernest Wishart, who was to give financial support to the *Calendar* and to found the publishing house of Wishart, which later became Lawrence and Wishart, publishers to the Communist Party.

After leaving Oxford Rickword supported himself by writing reviews for the *Daily Herald, Times Literary Supplement*, and *New Statesman*, and in 1924 he published a pioneering study of Rimbaud. At about that time, in collaboration with Higgins and Garman, he resolved to launch the *Calendar*. It is necessary to remember that the review was the product of a group of quite young men who, though dedicated and serious-minded, were also tinged with youthful iconoclasm. Unlike *Scrutiny* and many later journals, particularly in America, it had no base in the academy; nor was it produced by people who were close to the centres of power and influence in society, like the great reviews of the nineteenth century. It emerged, in fact, from the unlikely setting of the London literary Bohemia which Wyndham Lewis later satirized in *The Apes of God*. That novel featured some of the *Calendar*'s contributors; Edwin Muir appeared as 'Eddie Keith' and Roy Campbell as 'Zulu Blades', while Rickword himself made a brief appearance as 'Hedge-pinshot Pickwort'.

The *Calendar*'s importance was not primarily due to the publication of new poetry and fiction of high quality. In this respect it could not compare with some of its recent predecessors in England and America: the *English Review* under Ford Madox Ford, which published Lawrence's early poems and Wyndham Lewis's first short stories; or the various magazines in which Ezra Pound had a hand, such as *Blast*, which published the opening section of Ford's *The Good Soldier* and in its second and last number introduced Eliot's poetry to British readers, or the *Egoist* and *Little Review*, which serialized Joyce's *A Portrait of the Artist as a Young Man* and *Ulysses*, and Lewis's *Tarr*. In America the *Dial* published *The Waste Land*, and even if that poem's first British publication in Eliot's own *Criterion* was a special case, the *Criterion*, of which the *Calendar* disapproved, also published Yeats's 'The Tower'. The *Calendar* could not match this record with new creative work, though each issue included poems and stories. Of the poems by British writers the only ones that now seem of much interest or merit, apart from those by Rickword himself, are a few by Robert Graves, Edmund Blunden, Edwin Muir, and D. H. Lawrence. The Graves poems are interesting in that they show his transition from a fundamentally Georgian idiom to the polished, ironic, mythopoeic manner of his more mature verse.

In poetry the *Calendar*'s real achievement was in publishing a number of American poets before they were at all well known on either side of the Atlantic, such as Laura Riding (who was then beginning her close association with Graves), John Crowe Ransom, Allen Tate, and Hart Crane. With his usual prescience, Rickword had a good sense of the developing separateness of the American poetry from the English tradition, and he may have understood that the progress of poetic modernism was more advanced in America than in Britain (Eliot, after all, remained an American until 1927). Hart Crane's 'At Melville's Tomb', which must be his most famous short poem, was first published in the *Calendar*. Crane wrote: '*The Calendar* is a very decent quarterly, and I'm glad to get the "Melville" in print—not one magazine in America would take it.'

Of the fiction published in the *Calendar*, Lawrence's 'The Princess', serialized in the first three issues, is the most substantial representative. Not many of the short stories now seem of outstanding merit, apart from those by Liam O'Flaherty, A. E. Coppard, and William Plomer. Some studies in primitivism by T. F. Powys have a certain raw power, but not much else. Among the fiction by lesser-known writers, Iris Barry's 'An Historical Bride' is a pleasant piece of sub-Firbankian whimsy. It is very possible that the editors of the *Calendar* were simply unable to obtain enough short fiction of the quality they hoped for. In an interview in 1973 Rickword said that he admired Wyndham Lewis's short stories and wanted to publish some in the *Calendar* but had to settle instead for chunks of Lewis's polemical work in progress. The *Calendar* went in quite extensively for translated material, and published stories by Pirandello, Rudolf Kastner, and a number of Russians, of whom the best known today is Isaac Babel. Its policy of publishing Russian writing seems to have been prompted by S. S. Koteliansky, a recurring marginal figure in the literary life of the 1920s, who did many of the translations, including the memoirs of Dostoevsky's widow which were serialized over five numbers, and Chekov's play *The Wood Demon*, published in two instalments. One of the odder reflections of these Russian interests was a certain preoccupation with the Dostoevskyan mystagogue Vasili Rosanov, presumably under Koteliansky's influence. The *Calendar* published his translations of extracts from Rosanov's collection of aphorisms, *Solitaria*, and a long critical and biographical study of Rosanov. In 1927 Lawrence reviewed *Solitaria* in the *Calendar*; if Rosanov's name is known today it is probably because of Lawrence's review, later collected in *Phoenix*.

The *Calendar*'s interest in American poetry and Russian prose indicated an admirable internationalism. But the review's main impact was critical rather than creative. Its intention, and in large measure its achievement, was to establish more rigorous and responsible literary criticism. It did not open with a manifesto, but the first issue contained some rather gnomic notes by Rickword on the current state of literary culture and his hopes for the review:

> A preconceived idea is, as the artist knows, a tyrant dangerous to the proper organization of the impulse, definable in no other terms than those of the finished work, which compels him to his strange exertion. The same reticence is necessary even in the humble creation of a Review, in which activity, since it is to some degree an aesthetic one, there is virtue not in intentions but in achievement only. We lay down no programme as to *The Calendar*'s performance nor prophesy as to its character, since these things cannot interest our readers till they have a tangible existence, and then we shall be ready to join our own criticisms with theirs.

Later in these notes Rickword emphasizes the fact of social and cultural fragmentation: 'Today there is only the race, the biological-economic environment; and the individual. Between these extremes there is no class, craft, art, sex, sect or sub-division which, it seems to us, can claim privilege of the rest.' In this context Rickword asserts a role for the artist which is essentially late-Romantic: 'The artist, who can differ only in degree and in function from the rest of men, by revealing differences creates realities. It is through him that we can perfect our individuality.' An individualist view of literature emerges:

> The aim of writing is not to convince someone else (for that can never happen against the will) but to satisfy oneself. If, as well, the reader's pleasure is aroused by one of the many means which literature has to waken such a response, then the reader may make a gift of his assent or dissent to the conventicles which are founded on those wraiths, for the cycle of expression is complete without them.

The force of this obscure sentiment seems to be that one can appreciate literature without necessarily agreeing or disagreeing with the doctrines it contains, an idea close to that expressed by I. A. Richards in the discussion of 'pseudo-statements' in *Principles of Literary Criticism*, a book which Rickword reviewed admiringly in the second number of the *Calendar*. His own attitudes to literature and indeed to life seem to have been divided between an extreme individualism, with Nietzschean overtones, which was apparent in his interest in writers such as Rimbaud and Sade; and an Arnoldian concern with cultural health and intellectual standards. Rickword was only twenty-six when the *Calendar* was launched and it is not surprising that his ideas and beliefs were still not fully sorted out; the editorial note ends in an Arnoldian spirit, and it is this which influenced Leavis and coloured his highly influential view of the *Calendar*'s general achievement: 'In reviewing we shall base our statements on the standards of criticism, since it is only then that one can speak plainly without offence, or give praise with meaning.'

The most immediate influence on Rickword, however, was not Arnold but Eliot, and his view of Arnold may have been mediated by Eliot's invocation of him in the 'Introduction' to *The Sacred Wood*: 'What makes Arnold seem all the more remarkable is, that if he were our exact contemporary, he would find all his labour to perform again.' Rickword had reviewed *The Sacred Wood* in 1920, praising it as an example of the kind of rigorous, disinterested criticism which hardly existed in England at that time. He wrote a puzzled but highly intelligent review of *The Waste Land* in 1922; by the time he came to review Eliot's *Poems, 1909–1925* in the *Calendar* (2, 278–81) he had a better sense of what Eliot's poetry was about, and his discussion of it remains extraordinarily perceptive and just.

Rickword had a sure sense of what was relevant in the emergent literary culture of modernism, and he assimilated it rapidly and doubtless encouraged his contributors to. The *Calendar* was important in raising the public standards of reviewing and criticism; but it was at least as important in consolidating and publicizing the isolated achievements of modernism.

From the beginning, *The Waste Land* and *Ulysses* were taken for granted in its pages, not in a spirit of avant-garde defiance, but as major works of literature which intelligent readers either knew about, or should want to know about. In the first year of publication the *Calendar* published two essays on *Ulysses*: Bertram Higgins's 'The Natural Pander: Leopold Bloom and Others' and Edwin Muir's 'The Meaning of *Ulysses*' (1, 129–46, 347–55). This was only three years after the publication of *The Waste Land* and *Ulysses*, when the former was commonly regarded, as much in literary circles as elsewhere, as a hotch-potch of learned nonsense and quite possibly a hoax, while the latter was not legally obtainable in Britain and had the reputation of being both very dirty and largely unreadable.

Edwin Muir, in an acute essay called 'The Zeit Geist', compared Aldous Huxley ('our best example of the fashionable writer') with Joyce ('the artist expressing the age by an uncompromising opposition to it'), and described Eliot as a poet 'who in his poetry sets side by side the response of the poet who wishes to escape from his environment, and that of the critic of life who wishes to come to terms with it' (2, 112–18). Rickword remarked, in one of the casual asides that contained some of his most astute observations, that the prose of *Ulysses* was doing much of the work once done by poetry (3, 156). Joyce was a constant point of reference in the *Calendar*, and it was in dealing with Joyce that Rickword suffered a major disappointment, as Sylvia Beach recalls. When the *Calendar* was founded Rickword was keen to publish some of Joyce's 'Work in Progress'. He wrote offering 'the hospitality of our pages to Joyce, the greatest power of the present generation'. On Joyce's behalf Sylvia Beach offered Rickword the 'Anna Livia Plurabelle' episode. Rickword was delighted at this *coup*. Sylvia Beach describes the ludicrous aftermath:

> I got a delighted letter of acknowledgement from the editor; then a mortified, crestfallen one. The printers had refused to set up the passage beginning 'Two boys in their breeches' and ending with 'blushing and looking askance at her'. Very respectfully the *Calendar*'s editor asked Mr Joyce's permission to delete this passage from his text. Very reluctantly, I replied that Mr Joyce regretted the inconvenience over his contribution but could not discuss any alteration of his text—and would Mr Rickword please return it.

If Joyce had been published in the *Calendar*, as well as being frequently praised there, its reputation would have stood high with avant-garde readers. But the larger educated public might have been further alienated. The *Calendar* made assumptions about its readers' intellectual calibre and literary sophistication that would have been hard to meet in the mid-1920s. Uncertainty about its presumed readership was a central problem for the magazine, which may have been why its circulation declined so sharply. Malcolm Bradbury has quoted Rickword to the effect that the circulation of the *Calendar* began at between seven and eight thousand and dropped over the first year to between two and three thousand; and after the magazine became a quarterly the figure dropped to a thousand.

Rickword, Higgins, and Garman formed the nucleus of the *Calendar*'s critical team and contributed essays and reviews to practically every number. Another regular reviewer was John Holms, who had been an officer in the First World War and spent two years in a German prisoner-of-war camp. He appears as a charming if shadowy figure in the autobiographies of Edwin and Willa Muir and Peggy Guggenheim. Holms was well off enough not to need to work, though he desperately wanted to be a writer. He drank heavily, spent his time wandering idly round Europe like a character in Aldous Huxley or Scott Fitzgerald, and died at the age of thirty-four after an operation. During the short life of the *Calendar* he proved himself to be an excellent critic. Holms was a close friend of Edwin Muir, who described him as the most remarkable person he knew, and presumably introduced him to the *Calendar*. Muir himself was one of its most valued contributors of reviews and critical articles. At that time his writing was a good deal sharper and more incisive than in his later years, when his natural gentleness of temperament tended to muffle his fine critical intelligence. Writers of established reputation contributed occasionally; E. M. Forster wrote on 'Anonymity', and Aldous Huxley on Breughel. D. H. Lawrence was a fairly regular contributor; the *Calendar* published his essays 'Art and Morality' and 'Morality and the Novel', and some lively reviews, such as those of H. G. Wells's *The World of William Clissold*, and of selected American fiction, including Dos Passos's *Manhattan Transfer* and Hemingway's *In Our Time*. Despite a scattering of well-known names the *Calendar* was dependent for criticism on a quite small number of regular contributors. Eliot had assembled a larger team for the *Criterion*, as Leavis was later to do with *Scrutiny*.

The reviews in the *Calendar* were much more rigorous and intelligent than the bulk of the belletrist literary journalism of the time, though they had been anticipated by the work done by Eliot and other reviewers for the *Athenaeum* under Middleton Murry's editorship in 1919–20. The series of 'Scrutinies' of eminent living writers was the *Calendar*'s most sustained and systematic attempt at applying high and disinterested standards of criticism to fashionable reputations. These articles aroused resentment at the time, but they helped to establish the *Calendar*'s particular tone of unfaltering strictness. Rickword later edited two collections of them, with later additions, under the title of *Scrutinies* (London, 1928 and 1931), and they provided Leavis with a title and much else. Yet it is now evident that such criticism was not, and could not be, totally disinterested. The *Calendar*'s 'Scrutinies' were, in effect, a form of cultural politics aimed at overturning the literary idols of the pre-war (and pre-modernist) era, such as J. M. Barrie, Arnold Bennett, Bernard Shaw, John Masefield, and Walter de la Mare. They formed part of a campaign in the 1920s, to which Virginia Woolf's 'Mr Bennett and Mrs Brown' and Lawrence's attacks on Wells and Galsworthy also contributed. Some of the weaker victims underwent virtual demolition, as in Rickword's superb critique of Barrie: 'To go and see a Barrie play is like going to see a sheep in a cage in the Zoo; the bars, the "drama", are merely a device to encourage mutual self-esteem' (1, 41). On the other hand, Shaw is large enough to survive the telling and well-aimed shafts directed at him by C. H. Rickword (2, 50–4).

At the same time writers of broadly modernist tendency, including those who contributed to the *Calendar*, were not exempted from rigorous treatment where this seemed necessary. Wyndham Lewis was one such: Rickword was fairly severe about *The Art of Being Ruled* and Holms extremely so about *The Lion and the Fox* (3, 247–50; 4, 62–7). Lawrence, a writer of very different temperament, was given a justifiably harsh review of *The Plumed Serpent*, which wittily quoted one of his own dicta against him: ' "If you try to nail anything down in the novel, either it kills the novel, or the novel gets up and walks away with the nail". This novel is not wholly dead; rather, like the cow in the rhyme it has left its tail behind it, very full of tacks' (3, 79). Lawrence does not seem to have minded this review, or perhaps he never saw it, for he continued to contribute to the *Calendar*. On occasion the editors seem to have had differing attitudes to emerging writers; Rickword warmly praised Richards's *Principles of Literary Criticism* whereas Garman was dismissive of his *Science and Poetry* (1, 162–4; 3, 164–5).

The tone of the *Calendar* is still familiar in our critical language; mainly, I think, because of its influence on *Scrutiny*. There are many instances in the *Calendar* of what look like Leavisite procedures *avant la lettre*. For instance, Bertram Higgins writing about Masefield undertakes the detailed close reading of a passage of verse to enforce a total judgement: ' "Mournful, despairing, great, greater than speech". The tritely associative first pair of adjectives provide emotionalised comment where the narrative requires an image, and the comment is so deficient in vital force as to depress the curiosity stimulated by the "something" of the preceding line' (1, 223). Garman on Tom Moore anticipates *Scrutiny*'s tendency to 'place' minor writers in socio-cultural terms: 'He is an early specimen of a type now common—the social-artist and social-critic. Writing was valuable to him only as a passport into good society or as an activity in which he indulged as in a ball or a dinner party. His approach to literature was fundamentally as frivolous as his social conduct' (1, 484). It is interesting to see Rickword remark more or less in passing, 'it is clear that Pope could not have evolved his style without a knowledge of the processes by which Donne worked his transformations', which looks forward to a central argument of Leavis's *Revaluation*. Developing this idea, Rickword reveals the unassimilated influence of one of Eliot's famous formulations: 'In the finest seventeenth century poetry it is possible to say that the idea or thought is the immediate subject of expression; the feeling derives from the expression' (3, 321). Honorific references to Donne occur at regular intervals in the pages of the *Calendar*.

If the application of high and impersonal critical standards was the more obvious aspect of the *Calendar*'s activity, the other, closely related but less immediately apparent, was the establishing of a modernist poetic to underwrite those standards. The editors of the *Calendar* did not think of themselves as systematizers, and they may well have believed that the standards they strove for were no more than emanations of the natural intelligence; as Eliot had written, 'there is no method except to be very intelligent' (*The Sacred Wood*, p. 11). It is true that there is no overt system to be extracted from the *Calendar*, but there is a pattern of continuing and interrelated assumptions about literature (admittedly indebted to Eliot's poetry and criticism) which are still dominant in our own literary culture. Indeed, I see the *Calendar* as a *seminarium* of ideas which do not become really current until much later. Rickword several times insists that poetry should include a broad range of emotions, and that there is no longer any place for the 'poetic' as narrowly defined. He praises the so-called 'negative emotions' that he finds in Donne and Swift and the satires of Charles Churchill (1, 236–41). 'An expression, in prose or verse, is poetic when the object is immediately realized', he writes, in a way that echoes earlier pronouncements by Pound and Hulme (though their names are conspicuously absent from the *Calendar*).

Rickword insists that any feelings, however trivial and unpromising, can be made 'poetic': 'feelings not generally regarded with passionate interest will impel this interest when realized in poetic style not because the subject has been made more "important", blown-up, idealized, but because it has been exactly apprehended in its particular implications; without this any pretension to universal significance is a sham' (3, 158–9). This sentiment is now a commonplace of literary education, but it was not so in 1926. Related notions are the need for contemporary speech in poetry (2, 67) and the importance of irony as a means of reconciling seemingly opposed feelings and attitudes. Rickword quotes approvingly Richards's dictum that 'irony is a characteristic of poetry which is of the highest order', and adds: 'Certainly there is a high percentage of irony in the poetry which we most admire at the present time'; elsewhere he remarks: 'It is characteristic of the contemporary poet to put his money on each way. I mean that irony has come back to the attitude; it is the opportunism of the disinherited' (1, 164; 2, 67).

These ideas are amplified in one of the most interesting articles to appear in the *Calendar*, John Crowe Ransom's 'Thoughts on the Poetic Discontent' (1, 461–3). After indicating his dissatisfaction with poetic Romanticism and most poets of the nineteenth century, Ransom goes on: 'But the earlier and greater poets (Chaucer, Spenser, Shakespeare, Donne, Milton) along with or following their own share of lovely romantic adventures, turned back to the stubborn fact of dualism with a mellow wisdom which we may call irony. Irony may be regarded as the ultimate mode of the great minds—it presupposes the others.' Here irony is transformed from a mere matter of tone and attitude into a central principle of poetics, as it was to be developed much later by Ransom and his collaborators in the American New Criticism. Ransom's sense of the insufficiencies of Romanticism was echoed, if in less absolute terms, by the English contributors to the *Calendar*, rather in the spirit of Eliot's early observation: 'There may be a good deal to be said for Romanticism in life, there is no place for it in letters' (*The Sacred Wood*, p. 32). C. H. Rickword, for instance, begins a review of poems by Edmund Blunden (who had contributed to the first number of the *Calendar*) with the words, 'Mr Blunden is a long time sweating the romantic out of his system' (1, 366).

Resistance to Romanticism is conventionally regarded as 'classicism', and the *Calendar* made gestures to the classical ideal in some notes which are unsigned but probably by Edgell Rickword: 'The characteristics of a healthy criticism are invariably "classic", tending towards an ever greater rigidity of principle, and the canalization of the wide, shallow stream of taste' (3, 152). This suggests an intensification of Rickword's Arnoldian side, pointing towards an apotheosis of Hellenism, but the *Calendar* was, in fact, cautious about the notion of 'classicism', if only because its editors strongly disapproved of the *Criterion*'s brand of neoclassicism. Rickword felt that the vital Eliot of *The Sacred Wood* and *The Waste Land* was taking the wrong road, and he wrote a scathing parody of 'Whispers of Immortality' when Eliot became an Anglican. Interviewed in 1973 he said: 'The *Criterion* was a bit of a rag-bag. Eliot dug up a lot of old French critics, of an earlier generation, all pseudo-classicists. That was probably the result of his having been at the Sorbonne before the war.' The *Calendar*'s classicism was less ideological, consisting more in a conviction that the poet should be part of society and involved in its activities, not cut off in a romantic backwater or ivory tower. In one way this attitude looked back to an Augustan ideal; in another it anticipated Rickword's and Garman's later Marxist allegiance. It was itself irreconcilable with Rickword's own tendencies to late-Romantic individualism.

The writer of this same note takes a radical view of the importance of criticism:

> It is no longer useful to distinguish between an act of imagination and an act of criticism, where the first may, for all real purposes, be demanded by the second. Thus it is possible to say that the criticism in Mr Eliot's *Sacred Wood* not only is more valuable work than Mr Lawrence's latest novel, but takes precedence of it, makes it obsolete. (3, 154)

Wilde had mockingly proclaimed the superiority of the critic to the artist, but such extreme self-confidence about the critical function was uncommon in the 1920s, though comparable sentiments were later expressed in the heyday of *Scrutiny* and the New Criticism, and have been heard more recently in Structuralist quarters.

Some of the contributors to the *Calendar* were already well known, or later became so, but others remained irredeemably obscure. One such was C. H. Rickword about whom nothing appears to be known except that he was Edgell's cousin, and that he was killed in a motor-cycle accident while still quite a young man. He contributed a number of acerbic reviews, and two remarkable short essays on fiction, which anticipate much later critical discussions and problems; Malcolm Bradbury has called them 'a very early instance of the taking of modernist assumptions into the professional criticism of fiction.' The first is a review of *The Modern Novel* by Elizabeth A. Drew (3, 166-8), and the second is 'A Note on Fiction' (3, 226-33). C. H. Rickword rejects the familiar categories of character and plot as objective entities:

> Rhythm is a property of words, character a product that needs analysis before a satisfactory account of its effect can be given in terms of its

constituents, and a product, moreover, that invites extra-literary scrutiny
. . . 'character' is merely the term by which the reader alludes to the
pseudo-objective image he composes of his responses to the author's
verbal arrangements. (3, 166–7)

The form of a novel only exists as a balance of responses on the part of
the reader. Hence schematic plot is a construction of the reader's that
corresponds to that response and stands in merely diagrammatic relation
to the source. Only as precipitates from memory are plot or character
tangible; yet only in solution have either any emotive valency. (3, 226)

Like other *Calendar* contributors C. H. Rickword invokes *Ulysses* as a model
of the way literature should go, and he concludes his essay with some
remarks on the balance between events and consciousness in Joyce's novel:

Thus the authority and directness of objective presentation is secured
for the subjective narrative, Joyce's unit being the consciousness, not its
social crystallization the character. Dedalus and Bloom are but symbols
of disintegration; the imminent, never clearly apprehended Ulysses is the
hero of this Odyssey, whose significance lies wholly in the completed
action and its organic relation to the events of which it is composed.
(3, 233)

C. H. Rickword's brief but pregnant discussions point a long way ahead:
to the New Critics' discovery that novels as well as poems could be read in
terms of themes and images and symbols; and to Leavis's *Scrutiny* essays on
'the novel as dramatic poem'. More recently, and more extremely, poststructuralist discussions of novels as instances of self-referential textuality
seem to have the same relation to C. H. Rickword's early formulations as
the poetics of post-modernism do to those of classical modernism. The
argument in which he was so strong a partisan of one side is by no means
concluded; at the present time the criticism of John Bayley is still firmly
committed to the value and viability of the idea of 'character', as is Ian
McGilchrist's book *Against Criticism* (London, 1982); on the other hand,
another recent study, Thomas Docherty's *Reading (Absent) Character*
(Oxford, 1983) exposes the hollowness of 'character' as though this was a
completely new thought, but does so in terms that do not essentially go
beyond those proposed by C. H. Rickword in 1926.

In 'A Note on Fiction' C. H. Rickword speculates on the necessary
underlying quality of all literature, which he sees as some form of rhythm:
'a unity among the events, a progressive rhythm that includes and
reconciles each separate rhythm' and to which qualities like plot and
character are altogether secondary. In a sense this is very familiar, recalling
the Coleridgean insistence on the literary work as balancing and reconciling
opposites in an organic whole, which was central to the poetics of Richards
and Leavis and the New Critics. But the tone of C. H. Rickword's pursuit
of what he calls 'this basic, poetic quality', coupled with his analytical cast
of mind, suggests to me something of the Russian Formalists' pursuit of an
essential literariness. Elsewhere Edgell Rickword remarks that 'an element
of strangeness is necessary to beauty' (3, 321). His source is probably

Bacon's aphorism: 'There is no excellent beauty that hath not some strangeness in the proportion.' Yet one cannot but recall Shklovsky's formulation of the essence of literariness as lying in *ostraneniye* or 'making strange'. I mention this seemingly tenuous parallel because it is possible that Rickword and his collaborators may have known something of the contemporary Formalist movement in Russia through one of the *Calendar*'s Russian-reading contributors, Alec Brown. Reviewing Prince Mirsky's book on contemporary Russian literature, Brown makes a tantalizingly brief and casual reference to 'the formalists' useful clearing out of the critics' lumber-room, a work supplemented in England by Messrs Ogden and Richards in the theory of language and criticism' (3, 264).

The *Calendar* looked in two directions. In its critical thinking rather than its creative contributions it was in the vanguard of modernist poetics; in the 1920s its stance must have seemed subversively avant-garde. At the same time it was inspired by Arnoldian ideals of cultural health and the preservation of critical standards, which caused it to look back to a time when things were better ordered. In this aspect of its work the *Calendar* made formulations which a decade later were Scrutineering commonplaces. Reviewing Virginia Woolf's *The Common Reader*, Edgell Rickword invokes earlier periods when the writer had a fuller and more harmonious relationship with his environment and his readers:

> This happy state has been, in some considerable degree, the lot of the writers of any age remarkable for its literature, the Elizabethan, the Augustan, and the Victorian. In spite of internal dissension, the writers of these periods had a solid stratum to which finally they could refer to give value to their emotional utterances . . . Since then the reading public has split. (1, 321)

This was the diagnosis which the Leavises and their collaborators later made the basis of their literary and cultural criticism, and for a considerable time they were sustained by the hope and conviction that the right educational effort could have a reunifying effect on thought and culture. Rickword and the young socially marginalized intellectuals who ran the *Calendar* were not able to envisage such a development. Garman makes the same point about a fragmented audience and, like *Scrutiny* subsequently, looks back to the great nineteenth-century reviews: 'There is no longer a body of opinion so solid as that represented by *The Quarterly*, *The Edinburgh* and *Blackwood's*' (2, 48). These organs represented the *Calendar*'s ideal, but the eminent journalists and lawyers and men of affairs who ran them were close to the centres of cultural and political power and influence, and commanded a corresponding authority with their readers, of whatever ideological shading. None of this was true of the *Calendar*. *Scrutiny*, following up many of the *Calendar*'s approaches and analyses, made a highly successful connexion between criticism and education; with an academic base and a solid readership among people engaged in English studies, it survived for over twenty years. But after the first few issues *Scrutiny* dropped any attempt to publish creative work. Another review, *transition*, which was published in Paris, was wholly committed to the modernist avant-garde and made no claim to uphold critical standards; its contents were desperately uneven, but it too survived a good deal longer than the *Calendar*. Unlike the *Calendar* it was able to publish substantial extracts from Joyce's 'Work in Progress'.

The dilemma of the *Calendar* was that it was well aware of what the best modernist poetry and fiction were like but could not find enough of them to publish. Indeed the magazine's critical stance often seemed at odds with its creative contents; Rickword's friend W. J. Turner, whose verse appeared quite often, was only one of several traditionally inclined poetic contributors. The dilemma is most curiously illustrated in the editors' own poetry, which they rather imprudently published in generous selections. Rickword, of course, was a fine poet, whose verse and critical prose show similar qualities of sombre, convoluted, but elegant intellectual and emotional power. The same cannot be said of Higgins and Garman; their weakly traditional verse was in strange contradiction to their rigorous critical analyses. Higgins, who had no ear for metre or verse movement, seems to me not a poet at all; whereas Garman, a more fluent writer, may be called a poet, but a bad one. His poetry, collected in *The Jaded Hero* published by Wishart in 1927, is Nineties-ish, mellifluous and sentimental in a way that is untouched by the modernism he commended in his critical prose; 'damascened' is one of his favourite adjectives. In 1925 Garman reviewed Nancy Cunard's poem *Parallax*, and though he commented adversely on its excessively close imitations of *The Waste Land*, he concluded his review: 'one does, however, admire Miss Cunard's intention of using an idiom that is not worn out nor divorced by association from experience' (1, 248). But in the next issue he published a poem of his own called 'Antithesis' whose Swinburnean idiom can reasonably be called 'worn out'. The first stanza is representative:

> Dark streets with bloodshot eyes
> Run to a river of fire—
> Strings of a passionate lyre,
> Where curious fingers wandering, in surprise
> Wake melodies to glut the soul's desire.   (1, 270)

Precept and practice cannot always correspond, but seldom have they been so far apart. One assumes there was pyschological division as well as a marked lack of self-critical faculty in Garman (who was still a very young man), but the contradiction is not merely personal to him. It highlights the dilemma of the *Calendar*, and the general difficulty faced by British poets in the 1920s, where traditional idioms remained current for much longer than is now realized, and where the achievement of Eliot, though critically appreciated, either remained unassimilated or else was simply imitated, as by Nancy Cunard. Only in the American poets published in the *Calendar*, and indeed in Rickword himself, drawing in his own way on Donne and Rimbaud, is the possibility of a developing modernist idiom apparent.

The *Calendar* ceased publication in July 1927, for what appear to be a number of interrelated reasons: steadily dropping circulation, a lack of sufficient contributors, and a withdrawal of financial support by Wishart.

In the early 1930s its mantle was consciously assumed by Leavis, first in his anthology of material from its pages, *Towards Standards of Criticism*, and then in *Scrutiny* itself, to the first few issues of which Rickword and Garman contributed reviews. But there was only a tenuous continuity, and the *Calendar* team was dispersed. Bertram Higgins had returned to Australia and total obscurity. John Holms and Garman were part of the wealthy touring Bohemia of the time, and successively lovers of the American heiress and art collector Peggy Guggenheim, whose autobiography *Out of This Century* contains lively accounts of them. Holms died young, and Rickword and Garman became Communists. In the 1930s and 1940s Rickword edited journals closely associated with the Communist Party, *Left Review* and *Our Time*. In later interviews he tries to make his political development from *Calendar* days seem inevitable and even unremarkable, as a movement from cultural to political radicalism. The deeper implications of what it meant for a man of his intelligence and sensibility to be involved for so long, and to all appearances so loyally, with such an arid, repressive institution as the Communist Party of Great Britain, are politely evaded (it appears that Rickword quietly left the Party after the Hungarian revolution in 1956).

There is evidence, though, in some recollections of Rickword's life in the Party in the late 1940s by E. P. Thompson and David Holbrook, that, together with the poet Randall Swingler, he was under attack for professing too liberal and humanistic a form of Marxist–Leninism. His accusers were what Thompson has called the 'party's senior spokesman on cultural matters'; Emile Burns, John Lewis, and (most interestingly) Douglas Garman. By then Garman had become a fanatical hardline Stalinist. Holbrook, who was assistant editor of *Our Time*, has described Garman's part in an inquisition at Communist Party Headquarters in King Street some time in the late 1940s:

> I have a strong memory of Garman, with a deep sepulchral voice, in that compulsive guilty way Party fanatics had bollocking Edgell—he was feeble, bourgeois, tainted with reformism, ideologically unclear, etc. . . . Edgell was deeply hurt by this attack. Yet to my astonishment, he took it, and in the pub afterwards came up with some 'admissions' that he had been guilty of misdemeanours against the Revolution. Poor old Edgell was a bit of a masochist anyway.

This account offers sad evidence of how far Rickword, and Garman too for that matter, had moved since the days of the *Calendar* and its high Arnoldian ideals. Nevertheless, it remains Rickword's primary monument as poet, critic, editor, and instigatory literary intelligence, whose most important work was done before he was thirty. The *Calendar* clearly shows both the possibilities and the limitations of English literary culture in the 1920s, when modernism was being consolidated. It marks, too, the first extensive public practice of the kind of literary criticism that is still dominant in the English-speaking world.

NOTES

vii **the name of crisis** Graham Hough, review of *Criticism in the University*, *LRB*, 17 Oct. 1985. Once, long before, Professor Hough saw things differently. In 1963 he published an article, interestingly anticipating some of the arguments of this book, called 'Crisis in Literary Education' (*Sunday Times*, 17 Mar. 1963).

2 **Thoughtful Corporal belt** Arthur Koestler, *The Yogi and the Commissar* (London, 1945), p. 36.

6 **heyday of the Movement** See Blake Morrison, *The Movement: English Poetry and Fiction of the 1950s* (Oxford, 1980).

11 **to come would be to condone** Tony Gould, 'The Rebel Barons of Cambridge', *New Society*, 29 Jan. 1981.

11 **MacCabe's intelligence** ibid.

12 **aggressive piece of writing** Michael Mason, 'George Eliot, Joyce and Cambridge', *LRB*, 2–16 Apr. 1981.

13 **the first intellectual discussion** Raymond Williams, quoted in *Cambridge University Reporter*, 18 Feb. 1981, p. 347.

13 **top of the list for an appointment** Howard Erskine-Hill, quoted in 'Cambridge Scholars Wage Literal Warfare', *THES*, 23 Jan. 1981.

14 **corporate vacuity and vanity** Frank Kermode, *Cambridge University Reporter*, 18 Feb. 1981, 334.

14 **subjectivism in critical matters** Erskine-Hill, 'Scholarship as Humanism', *Essays in Criticism*, 29 (1979), 33–52.

14 **Cambridge, of course**, Kermode, quoted in Imre Salusinsky, *Criticism in Society* (London, 1987), p. 105.

14 **indifferently decent first book** ibid. 120.

15 **truly brilliant people** Gould, *New Society*, 29 Jan. 1981.

15 **quietly significant contributions** Beer, *Cambridge University Reporter*, 18 Feb. 1981, 353–5.

16 **causes within the Faculty** Wright, ibid. 351.

17 **fissiparous disciplines** 'Isolated Islands of Discontent', *THES*, 13 Feb. 1981.

18 **materialist poetics** Peter Widdowson, 'Introduction: The Crisis in English Studies', in Widdowson (ed.), *Re-Reading English* (London, 1982), p. 14.

18 **think of this, then?** Tony Davies, 'Common Sense and Critical Practice: Teaching Literature', ibid. 34.

18 **textual and authorial** Davies, ibid. 38.

19 **attitudinizing in its place** Tom Paulin, 'Faculty at War', *LRB*, 17–30 June 1982.

19 **monstrous non-subject** Paulin, letter, *LRB*, 19 Aug.–2 Sept. 1982.

19 **questions demand discussion** Widdowson, letter, *LRB*, 30 Dec. 1982–19 Jan. 1983.

20 **another attack** Claude Rawson, 'The Crisis, and How Not to Solve it', *TLS*, 10 Dec. 1982.

20 **liberal paternalism** Anthony Easthope, letter, *TLS*, 31 Dec. 1982.

20 **review of *Re-Reading English*** Nicholas Tredell, 'Hegemony by Other Means', *PNR*, No. 30 (1982).

20 **a subsequent article** Tredell, 'The Politicization of English', *PNR*, No. 37 (1984).

20 **another letter from Easthope** letter, *PNR*, No. 40 (1984).

21 **weakly argued and badly written** letter, ibid.

21 **ideologically unacceptable** letter, *PNR*, No. 42 (1984).

21 **a subsequent letter** *PNR*, No. 44 (1985).

21 **kind of literary Rip Van Winkle** Helen Gardner, *In Defence of the Imagination* (Oxford, 1982), p. 2.

23 **feel and think** ibid. 118.

23 **antediluvian almost on publication** Frank Kermode, *Essays on Fiction 1971–82* (London, 1983), p. 3.

23 **a detailed reply** 'On Being an Enemy of Humanity', *Raritan*, 2 (1982), 87–102.

24 **power over the imagination** *In Defence of the Imagination*, pp. 135–6.

24 **book so offends her** 'On Being an Enemy of Humanity', 99.

28 **these studies** See Stephen Potter, *The Muse in Chains* (London, 1937); E. M. W. Tillyard, *The Muse Unchained* (Cambridge, 1958); D. J. Palmer, *The Rise of English Studies* (Oxford, 1965); Margaret Mathieson, *The Preachers of Culture: A Study of English and its Teachers* (London, 1975).

   Marxist accounts include Brian Doyle, 'The Hidden History of English Studies', in *Re-Reading English*; Chris Baldick, *The Social Mission of English Criticism 1848–1932* (Oxford, 1983); and 'The Rise of English', in Terry Eagleton, *Literary Theory: An Introduction* (Oxford, 1983), though this chapter contains substantial inaccuracies. Doyle's work has been expanded in a valuable unpublished Ph.D. thesis, 'English and Englishness: A Cultural History of English Studies in British Higher Education 1880–1980' (Council for National Academic Awards, Thames Polytechnic, London, 1986). A book by Doyle on English studies, presumably based on this thesis, has been announced

for publication. There is a very useful history of American developments in Gerald Graff, *Professing Literature: An Institutional History*
(Chicago, 1987).

29 **rise of cultural nationalism** Patrick Parrinder, *Authors and Authority:
A Study of English Literary Criticism and its Relation to Culture 1750–1950*
(London, 1977), p. 21.

29 **Hindu or Hebrew poetry** Isaiah Berlin, *Vico and Herder: Two Studies
in the History of Ideas* (London, 1977), p. 196.

30 **autobiography of a nation, life of our nation** both phrases quoted
by Palmer, *Rise of English Studies*, 39.

30 **won by England** *The Letters of Gerard Manley Hopkins to Robert Bridges*,
ed. C. C. Abbott (London, 1955), p. 231.

30 **remarkable Government publication** *The Teaching of English in England* (London, 1921); henceforth referred to as the 'Newbolt Report',
the name by which it is generally known.

30 **we live and work** ibid. 20.

31 **men of our own race and culture** ibid. 13–14.

33 **God and the imagination are one** Wallace Stevens, 'Final Soliloquy
of the Interior Paramour'.

33 **replaced by poetry** Matthew Arnold, 'The Study of Poetry', in *Essays
in Criticism: Second Series*.

34 **ambassador of poetry** Newbolt Report, 259.

34 **without saving the State** George Gordon, *The Discipline of Letters*
(Oxford, 1946), p. 12. Gordon's hostile attitude to the Newbolt Report
and its high Arnoldian claims for literature has been lately subject to
a curious process of transmitted error. In the course of his inaugural
lecture Gordon sarcastically summarized the sentiments he was
opposed to as the belief that 'England is sick, and that English
literature must save it . . . save our souls and save the state.' Chris
Baldick quotes the whole passage, remarking on Gordon's 'biting
scorn' (*Social Mission of English Criticism*, 105). Eagleton takes the
passage from Baldick but overlooks the irony and scorn; he summarizes
it in his *Literary Theory* (p. 23) as if Gordon actually believes that
'literature must save us'. At least two subsequent writers have passed
on Eagleton's misapprehension: John Bayley (in *The Order of Battle at
Trafalgar and Other Essays* (London, 1987), p. 22) and Raymond Tallis
(in *In Defence of Realism* (London, 1988), p. 167). Thus, there is a
spreading impression that the unfortunate Gordon professed the
sentiments that he most detested. Two morals are suggested by this
confusion: (i) irony is liable to mislead hasty readers; (ii) where
possible, original sources for quotations should be given.

34 **fragmentary and deceptive** L. C. Knights, 'In Search of Fundamental Values', *The Critical Moment: Literary Criticism in the 1960s. Essays
from the London Times Literary Supplement* (New York, 1964), pp. 75–81.

36 **making principles operative** Newbolt Report, 49.

36 **physical and the moral sphere** J. C. Schiller, *On The Aesthetic Education of Man*, ed. and trans. E. M. Wilkinson and L. A. Willoughby (Oxford, 1967), p. 215.

37 **other of his functions** ibid. 155.

37 **dynamics of aesthetic purpose** René Wellek and Austin Warren *Theory of Literature* (London, 1949), p. 252.

37 **conditions of aesthetic experience** Helen Gardner, *The Business of Criticism* (Oxford, 1959), p. 13.

38 **By rhetoric I mean** *The Correspondence of Gerard Manley Hopkins and Richard Watson Dixon*, ed. C. C. Abbott (London, 1955), p. 141.

38 **encouraging clear expression** Alastair Fowler, 'A Critical Point for Literature', *THES*, 8 Mar. 1985.

39 **should not be taught** Newbolt Report, 150.

41 **long since dead** *The Letters of Sir Walter Raleigh*, ii (London, 1926), p. 396.

41 **movement for teaching English** ibid. 352.

42 **the English-speaking world** Gordon, *Discipline of Letters*, 5

43 **Eliot as a teacher** I. A. Richards, 'On TSE', in Allen Tate (ed.), *T. S. Eliot: The Man and his Work* (London, 1967), p. 3.

44 **going into church** James Reeves, 'Cambridge Twenty Years Ago', in Richard March and Tambimuttu (edd.), *T. S. Eliot* (London, 1948), p. 38.

44 **interesting account of those years** M. C. Bradbrook, 'I. A. Richards at Cambridge', in Reuben Brower, Helen Vendler, and John Hollander (edd.), *I. A. Richards: Essays in His Honour* (New York, 1973), pp. 61–72.

44 **bland, traditionalist humanism** Raymond Williams, *Writing in Society* (London, n.d., c.1984), p. 182.

44 **experimentation and inquiry** ibid. 190.

46 **tension in which he lived** Michael Tanner, 'Some Recollections of the Leavises', in Denys Thompson (ed.), *The Leavises: Recollections and Impressions* (Cambridge, 1984), p. 135.

46 **a tragic dimension** M. C. Bradbrook, '"Nor Shall my Sword": The Leavises' mythology', in *The Leavises*, 32.

47 **sinuous, lithe and unheeding** George Steiner, *Language and Silence: Essays 1958–1966* (London, 1967), p. 249.

48 **corrupt dilettanti** John Wain, *Sprightly Running* (London, 1963), p. 176.

48 **sometimes tempestuous sea** ibid. 174.

50 **discussed at length elsewhere** See 'Leavis and Eliot: The Long

Road to Rejection', in Bergonzi, *The Myth of Modernism and Twentieth Century Literature* (Brighton, 1986), pp. 85–112.

50 **complex of agrarian autonomism** Steiner, *Language and Silence*, 265.

52 **a blinded civilization** Francis Mulhern, *The Moment of 'Scrutiny'* (London, 1979), p. 267.

53 **as a religious ritual** Howard Felperin, *Beyond Deconstruction: The Uses and Abuses of Literary Theory* (Oxford, 1985), pp. 8–9.

54 **and works havoc** F. R. Leavis, '"Believing in" the University', *The Human World*, May–Aug. 1974, p. 104.

55 **turn him into a philosopher** 'Literary Criticism and Philosophy', in Leavis, *The Common Pursuit* (London, 1952), pp. 211–22.

55 **task for every humanist** René Wellek, *A History of Modern Criticism 1750–1950*, v, *English Criticism 1900–1950* (New Haven, 1986), p. 264.

57 **one of Pound's late Cantos** CIV; *The Cantos of Ezra Pound* (London, 1975), p. 745.

58 **sets them in a fresh light** Helen Gardner, 'Clive Staples Lewis', *Proceedings of the British Academy*, 51 (1965), p. 423.

59 **domestic, thrifty, honest** C. S. Lewis, *The Allegory of Love: A Study in Medieval Tradition* (London, 1936), p. 321.

59 **middle-class Englishmen** Lewis was an Ulsterman by birth, but he presented a resolutely English persona, emphasized by his nickname of 'Jack'.

59 **universities on American soil** Donald Davie, *These the Companions: Recollections* (Cambridge, 1982), p. 159.

60 **is salt water** Lewis, *Rehabilitations and Other Essays* (London, 1939), p. 82.

61 **who do not share it** id., *Surprised by Joy* (paperback edn., London, 1978), p. 86.

61 **that I see and love** id., *A Preface to Paradise Lost* (London, 1942), p. 130.

62 **is no longer possible** id., *An Experiment in Criticism* (Cambridge, 1961), p. 129.

62 **some authors to others** Robert Graves, *Goodbye to All That* (Harmondsworth, 1960), p. 240.

62 **successor in the Merton chair** John Carey, *Original Copy: Selected Reviews and Journalism 1969–1986* (London, 1987), pp. 25–9.

63 **nature of the cry** Lewis and E. M. W. Tillyard, *The Personal Heresy: A Controversy* (London, 1939), pp. 9–10.

63 **gives to the right reader** ibid. 114.

63 **which prevents enjoyment** ibid. 120.

63 **every poem that endures** ibid. 16.

63 **advocates of the New Pragmatism** See W. J. T. Mitchell (ed.), *Against Theory: Literary Studies and the New Pragmatism* (Chicago, 1985).

64 **privilege, of individuality** Lewis, *Experiment in Criticism*, 140.

64 **remarks on fantasy and realism** ibid. 50–73.

65 **ideal happiness** id., *Allegory of Love*, 304.

67 **giving the public what it wanted** id., *Rehabilitations*, 107.

67 **happens to interest them** id., *The Personal Heresy*, 112–13.

68 **literature does not exist** Eagleton, *Literary Theory*, 197.

68 **are absolutely debarred** Elizabeth W. Bruss, *Beautiful Theories: The Spectacle of Discourse in Contemporary Criticism* (Baltimore, 1982), p. 69.

68 **claims upon literature** E. D. Hirsch, jun., *The Aims of Interpretation* (Chicago, 1978), p. 135.

69 **pretty arbitrary selection** Knights, *Scrutiny*, 8 (June 1939), 91.

69 **before the Civil War** Catherine Belsey, 'Anti-Imperative: Questioning the Old Order', *PNR*, No. 48 (1985).

71 **appropriately equipped minority** 'It was a subject for the *élite*, not for the masses. This was Raleigh's view.' Helen Gardner, *Literary Studies: An Inaugural Lecture* (Oxford, 1967), p. 12.

71 **in our own day** See Paul de Man, 'The Return to Philology', *TLS*, 10 Dec. 1982.

72 **This poise is perfect** Louis MacNeice, 'To a Communist'.

73 **they are also retarding** Matthew Arnold, *The Last Word*, ed. R. H. Super, (Ann Arbor, 1977), p. 177.

74 **plurality of writings** Colin MacCabe, *Towards a Modern Trivium: English Studies Today* (Glasgow, 1982), p. 18.

80 **lecturing on the modern novel** Graff, *Professing Literature*, 124.

80 **a session of practical criticism** Anthony Burgess, 'The Writer Among Professors', *TLS*, 10 Dec. 1982.

80 **blowing his own nose** Lewis, *Rehabilitations*, 91.

86 **philosophical sense of the term** de Man, 'The Return to Philology'.

86 **'The Rhetoric of Temporality'** in id., *Blindness and Insight: Essays in the Rhetoric of Contemporary Criticism* (2nd edn., London, 1983), pp. 187–228.

89 **version of aestheticism** 'Arnold and Pater', in T. S. Eliot, *Selected Essays* (London, 1949), pp. 393–405.

89 **First World War** See Paul Fussell, *The Great War and Modern Memory* (London, 1975).

89 **truth, beauty and goodness** Gardner, *Business of Criticism*, 21.

89 **Beauty is difficult** LXXIV; *The Cantos*, 444 ff.

90 **That paralysing apparition** I. A. Richards, *Principles of Literary Criticism* (London, 1924), p. 19.

90 **was wont to admit** Peter Jones, 'A Critical Outline of Collingwood's Philosophy of Art', in Michael Krausz (ed.), *Critical Essays on the Philosophy of Collingwood* (London, 1972), pp. 62–3.

90 **combines evaluation and description** L. Wittgenstein, *Lectures and Conversations on Aesthetics, Psychology and Religious Belief*, ed. Cyril Barrett (Oxford, 1966), pp. 5–11.

90 **Papini's gibe** Richards, *Principles*, 255 n.

91 **commentator on Croce** M. E. Moss, *Benedetto Croce Reconsidered* (Hanover, N. H., 1987).

91 **mostly dull jargon** D. H. Lawrence, *Selected Literary Criticism*, ed. Anthony Beal (New York, 1956), p. 118.

92 **interested in 'sentiment'** Wellek, *English Criticism 1900–1950*, 251.

92 **always and necessarily intuitive** Krystyna Pomorska, 'Russian Formalism in Retrospect', in L. Matejka and K. Pomorska (edd.), *Readings in Russian Poetics* (Ann Arbor, 1978), p. 275.

92 **'Broad Genre' theory** Hirsch, *Aims of Interpretation*, 116–18.

93 **Geneva School** See J. Hillis Miller, 'The Geneva School', *Critical Quarterly*, 8 (1966), 305–21.

93 **intellectual and spiritual betters** Gardner, *Business of Criticism*, 16.

95 **discussion and dispute** Graff, *Professing Literature*, 252.

95 **not towards something else** Michael Edwards, 'Theory?' *PNR*, No. 48 (1985).

96 **'principles' rather than 'theory'** Christopher Ricks, 'In Theory', *LRB*, 16 Apr.–6 May 1981.

96 **a comparable distinction** Stanley Fish, 'Consequences', in Mitchell (ed.), *Against Theory*, 116.

98 **not want to READ** The quotation comes from the non-paginated Preface to *Signs of the Times*, which was published *c.*1971 without bearing date or publisher's imprint.

99 **pleasure and instruction** Kermode, *Essays on Fiction*, 3.

100 **led to a literary revolution** Veronica Forrest-Thomson, *THES*, 2 Feb. 1973.

100 **'Copernican' revolution** Belsey, *Critical Practice* (London, 1980), p. 130.

101 **his inaugural lecture** 'Modernism, Antimodernism and Postmodernism', in David Lodge, *Working with Structuralism: Essays and Reviews on Nineteenth and Twentieth Century Literature* (London, 1981), pp. 3–16.

102 **mystification and intimidation** ibid. p. ix.

102 **post-Saussurean perspective** Belsey, *Critical Practice*, 46.

102 **been examined sharply** 'Catherine Belsey and Classic Realism', in Patrick Parrinder, *The Failure of Theory—Essays on Criticism and Contemporary Fiction* (Brighton, 1987), pp. 18–29.

103 **neither animate nor conscious** Roger Poole, 'Generating Believable Entities: Post Marxism as a Theological Enterprise', *Comparative Criticism*, 8 (1985), 69.

103 *cause a new reality* Terence Hawkes, *Structuralism and Semiotics* (London, 1977), p. 149.

104 **not objectivity and truth** ibid. 156.

104 **pathologist of modern literary theory** Raymond Tallis, *Not Saussure: A Critique of Post-Saussurean Literary Theory* (London, 1988), p. 260 n.

104 **North American structuralism** Hawkes, *Structuralism and Semiotics*, 174 n.

105 **becomes a hegemonic form** Anthony Easthope, *Poetry as Discourse* (London, 1983), 65.

105 **open to variation** ibid. 64.

106 **literary criticism of Shakespeare** Derek Longhurst, ' "Not for all time, but for an Age": An Approach to Shakespeare Studies', in *Re-Reading English*, 152.

106 **have elsewhere argued** See 'The Terry Eagleton Story', in Bergonzi, *The Myth of Modernism*, 188–209.

106 **take the boy out of Cambridge** Felperin, *Beyond Deconstruction*, 57.

106 **should 'piss off'** Hawkes, letter, *LRB*, 21 Nov. 1985.

107 **to a star** Baldick, 'Talking among Themselves', *TLS*, 6 Nov. 1987.

108 **guilty political context** Eagleton, 'The Poetry of E. P. Thompson', *Literature and History*, 5 (Autumn 1979), 141–2.

109 **contradiction in terms** Marjorie Perloff, 'An Intellectual Impasse', *Salmagundi*, No. 72 (Fall 1986), 129.

109 **of cold showers** Nicolas Tredell, letter, *PNR*, No. 40 (1984).

109 **have misunderstood Derrida** Christopher Norris, *Derrida* (London, 1987).

110 **happens to fall on them** Lodge, *Write On: Occasional Essays 65–85* (London, 1986), p. 113.

110 **time, psyche or history** Geoffrey Thurley, *Counter-Modernism in Current Critical Theory* (London, 1983), p. 162.

111 **acted as a red rag** A. D. Nuttall, 'Solvents and Fixatives: Critical Theory in Transition', *MLR*, 82 (1987), 274.

112 **an almost popular appeal** Tallis, *Not Saussure*, 3–4.

113 **accounts of the ideogram** Easthope, *Poetry as Discourse*, 140.

114 **erasure of the world** Robert Scholes, *Textual Power: Literary Theory and the Teaching of English* (New Haven, 1985), p. 92.

115 **But I said nothing** Nuttall, 'Solvents and Fixatives', 276.

115 **are not to be trusted** Parrinder, *Failure of Theory*, p. ix.

115 **largely Marxist collection** Frank Gloversmith (ed.), *Theory of Reading* (Brighton, 1984).

115 **made the issue painfully acute** See Jacques Derrida, 'Like the Sound of the Sea Deep within a Shell: Paul de Man's War', *Critical Inquiry*, 14 (1988), 590–652.

116 **sensible body of doctrine** Nuttall, 'Solvents and Fixatives', 274.

118 **sensitive discussion of Williams** Parrinder, *Failure of Theory*, 72–84.

118 **of the class struggle** Eagleton, 'Two Approaches in the Sociology of Literature', *Critical Inquiry*, 14 (1988), 472.

118 **readers can respond to** Kiernan Ryan, 'Towards a Socialist Criticism: Reclaiming the Canon', *LTP: Journal of Literature, Teaching, Politics*, No. 3 (1984), 4–17.

119 **find a *rapprochement*** See Michael Ryan, *Marxism and Deconstruction* (Baltimore, 1982).

121 **widely different meanings** Malcolm Bowie, 'Jacques Lacan', in John Sturrock (ed.) *Structuralism and Since* (London, 1979), p. 145.

121 **L. Ron Hubbard of psychoanalysis** Tallis, 'The Strange Case of Jacques L.', *PNR*, No. 60 (1987).

121 **enquiry traditionally rests** Bowie, 'Jacques Lacan', 147.

122 **original ideas and texts** ibid. 149.

122 **formally opposed categories** Frederick Crews, *Skeptical Engagements* (New York, 1986), p. 170.

122 **practices engaged in by feminists** Kathleen McLuskie, 'The Patriarchal Bond: Feminist Criticism and Shakespeare', in Jonathan Dollimore and Alan Sinfield (edd.), *Political Shakespeare: New Essays in Cultural Materialism* (Manchester, 1985), p. 88. For a more systematic discussion of this multiplicity of practices see Elaine Showalter, 'Feminist Criticism in the Wilderness', in David Lodge (ed.), *Modern Criticism and Theory: A Reader* (London, 1988), pp. 330–53.

123 **arguments in America** Graff, *Professing Literature*, 260.

125 **There are, broadly speaking** Tredell, 'Post-Theory', *PNR*, No. 41 (1984).

126 **a recent paper** Lodge, 'After Bakhtin', in Nigel Fabb and others (edd.), *The Linguistics of Writing: Arguments Between Language and Literature* (Manchester, 1987), pp. 89–102.

126 **real or hypothetical Other** Lodge, 'Lawrence, Dostoevsky, Bakhtin: D. H. Lawrence and Dialogic Fiction', *Renaissance and Modern Studies*, 29 (1985), 17.

127 **instead of having desperately** ibid.

129 ***obscurantisme terroriste*** John R. Searle, review of Culler, *On Deconstruction*, in *New York Review of Books*, 27 Oct. 1983.

130 **set of perfunctory dualisms** Peter Dews, *Logics of Disintegration: Post-Structuralist Thought and the Claims of Critical Theory* (London, 1987), p. xv.

131 **a *written* Constitution** Norris, *Derrida*, 199.

131 **beyond man and humanism** Jacques Derrida, *Writing and Difference* (London, 1976), p. 292.

132 **intellectual nihilist** Crews, *Skeptical Engagements*, 171.

132 **frivolity to the obscurity** Tallis, *Not Saussure*, 226.

133 **Reality which matters to us** Bernard Harrison, 'Deconstructing Derrida', *Comparative Criticism* 7 (1985), 21.

133 **at worst trivial** Geoffrey Hartman, *Saving the Text: Literature/Derrida/Philosophy* (Baltimore, 1981), p. 22.

134 **self-congratulatory hermeticism** Crews, *Skeptical Engagements*, 122.

134 **cruel parody** Tallis, *Not Saussure*, 24–5.

134 **myth of art has itself** Allan Megill, *Prophets of Extremity: Nietzsche, Heidegger, Foucault, Derrida* (Berkeley, 1985), p. 333.

135 **a limited number of motifs** ibid. 330.

135 **have been in part achieved** ibid. 345.

135 **or changing ourselves** ibid.

136 **problems of professionalization** Salusinsky, *Criticism in Society*, 17–18.

136 **returned to the attack** Searle, *New York Review of Books*, 27 Oct. 1983.

137 **metaphorical through and through** Norris, *Derrida*, 169–70.

137 **found in Kant** ibid. 162.

138 **in a book like this** ibid. 14–15.

139 **argumentative rigour** ibid. 140.

139 **resources of his writing** ibid. 204.

140 **negative theology** Edward Said, *The World, the Text and the Critic* (London, 1984), p. 184.

140 **metaphysics of absence** Tredell, 'Post-theory', *PNR*, No. 41 (1984).

141 **all work in universities** Kermode, 'The Decline of the Man of Letters', *Partisan Review*, 52 (1985), 203.

142 **receptiveness and disinterestedness** Gardner, *Business of Criticism*, 13.

143 **judging if it works well** Bayley, *Order of Battle at Trafalgar*, 80.

144 **our own imaginative life** Gardner, *Business of Criticism*, 148.

144 **valuable, or not valuable** Richards, *Principles*, 23.

145 **would scorn to produce** Thurley, *Counter-Modernism*, 38.

148 **players look curiously on** Lodge, *Write On*, 40.

149 **list of deficiencies** Richards, *Practical Criticism* (London, 1929), 311.

151 **nature of literary canons** See Robert von Halberg (ed.), *Canons* (Chicago, 1984).

151 **'Institutional Control of Interpretation'** in Kermode, *Essays on Fiction*, 168–84.

152 **in fact is timidity** Donald Davie, 'Criticism and the Academy', in Gerald Graff and Reginald Gibbons (edd.), *Criticism in the University* (Evanston, 1985), p. 175.

155 **reading English at Manchester** Anthony Burgess, *Little Wilson and Big God* (Harmondsworth, 1988), pp. 167 ff.

157 **exam-passing essays** Lodge, *Nice Work* (London, 1988), pp. 35–6.

157 **similar conflict of interest** Hirsch, 'Back to History', in *Criticism in the University*, pp. 189–97.

158 **the rest would be silence** Lodge, *Changing Places: A Tale of Two Campuses* (London, 1975), p. 35.

159 **a pain in the ass** ibid. 38.

159 **is another encoding** Lodge, *Small World: An Academic Romance* (London, 1984), p. 25.

159 **lawyers, politicians, journalists** ibid. 28.

159 **ended up empty-handed** Lodge, *Changing Places*, 12.

160 **jobs are hereditary** ibid. 52.

161 **and those who read it** Newbolt Report, 237.

161 **kinds of doctoral manufacture** Leavis, 'Research in English', in *The Critical Moment*, 92.

161 **even if they could pass** ibid. 97.

164 **about some literary work** Lewis, *Experiment in Criticism*, 6–7.

164 **scholarly output** Gardner, *Literary Studies*, 22.

167 **paperback research** Hawkes, letter, *LRB*, 21 Nov. 1985.

167 **knowledge in English** Hirsch, 'Derrida's Axioms', *LRB*, 21 July 1983.

168 **reply was 'Yes'** Edwards, *PNR*, No. 48 (1985).

168 **theatre of Molière** Perloff, 'An Intellectual Impasse'.

169 **theorists and critics?** Bruss, *Beautiful Theories*, 79.

169 **de Man is reported** cited by Gibbons, 'Academic Criticism and Contemporary Literature', *Criticism in the University*, 29.

172 **needs of the Tripos course** quoted in *Cambridge University Reporter*, 362.

173 **candidate's personal response** Sinfield, *Political Shakespeare*, 140.

174 **literary value becomes irrelevant** Belsey, 'Literature, History, Politics', in Lodge (ed.), *Modern Criticism and Theory*, 409.

174 **from invoking 'language'** Miller, Presidential Address, *PMLA* 102 (May 1987).

175 **Always historicize!** Fredric Jameson, *The Political Unconscious*, (London, 1981), p. 9.

175 **All art is . . . historical** Gardner, *Business of Criticism*, 17.

175 **in a different culture** *The Complete Psychological Works of Sigmund Freud*, xxi (London, 1961), p. 89.

175 **interpret Shakespeare plays** See *Political Shakespeare*; and John Drakakis (ed.), *Alternative Shakespeares* (London, 1985).

176 **embody universal truths** *Political Shakespeare*, 135.

176 **the other way round** Edward Pechter, 'The New Historicism and its Discontents', *PMLA* 102 (May 1987).

177 **discussions of Romantic literature** See Marilyn Butler, *Romantics, Rebels, and Reactionaries* (Oxford, 1981), and Jerome J. McGann, *The Beauty of Inflections* (Oxford, 1985).

179 **one on Jane Austen** 'I was recently asked to contribute a monograph on Jane Austen to a radical series whose object was to re-analyze the canon from a left perspective. I offered to take on Gissing instead, and received the rather shamefaced response that Gissing was not to be included in the series. The acid test seems to be whether or not the writer was studied at A-level. Even demystification of the canon must stay strictly within its boundaries.' Terry Lovell, *Consuming Fiction* (London, 1987), pp. 172–3 n.

180 **primarily to be stored** '. . . the book expansion also indicates a very large increase in book *storage*: the institutional buying of public, school, university and industrial or scientific libraries is by no means all buying for use.' Malcolm Bradbury, *The Social Context of Modern English Literature* (Oxford, 1971), p. 218.

180 **I feel sick** Stefan Collini, 'Viewpoint: Research in the Humanities', *TLS*, 3 Apr. 1987.
   As I was preparing the book for the press I came across eloquent support for the argument of this Chapter in a paper by Sir Keith Thomas. He writes: 'The most influential thing that literary critics do nowadays is shape public taste by contributing to commercial publications, like the *TLS*, the *THES*, the *London Review of Books* and the Sunday newspapers, and by writing prefaces to Penguin Classics and World's Classics and helping to determine what titles are included in such series. But the triumph in this century of the research ethic means that many teachers are contemptuous of such activities. They write

primarily for each other and they are more concerned to produce future scholars and to win professional accolades for themselves than to educate a wider public. Is it too much to say that we are now members of a self-perpetuating interest group of scholars who have half forgotten their original social function and whose professional status is based on a misleading analogy between their activities and those of the physical scientists?' *THES*, 2 Dec. 1988.

181 **teach the cultural text** Scholes, *Textual Power*, 33.

184 **by a central power** Scholes, 'Aiming a Canon at the Curriculum', *Salmagundi*, No. 72 (Fall, 1986), 116.

184 **subscribe to wholeheartedly** Hirsch, 'Responses to Robert Scholes', ibid. 120.

185 **an axe to shatter the frozen sea** Franz Kafka, *Letters to Friends, Family and Editors* (London, 1978), p. 16.

185 **find *Othello* or *Lear* frightful** T. S. Eliot, 'Contemporanea', *Egoist*, June–July 1918.

187 **no literary sensibility** Davie, 'Criticism and the Academy', 174.

190 **its available facsimile** Williams, *Writing in Society*, 189.

192 **actual material of study** ibid. 211.

195 **the book vanishes** Percy Lubbock, *The Craft of Fiction* (London, 1926), p. 273.

195 **provide a working answer** Jameson, *Fables of Aggression: Wyndham Lewis, the Modernist as Fascist* (Berkeley, 1979), p. 7.

202 **Bradbury's story** in his *Who Do You Think You Are?* (London, 1976).

203 **genuine and valuable criticism** Morris Dickstein, 'Journalism and Criticism', *Criticism in the University*, pp. 147–58.

203 **not for the general public** Victoria Glendinning, 'The Book Reviewer: the Last Amateur?' in A. N. Wilson (ed.) *Essays by Divers Hands* (Transactions of the Royal Society of Literature, Woodbridge, 1986), p. 187.

204 **in university administration** Noel Annan, *Leslie Stephen* (London, 1951), p. 35.

205 ***Calendar* young man** *Collected Letters of D. H. Lawrence*, ed. H. T. Moore (London, 1962), ii. 968.

207 **in America would take it** *Letters of Hart Crane*, ed. Brom Webber (Berkeley and Los Angeles, 1952), p. 259.

207 **polemical work** Alan Young and Michael Schmidt, 'A Conversation with Edgell Rickword', *Poetry Nation* i (1973), 73–89.

208 **give praise with meaning** 'Comments and Reviews', *The Calendar of Modern Letters* i (1925), 70–1. The source of subsequent quotations from the *Calendar* is indicated parenthetically by volume and page number.

208 **perceptive and just** Edgell Rickword, *Essays and Opinions 1921–1931*, ed. Alan Young (Cheadle, 1974), pp. 42–4.

209 **please return it** Sylvia Beach, *Shakespeare and Company* (New York, 1959), p. 169.

209 **dropped to a thousand** Malcolm Bradbury, 'A Review in Retrospect', *The Calendar* (repr. London, 1966), i. p. x.

213 **Sorbonne before the war** interview with A. Young and M. Schmidt, 78–9.

213 **criticism of fiction** Bradbury, *Possibilities* (London, 1973), p. 86.

217 **Rickword's life in the Party** David Holbrook, 'Edgell Rickword: Politics and Poetry', and E. P. Thompson, 'Edgell Rickword', *PNR*, No. 9 (1979), Supplement, pp. xxv–xxviii; D. Holbrook, letter to author, 19 Sept. 1984.

SELECTIVE BIBLIOGRAPHY

(Place of publication is London unless otherwise stated)

ANNAN, NOEL, *Leslie Stephen* (1951).
BAKHTIN, MIKHAIL, *The Dialogic Imagination* (Austin, 1981).
—— *Problems of Dostoevsky's Poetics* (Manchester, 1984).
BALDICK, CHRIS, *The Social Mission of English Criticism 1848–1932* (Oxford, 1983).
BARTHES, ROLAND, *Writing Degree Zero* (1967).
—— *Mythologies* (1972).
—— *S/Z* (1975).
—— *The Pleasure of the Text* (New York, 1975).
—— *Image–Music–Text* (New York, 1977).
—— *Camera Lucida* (1982).
BAYLEY, JOHN, *The Order of Battle at Trafalgar and Other Essays* (1987).
BEACH, SYLVIA, *Shakespeare and Company* (New York, 1959).
BELSEY, CATHERINE, *Critical Practice* (1980).
BENNETT, TONY, *Marxism and Formalism* (1979).
BENTLEY, ERIC (ed.), *The Importance of Scrutiny* (New York, 1964).
BERLIN, ISAIAH, *Vico and Herder: Two Studies in the History of Ideas* (1977).
BRADBURY, MALCOLM, *The Social Context of Modern English Literature* (Oxford, 1971).
—— *Possibilities: Essays on the State of the Novel* (1973).
—— *Who Do You Think You Are?* (1976).
BROOKE-ROSE, CHRISTINE, *A Rhetoric of the Unreal* (Cambridge, 1981).
BROOKS, CLEANTH and WARREN, ROBERT PENN, *Understanding Poetry* (New York, 1938).
BRUSS, ELIZABETH W., *Beautiful Theories: The Spectacle of Discourse in Contemporary Criticism* (Baltimore, 1982).
BURGESS, ANTHONY, *Little Wilson and Big God* (Harmondsworth, 1988).
BUTLER, MARILYN, *Romantics, Rebels, and Reactionaries* (Oxford, 1981).
CAREY, JOHN, *Original Copy: Selected Reviews and Journalism 1969–1986* (1987).
COLLINGWOOD, R. G., *The Principles of Art* (Oxford, 1938).
CRANE, HART, *Letters*, ed. Brom Webber (Berkeley, 1952).
CREWS, FREDERICK, *Skeptical Engagements* (New York, 1986).
The Critical Moment: Literary Criticism in the 1960s: Essays from the London Times Literary Supplement (New York, 1964).
CROCE, BENEDETTO, *Aesthetic* (1953).
CULLER, JONATHAN, *Structuralist Poetics* (1975).
—— *The Pursuit of Signs* (1981).
DAVIE, DONALD, *These the Companions: Recollections* (Cambridge, 1982).
DE MAN, PAUL, *Blindness and Insight: Essays in the Rhetoric of Contemporary Criticism* (2nd edn., 1983).

DERRIDA, JACQUES, *Of Grammatology* (Baltimore, 1976).
—— *Writing and Difference* (1978).
—— *Positions* (1981).
—— *The Post Card: From Socrates to Freud and Beyond* (Chicago, 1987).
DEWS, PETER, *Logics of Disintegration: Post-Structuralist Thought and the Claims of Critical Theory* (1987).
DOLLIMORE, JONATHAN and SINFIELD, ALAN (edd.), *Political Shakespeare: New Essays in Cultural Materialism* (Manchester, 1985).
DONOGHUE, DENIS, *Ferocious Alphabets* (1981).
DRAKAKIS, JOHN (ed.), *Alternative Shakespeares* (1985).
EAGLETON, TERRY, *Criticism and Ideology*, (1976).
—— *Marxism and Literary Criticism* (1976).
—— *Literary Theory: An Introduction* (Oxford, 1983).
—— *The Function of Criticism* (1984).
EASTHOPE, ANTHONY, *Poetry as Discourse* (1983).
ELIOT, T. S., *Selected Essays* (1932).
EMPSON, WILLIAM, *Seven Types of Ambiguity* (1930).
ERLICH, VICTOR, *Russian Formalism: History-Doctrine* (New Haven, 1981).
FABB, NIGEL and others (edd.), *The Linguistics of Writing: Arguments Between Language and Literature*: (Manchester, 1987).
FEKETE, John, *The Critical Twilight* (1977).
FELPERIN, HOWARD, *Beyond Deconstruction* (Oxford, 1985).
FISCHER, ERNST, *The Necessity of Art: A Marxist Approach* (Harmondsworth, 1963).
FOUCAULT, MICHEL, *The Order of Things* (1970).
FREUD, SIGMUND, *Complete Psychological Works* xxi (1961).
FRYE, NORTHROP, *Anatomy of Criticism* (Princeton, 1957).
FUSSELL, PAUL, *The Great War and Modern Memory* (1975).
GARDNER, HELEN, *The Business of Criticism* (Oxford, 1959).
—— *Literary Studies: An Inaugual Lecture* (Oxford, 1967).
—— *In Defence of the Imagination* (Oxford, 1982).
GORDON, GEORGE, *The Discipline of Letters* (Oxford, 1946).
GLOVERSMITH, FRANK, (ed.), *Theory of Reading* (Brighton, 1984).
GRAFF, GERALD, *Literature Against Itself* (Chicago, 1979).
—— *Professing Literature: An Institutional History* (Chicago, 1987).
—— and GIBBONS, REGINALD (edd.), *Criticism in the University* (Evanston, 1985).
GROSS, JOHN, *The Rise and Fall of the Man of Letters* (1969).
GROSSMAN, JUDITH, *Her Own Terms* (New York, 1988).
HALBERG, ROBERT VON (ed.), *Canons* (Chicago, 1984).
HARTMAN, GEOFFREY, *Saving the Text: Literature/Derrida/Philosophy* (Baltimore, 1981).
HAWKES, TERENCE, *Structuralism and Semiotics* (1977).
HAWTHORN, JEREMY (ed.), *Criticism and Critical Theory* (1984).
HEATH, STEPHEN and others (edd.), *Signs of the Times: Introductory Readings in Textual Semiotics* (Cambridge, c.1971).
HIRSCH, E. D., jun., *Validity in Interpretation* (New Haven, 1967).
—— *The Aims of Interpretation* (Chicago, 1978).

HIRSCH, E. D., jun., *Cultural Literacy* (New York, 1988).
JAMESON, FREDRIC, *The Prison House of Language* (Princeton, 1972).
—— *Fables of Aggression: Wyndham Lewis, the Modernist as Fascist* (Berkeley, 1979).
—— *The Political Unconscious* (1981).
JARRELL, RANDALL, *Poetry and the Age* (1973).
KERMODE, FRANK, *The Sense of an Ending* (1967).
—— *The Genesis of Secrecy* (1979).
—— *Essays on Fiction 1971–82* (1983).
KRAUSZ, MICHAEL (ed.) *Critical Essays on the Philosophy of Collingwood* (1972).
LACAN, JACQUES, *Écrits* (1977).
LAWRENCE, D. H., *Selected Literary Criticism*, ed. Anthony Beal (1956).
—— *Letters*, ed. H. T. Moore (1962).
LEAVIS. F. R., *New Bearings in English Poetry* (1932).
—— *For Continuity* (Cambridge, 1933).
—— *Revaluation* (1936).
—— *Education and the University* (1943).
—— *The Great Tradition* (1948).
—— *The Common Pursuit* (1952).
—— *D. H. Lawrence: Novelist* (1955).
LEAVIS, Q. D., *Fiction and the Reading Public* (1932).
LENTRICCHIA, FRANK, *After the New Criticism* (1980).
LERNER, LAURENCE (ed.), *Reconstructing Literature* (Oxford, 1983).
LEWIS, C. S., *The Allegory of Love* (1936).
—— *Rehabilitations and Other Essays* (1939).
—— *A Preface to Paradise Lost* (1942).
—— *An Experiment in Criticism* (Cambridge, 1961).
—— *Surprised by Joy* (paperback edn., 1978).
—— and TILLYARD, E. M. W., *The Personal Heresy: A Controversy* (1939).
LODGE, DAVID, *Language of Fiction* (1966).
—— *Changing Places: A Tale of Two Campuses* (1975).
—— *The Modes of Modern Writing: Metaphor, Metonymy and the Typology of Modern Literature* (1977).
—— *Working with Structuralism: Essays and Reviews on Nineteenth and Twentieth Century Literature* (1981).
—— *Small World: An Academic Romance* (1984).
—— *Write on: Occasional Essays '65–'85* (1986).
—— *Nice Work* (1988).
—— (ed.), *Modern Criticism and Theory: A Reader* (1988).
LONSDALE, ROGER (ed.), *The New Oxford Book of Eighteenth-Century Verse* (Oxford, 1984).
LOVELL, TERRY, *Consuming Fiction* (1987).
LUBBOCK, PERCY, *The Craft of Fiction* (1926).
MARCH, RICHARD and TAMBIMUTTU (edd.), *T. S. Eliot* (1948).
MATEJKA, L. and POMORSKA, K. (edd.), *Readings in Russian Poetics* (Ann Arbor, 1978).
MATHIESON, MARGARET, *The Preachers of Culture: A Study of English and its Teachers* (1975).

MEGILL, ALLAN, *Prophets of Extremity: Nietzsche, Heidegger, Foucault, Derrida* (Berkeley, 1985).

MITCHELL, W. J. T. (ed.), *Against Theory: Literary Studies and the New Pragmatism* (Chicago, 1985).

MORRISON, BLAKE, *The Movement: English Poetry and Fiction of the 1950s* (Oxford, 1980).

MOSS, M. E., *Benedetto Croce Reconsidered* (Hanover, NH, 1987).

MULHERN, FRANCIS, *The Moment of 'Scrutiny'* (1979).

MACCABE, COLIN, *James Joyce and the Revolution of the Word* (1978).

—— *Towards a Modern Trivium: English Studies Today* (Glasgow, 1982).

MACDIARMID, LUCY, *Saving Civilization: Yeats, Eliot and Auden Between the Wars* (1984).

MCGANN, JEROME J., *The Beauty of Inflections* (Oxford, 1985).

NORBROOK, DAVID, *Poetry and Politics in the English Renaissance* (1984).

NORRIS, CHRISTOPHER, *Deconstruction: Theory and Practice* (1982).

—— *The Contest of Faculties: Philosophy and Theory After Deconstruction* (1985).

—— *Derrida* (1987).

NUTTALL, A. D., *A New Mimesis* (1983).

PALMER, D. J., *The Rise of English Studies* (Oxford, 1965).

PARRINDER, PATRICK, *Authors and Authority: A Study of English Literary Criticism and its Relation to Culture 1750–1950* (1977).

—— *The Failure of Theory: Essays on Criticism and Contemporary Fiction* (Brighton, 1987).

POTTER, STEPHEN, *The Muse in Chains* (1937).

POUND, EZRA, *The Cantos* (1975).

RALEIGH, SIR WALTER, *Letters* (1926).

RAVAL, SURESH, *Metacriticism* (Athens, Ga., 1981).

RICHARDS, I. A., *Principles of Literary Criticism* (1924).

—— *Science and Poetry* (1926).

—— *Practical Criticism* (1929).

RICKS, CHRISTOPHER, *The Force of Poetry* (Oxford, 1984).

RICKWORD, EDGELL, *Essays and Opinions 1921–1931*, ed. Alan Young (Cheadle, 1974).

ROBINSON, IAN, *The Survival of English* (Cambridge, 1974).

ROBSON, W. W., *Critical Essays* (1966).

—— *The Definition of Literature and Other Essays* (Cambridge, 1982).

RYAN, MICHAEL, *Marxism and Deconstruction* (Baltimore, 1982).

SAID, EDWARD, *The World, the Text and the Critic* (1984).

SALUSINSKY, IMRE, *Criticism in Society* (1987).

SCHILLER, J. C., *On the Aesthetic Education of Man*, ed. and trans. E. M. Wilkinson and L. A. Willoughby (Oxford, 1967).

SCHOLES, ROBERT, *Textual Power: Literary Theory and the Teaching of English* (New Haven, 1985).

STEINER, GEORGE, *Language and Silence: Essays 1958–1966* (1967).

STURROCK, JOHN (ed.), *Structuralism and Since* (1979).

TALLIS, RAYMOND, *In Defence of Realism* (1988).

—— *Not Saussure: A Critique of Post-Saussurean Literary Theory* (1988).

TATE, ALLEN (ed.), *T. S. Eliot: The Man and his Work* (1967).

236 Selective Bibliography

The Teaching of English in England (The 'Newbolt Report', 1921).

THOMPSON, DENYS, *Reading and Discrimination* (1934).

—— (ed.), *The Leavises: Recollections and Impressions* (Cambridge, 1984).

THURLEY, GEOFFREY, *Counter-Modernism in Current Critical Theory* (1983).

TILLYARD, E. M. W., *The Muse Unchained* (Cambridge, 1958).

WAIN, JOHN, *Sprightly Running* (1963).

WATSON, GEORGE, *Modern Literary Thought* (Heidelberg, 1978).

WELLEK, RENÉ, *A History of Modern Criticism* , v, *English Criticism 1900–1950* (New Haven, 1986).

—— and Austin Warren *Theory of Literature* (1948).

WIDDOWSON, PETER (ed.), *Re-Reading English* (1982).

WILLIAMS, RAYMOND, *Culture and Society 1780–1950* (1958).

—— *Writing in Society* (n.d., c.1984).

WILSON, A. N. (ed.), *Essays by Divers Hands* (Transactions of the Royal Society of Literature, Woodbridge, 1986).

WITTGENSTEIN, LUDWIG, *Lectures and Conversations on Aesthetics, Psychology and Religious Belief*, ed. Cyril Barrett (Oxford, 1966).

INDEX